CORPORATE CRIME

CORPORATE CRIME

Editor
Prakash Talwar

ISHA

ISHA BOOKS
DELHI-110033

Corporate Crime

Rs. 720

ISBN: 81-8205-346-3

Published in 2006 in India by
Isha Books
D-43, Prithviraj Road,
Adarsh Nagar, Delhi-110033
e-mail : ishabooks@hotmail.com

Laser Typesetting at : Shiva Infosystem, Delhi
Printed at : Mehra Offset Press, Delhi

Preface

Corporate crime refers to criminal practices by individuals that have the legal authority to speak for a corporation or company. These can include presidents, chief executive officers, managers, directors and chairmen, sales people, agents, or anyone within a company that has authority to act on behalf of the firm. Examples of criminal behaviour in most jurisdictions include: antitrust violations, fraud, damage to the environment in violation of environmental legislation, exploitation of labour in violation of labour laws, and failure to maintain a fiduciary responsibility towards shareholders.

This book provides a detailed account of the nature, causes and consequences of various forms of corporate crimes. It assesses the potential for the legal control of corporate criminality as informed by insights gleaned from an understanding of why such crimes occur. Corporate crime features on various undergraduate and postgraduate criminology and criminal justice courses across the country, which makes this comprehensive book highly appropriate for law and criminology students. It is also an insightful text appropriate for a wider academic audience and discusses the legal, sociological and criminological dimensions of corporate crime in detail.

Editor

Contents

1
Introduction

Corporate crime refers to criminal practices by individuals that have the legal authority to speak for a corporation or company. These can include presidents, managers, directors and chairmen, sales people, agents, or anyone within a company that has authority to act on behalf of the firm. Examples of criminal behaviour in most jurisdictions include: antitrust violations, fraud, damage to the environment in violation of environmental legislation, exploitation of labour in violation of labour laws, and failure to maintain a fiduciary responsibility towards shareholders.

Corporate accountability refers to being accountable to the stakeholders of the organization. These stakeholders may include shareholders, employees, customers, suppliers, the local community, and the country(s) that the firm operates in. In most jurisdictions, a body of corporate law has been developed to formalize these requirements. Joel Bakan argued that as corporations increase profitability, they often engage in criminal activity.

Corporate Environmental Crime

The term 'corporate environmental crime', which may be defined as any environmental crime that has been committed by any corporate body. The importance of the inquiry was to hear from a range of corporate bodies and their representatives on the present environmental criminal justice system, while at the same time recognising that an environmental sentence for a corporate body is at present limited to a fine. The reasons for committing corporate environmental crimes are also varied.

The crime may occur because the business concerned is ignorant of its environmental obligations. It may also occur all too often as a result of negligent behaviour, for example, where businesses are poorly managed, staff are inadequately trained or equipment and infrastructure has not been maintained to the required standard, allowing a pollution incident to occur. But perhaps the most depressing cause is when corporate environmental crime is the result of a deliberate and intentional illegal act, a decision taken in the full knowledge that the act is illegal and will result in environmental harm.

Bhopal-type Disaster

It is only a matter of time before the world is shocked and sickened by another Bhopal-type industrial disaster. This is because the global economic forces that led Union Carbide to build and operate its ill-fated factory in Bhopal have not gone away - they have only become stronger. The fact that after 20 years of the Bhopal disaster, survivors are forced to drink poisoned water, contaminated by stockpiles of abandoned chemicals, clearly reflects the apathy of Corporations and Governments towards communities and the environment.

The lessons of Bhopal are still waiting to be learned. In fact, a 1000 Bhopals are happening in slow motion across India - destroying the environment and poisoning people with impunity. Environmental disasters, both chronic and immediate, induced by irresponsible corporate practices are becoming more frequent. Transnational corporations have learned to downplay damage, and focus attention and liability on the local company to elude full criminal and civil liability. To curb these abuses, governments must act on a global basis to ensure that both transnational and national corporations are held liable for their actions, particularly in countries like ours where companies operate in less regulated environments.

Not all companies operating in both the developing and developed world fit this description. But many certainly do. Some routinely fail to respond in an adequate manner to incidents, fail to compensate and assist impacted communities, fail to meet their obligations to clean up damaged environments and violate the rights of workers and local residents by not monitoring or disclosing essential information concerning their products and processes. Bhopal is an icon for the need to change the way corporations operate globally in rich and poor nations. Their safety measures designed to prevent a gas leak had either malfunctioned or were otherwise inadequate; the safety siren intended to alert the community should an accident occur was turned off. This is particularly irresponsible in light of the fact that storage of the chemical being manufactured - methyl isocyanate (MIC) - is known to be extremely dangerous.

In the aftermath of the disaster, Union Carbide refused to provide full information regarding the nature of the poisoning which meant that doctors were unable to properly treat those exposed. Such behavior is no less than criminal, but it is becoming increasingly difficult to seek justice and to hold these companies accountable and liable for their crimes. Union Carbide managed to escape its obligations for the Bhopal disaster by deflecting responsibility on to the Indian government. It constantly downplayed the damage to the people and environment of Bhopal to limit its liability, demonstrating its utter moral bankruptcy in the process. Finally, the company simply fled from India, abandoning the factory and fobbing off the devastated population with a paltry 'final' settlement of just US$370-533 per person.

In 2001, Union Carbide shed its name by merging with the multinational Dow Chemical for US$9.3 billion. This made Dow the largest chemical company in the world. Yet despite buying Union Carbide's assets - and its liabilities - Dow has refused to accept moral responsibility for the actions of Union Carbide in Bhopal, or even to be accountable for the actions of the company it took over.

Dow refuses to accept responsibility for the on-going health problems in Bhopal. Nor has it attempted to deal with the large stockpiles of dangerous poisons left behind by Union Carbide or the toxic legacy that is still ruining people's lives. Yet it nevertheless claims that it has "done what it needs to do to pursue the correct environment, health and safety programs."

This incredible claim clearly reflects the double standards that many corporations operate under. For example, Former Attorney to the US Senate, Curtis Moore, stated: "A Bhopal type event in the United States... would have been cleaned up by now, no question about it. If the company didn't want to clean it up then the government would have done it, and given the bill for three times the cost of clean-up to the company. Every corporate executive in the USA knows that those are the sorts of liability that are attached to releasing chemical poisons."

The ongoing Bhopal disaster shows how important it is that corporations across all industrial sectors guarantee paramount safety standards wherever they operate in the world. Greenpeace - which has been working with Bhopal survivor groups is campaigning to ensure that corporations are held liable for their actions, for both compensation to victims of pollution and for environmental clean-up. We believe that all human beings around the world have the right to live in a clean, safe and healthy environment.

GLOBALIZATION AND ENVIRONMENTAL CRIME

Their power is huge, and their rights typically supercede the rights of individuals in society. Multinational corporations intentionally release 3.5 billion pounds of industrial toxins, and 1 to 2 billion pounds of pesticides every year in the United States alone. Disease to children associated with exposure to environmental chemicals costs society between $48 billion and $64 billion per year.

Every year preventable exposures to toxins sicken and kill thousands of people in the United States and the world. Per Philip Landrigan, chairman of community medicine at the Mount Sinai School of Medicine in New York City, "these hazards must be confronted. They cannot be wished away. Reduction of exposures to chemical toxins will prevent thousands of deaths and will improve the quality of hundreds of thousands of lives". Indeed, environmental crimes cost huge amounts in terms of life and property. But unlike other kinds of crime, "environmental crime harms society as a whole".

After the Civil War, railroads became the first powerful industry in the United States. With the help of the young lawyer Abraham Lincoln, the railroads successfully argued that the Fourteenth Amendment (the former slaves' equal protection clause) could serve as a shield to avoid paying taxes as a corporation. In doing so, the industry became in essence an "artificial" person, replete with the same benefits as a "natural" person.

Furthermore, in addition to tax and other more obvious benefits, "it was held that a corporation had no 'mind' and therefore could not be prosecuted for willful intent, and further, that it had no 'body' and could not be subjected to imprisonment". By the end of 19th century, corporations had transformed the law and evolved into powerful entities, in essence changing the balance of power from the individual person to the corporation. "So rather than our defining them, they became the authority to define us".

As standardization and mass production began to re-organize work, there occurred a deterioration in working conditions. "The massive industrialization that transformed the cities of the nation created a heightened awareness of the dangers of the new society that was increasingly seen as threatening and dangerous".

By the 1920's, "the glimmerings of a massive crisis for industry could be discerned by the fact that workers themselves were beginning to bring cases of disease to the courts in the form of liability suits" which soon "reached epidemic proportions". The National Safety Council (a private organization) produced an independent report which revealed that safety standards were rarely met and predisposed workers "in a high degree" to sickness.

Ultimately, industry suppressed the report. "The final resolution of this confrontation reflects the enormous influence that private industry had on ostensibly objective scientific research as early as the 1930's". The Stock Market Crash and Great Depression were catalysts for discussion on social responsibility and industrial disease, which emerged "as a highly politicized issue; for upon this seemingly academic debate would hinge the economic survival of families". As greater numbers of workers turned to the courts for redress, their individual suffering evolved into a national crisis. Courts, labor unions, and even the insurance industry became embroiled in the battle.

A mutual agreement to establish a workers' compensation system whereby workers gave up their right to civil remedy in exchange for no fault compensation became established. This system "further undermined popular understanding of workplace injuries as a responsibility of employers by establishing a no-fault system, in which culpability for an accident was no longer an issue".

Rather than looking at the specific actors and acts as they were related to industrial injury and death (and thus enhancing the ability to remedy such actions), attention shifted, allowing corporations with bad records to escape scrutiny and accountability on a massive scale. In addition, the new system removed "the issue of accidents from the courts and therefore from public view". Nevertheless, corporations began looking for more lucrative places to do business – where cheap labor was rife, environmental and labor laws were non-existent, or where communities did not have the collective strength to fight powerful polluters.

Erich Goode describes corporate crime whereby executives and officers engage in illegal actions intend "to further the interests of that corporation" – actions which thereby become "actions taken on *behalf* of the corporation". Because individuals in an organization act within a corporate social structure, often the organization and/or industry climate plays a role in whether an actor commits a crime on behalf of the organization. But if corporate culture secretly rewards such behavior, is that behavior actually deviant? Goode posits that corporate crime is a form of deviant behavior when actions include the harm of people, sanctions against the actor and/or company, and the discrediting of the corporate actor. In sum, corporate crime is "an important form of organizational deviance".

Justification of Corporate Crime

Some scholars posit that deliberate decision-making is the cause of corporate crime and deviance. "Corporate crime and violence are often the result of calculated, rational discussions made by people who clearly would be deterred by stronger penalties and enforcement". Corporate norms, institutional climate, social control, and the perceived cost/ benefits of various solutions can be viewed as contributory elements. Of note, "the most striking aspect of corporate transgression is that it is committed not by dangerous, criminally-oriented mavericks but by eminent members of the business community who break the rules ostensibly in the interests of their companies and their own interests". Whether individual choice or corporate pressure (or both), it is important that research further examine social control from within the organization, which leads to corporate deviance in the form of environmental crime.

Factors of Environmental Crime

If a corporate actor's deviant acts are "successful" (escapes detection and/or punishment), "this adaptation may become normative for others in a similar social context". People do not ordinarily engage in deviant and harmful conduct, however, "until they have justified to themselves the rightness of their actions" in a process of moral justification, whereby "detrimental conduct is made personally and socially acceptable by portraying it in the service of valued social or moral purposes". Rationalization has also been identified as a license for departure from social rules "as actors convince themselves that in their particular circumstances, an exception is acceptable".

Societal factors also create a climate favorable for international environmental crime. Factors such as differential costs or values, enforcement and regulatory failure, and trends toward trade liberalization and deregulation create a power differential favorable to corporate polluters. As well, the growing involvement of countries in multilateral environmental agreements has contributed to the increasing rates of international environmental crime.

International environmental crime is defined as "the deliberate evasion of environmental laws and regulations by individuals and companies in the pursuit of personal financial benefit, where the impacts are transboundary or global". It is estimated that the economic cost of international environmental crime is between $20 and $40 billion a year. Furthermore, it is highly likely that international environmental crime will "continue to expand in the coming decades". As seen during the Industrialization period in the U.S., Third World countries on the path toward industrialization are beginning to witness a rise in similar industrial health issues of illness, injury, and death.

Furthermore, "corporate crime has become more institutionalized, more legitimate, and more intense with the advent of globalization". The sophistication of corporate polluters' strategies have thus evolved to a new standard, far exceeding the ability of individuals and poorer nations to respond effectively. Corporate crime can be viewed as the "flipside of economic growth," whereby globalization contributes to "global anomie, dysnomie and ultimately economic misconduct by activating the potential of crime through opportunity, motive and weakened social controls".

Clearly, an economic advantage exists when corporations move from a First World country to a Third World country, as the cost of labor is cheaper, laws are less stringent and regulated erratically, government corruption is perhaps rampant, and the economic differential between the powerful and the poor in society are greater. As laws in the U.S. become more stringent,

American corporations are forced to comply at home. However, "amid promises of cleaning up their act in the Western countries, corporations are rapidly shifting their dirty work to the South where resistance is either weaker or less visible". Large populations "have become more vulnerable to exploitation, criminal victimization, and recruitment in illicit enterprises or rebel and fundamentalists groups," which make them prime targets for exploitative multi-national corporations with a design to pollute the environment.

Investigating and prosecuting corporate environmental crime in developing countries is extremely challenging and "normative standards and control mechanisms are weak or completely absent exactly where they are needed the most". Third World laws are often no match for multinationals experienced in public relations, political maneuvering and successful exploitation of resources. "Even where environmental laws exist, local police forces are often uneducated about environmental concerns or influenced by corrupt officials" (Schmidt, 2004: A98). Often corporate polluters will incorporate the cost of violation penalties into the cost of doing business, rather than correct the problem.

Further, financial aid to poor countries has declined and "whatever assistance is offered comes with strings attached, including the reduction of state intervention...these policies further undercut food security, cause poverty and increase economic and power asymmetries" making these populations yet more vulnerable to polluters.

In the pursuit of a "global economy," countries have been persuaded or forced to sign agreements which include stipulations such as reduction of governmental intervention in the regulation of business (regardless of any detrimental effect or ill-fit of such a model for that particular country). There is often a negative effect of imposed western agendas through the IMF, World Bank, European Union, etc., who press debt-ridden countries to seek additional loans (to pay off old ones) from banks in industrialized nations. Often attached to the loan are stipulations that Structural Adjustment Programs (SAPs) be introduced which favor privatization and foreign investment, often at great societal and environmental cost to the country.

American officials have encouraged expansion of trade, and exportation of waste to developing countries, which are "vastly underpolluted" per one government official. The promises of globalization have indeed fallen short; an abrupt and dramatic shift in political and economic symmetry is the result, yet further opening the floodgates of poor Third World countries to multinational corporations who make it standard practice to pollute at any cost.

Often in developing countries, corporations can run amuck with few restrictions to regulate environmental contamination and the poisoning of people. Furthermore, "under Chapter 11 of NAFTA, corporations can sue nation states whose laws protecting their people and the environment violate corporate free trade rights". This clause has been written for and utilized to benefit American corporations in recent years. For example, Bechtel sued the Bolivian government in 2003 for violating the company's free trade rights to privatize water in Cochabamba, Bolivia, despite the violent protest of local citizens to maintain a clean, safe and affordable public water source.

The economically poor Bolivian government can hardly hold its own against the huge multinational conglomerate Bechtel. Situations such as these force financially dependant countries to accept whatever terms such corporations deem suitable to their own needs, including removal of the country's own natural resources, cavalier environmental dumping and the poisoning of its citizens.

In 1970 when the Clean Air Act became law, industrial polluters found that they could no longer freely contaminate the air without consequences. "The corporate response...was to deny problems, deny responsibility, resist controls and [threaten] to relocate production if hostile measures were implemented". Later other federal environmental laws were added, including the Clean Water Act, Resources Conservation and Recovery Act (RCRA) and Superfund Amendments Reauthorization Act of 1986 (SARA), partly as a result of a widespread environmental crisis topped by several catastrophic environmental disasters in American residential communities. Industry found that they had to either comply with the laws (which might necessitate expensive capital improvements) or find ways to escape liability. Many corporations developed a series of tactics to avoid liability, and such tactics quickly became popular in industrial circles.

The growing list of tactics used by corporations to manipulate public perception regarding deviant corporate practices include (but are not limited to), falsification of data; creation of front groups to convince the public that the products are safe and society needs them; the discrediting of independent scientists; manipulation of research results and data; co-optation of researchers to control research agenda and outcome; attribution of blame; co-optation of local oppositional leaders; moral justification; euphemistic labeling; disregarding and/or distorting the consequences; diffusion of responsibility; positioning of the corporation as a faultless victim; advantageous comparison; displacement of responsibility; and dehumanization.

When people engage in harmful corporate activity for personal gain or social inducements, they may also attempt to minimize the harm caused. "In addition to selective inattention and cognitive distortion of effects, the misrepresentation may involve active efforts to discredit evidence of the harm that is caused". Other tactics may include the funding of scientific studies and control of outcome; hiring of former industry regulators; carefully-framed public relations campaigns; donations to local groups in and around contaminated communities in an effort to buy goodwill; community beautification projects; the arrangement of industry awards for the polluting company; manipulation of data through mathematical and other methods; community "education campaigns"; and blaming the victims.

Strategies of corporations confronted with a negative public opinion are widely known and widely practiced within industry. Such strategies include changing public perception (rather than performance) through "education" and public relations campaigns, framing of arguments, and sanitized language. "The strategy of delivering carefully prepared responses to environmental concern is generally designed to confuse the argument, dissipate protest and so postpone action". Additionally, if pollution is proven to be intentional, "cleanup costs would not be covered by insurance, and polluters would be liable to civil suits by those they injured". Euphemistic labeling is also used as another tool to cover up reprehensible activities or confer a respectable status upon the company. "Through sanitized and convoluted verbiage, destructive conduct is made benign and those who engage in it are relieved a sense of personal agency".

When confronted with heavy industrial contamination in residential communities and with a company who has no intention of addressing the contamination other than enlisting the assistance of public relations experts, community members must often engage in direct confrontation and protest. Those who have never had a political interest are often forced into direct response to what they perceive as an intolerable situation. An organized interest will evolve, and develop into what is called "grassroots" activism. "Grassroots environmentalists...are usually engaged at the local level in a power struggle with one corporation or another, directly challenging the corporation's right to poison the local environment". Activists will often link with experienced organizers to develop a sophisticated network, and to confront the corporate polluter and attempt to instill accountability and remedy.

Organizers encourage people in contaminated communities to recognize that their enemy is...the corporations who profit from [the production of toxins] and government agencies who fail to protect people from them. Without a particular political agenda, their local, place-based analysis brings to light concrete linkages between community, environmental and labour concerns. The majority of communities suffering the effects of deviant environmental corporate practices are predominantly comprised of the poor, the elderly, and people of color. These communities are often targeted because they are often unable to fight back. By the 1990's organizations in Louisiana and around the country were documenting the fact that a disproportionate number of chemical plants were being placed in minority communities. Greenpeace found that the percentage of vinyl chloride...plants situated in minority communities in Louisiana was '237 percent greater than the national average.'

"Holding corporations accountable for their crimes will involve the solidarity of victimized communities and their supporters worldwide". There is no packaged formula to confront corporate polluters who knowingly violate laws and standards by choice. Careful research, the sharing of information between groups struggling to confront industry at the grassroots level, support from outsiders to grassroots activists, the reigning in of corporate power, the linking of grassroots activist groups nationally and internationally, the careful review of international laws and standards, and a review of the stipulations associated with trade agreements will certainly be a solid step toward remedy.

As well, exposing public relations tactics as such will help isolate egregious polluters from more scrupulous industrialists. Additionally, the environmental movement has been "caught up in endless unsuccessful attempts to regulate corporate behavior around the edges, never tackling the central issue, which is the illegitimacy of corporate power"

2

Economic and Organised Crime

Economic crime is changing and increasing has led to frequent calls for Justice systems around the world to respond with dramatic new investigatory and prosecutorial powers. For example, there have been calls for increased freedom for police in conducting uncover operations, measures to trace and seize the proceeds of crime and laws to make membership in a criminal "organization" a crime per se.

On the surface, crimes motivated by profit are different from those driven by passion, peer pressure or simple perversity of human nature. The lure of profit is presumed "rational" and profit-driven events therefore seem predictable. That also seems to suggest at least part of the appropriate response—if there is financial motive, it can be removed; and if there is monetary damage, it can be compensated. This assumes that the offender is a cost-benefit calculator who weighs the probable consequences against the possible gain. In that way, the profit-driven criminal can be assumed to behave in a way analogous to the profit-maximizing corporation.

A legitimate corporation first seeks survival. Then it may seek to satisfy the shorter term financial goals of its senior employees as well as its investors, something distinct from the long-term profit goals of the corporate per se. Then perhaps it might seek to expand its sphere of indirect commercial influence, engage in political lobbying or raise corporate prestige through community and cultural affairs. These cannot be simply lumped into an attempt to maximize corporate "goodwill." To the extent that a steady stream of profit is necessary to achieve most or all of these results, it will not necessarily correspond to a theoretical maximum - some notion of a satisfactory profit rate will suffice. Therefore, the corporation's profit goals are more likely to be expressed in terms, not of maximizing the difference between cost and revenue in the short run, but of generating the stream of net revenues to permit survival, expansion and development over the long run.

Indeed, if a legitimate firm were really a simple profit maximizer, there would be no reason for it to stay legitimate - yet obviously only a small percentage of entrepreneurs and corporations cross the line. Much the same applies to a criminal "firm." Certainly profit is part of the calculation. But the notion that everything is subordinated to the hunt for a maximum of profit is very misleading. Even in profit-driven crimes, many other factors can be at play to determine actions - jealousy, ego enhancement, the search for prestige among peers, or the desire for increased status which in turn might be enhanced more by displays of generosity than cold-blooded pursuit of more wealth. Thus, a criminal firm, too, operates within a social matrix in which all manner of other, not strictly economic, criteria figure in its decision rules.

Impact of Globalization

Globalization is the modern term for a process that began at least as far back as the time of Marco Polo, if not before, by which information about trade and financial opportunities spreads across national and/or regional frontiers, and goods and money shortly follow. Globalization is a factor in crime since criminal entrepreneurs, like legitimate business people, expand their geo-political horizons to conform to the opportunities resulting from greater ease of long-distance communication and travel. This is not to suggest that the broad geo-economic context in which crime occurs is no different today than, say, at the end of the Second World War. There are real differences.

One is scale - more people, more goods and more income. This, though, is a long-term trend. Even rapid acceleration of growth rates dates at least back to the early 19th century. It is hard to see how it translates into a qualitative change in the current criminal threat. Certainly there is more economic crime today, but there is also much more legal economic activity, and there is no proof the first is growing faster than the second. A second difference is complexity of economic interrelations - the fact that more and more economic activity takes place in a market-driven context. But this, too, is a longterm historical trend, it is just as true inside countries as well as outside, and it therefore has only an indirect link at best to "globalization," whatever that may mean.

A third factor frequently cited as part of the trend to "globalization" is the seemingly remarkable propensity for people today to move across borders. What seems to be forgotten is that the passport was not generalized until after the First World War. Until then the main impediment to travel was the likelihood of being robbed and murdered, together with the fact that most people had neither the inclination nor the income to try. Those who utter platitudes about today's borderless world should try to cross the US-Mexico frontier during a trade dispute or drug alert. The frequently cited example of the EC is remarkable precisely because it is so exceptional.

Furthermore, there is a prevalent idea that a world in which people are increasingly free to travel (relative to the situation 50 years ago, but not to previous centuries) is also a world in which it is easier for serious economic criminals to escape. Each octogenarian Nazi war criminal unearthed serves to belie this simplistic belief. Similarly, the recent tendency of the US government to authorize transnational kidnapping to bring (mainly drug) offenders to American justice suggests that secure places to hide are getting harder to find. Counterfeit is now considerably harder to use. In the past, it relied on information asymmetries (e.g. the fact that births and deaths might not correlate and drivers' license applications were not matched with social security numbers). But today technology has considerably reduced those information asymmetries. It has made crime more difficult, not less. Thus, the real issue is not a (non-existent) borderless world or the (genuine) growing ease of international travel, but the ability to enforce law across borders - which is scarcely a new problem.

Modern Information Technology

Modern communications and transportation technology have a major impact on economic exchanges (illegal as well as legal). But the effects of electronic communication and mass-based, cheap and rapid international transport of goods and people today are, quite likely, no greater and arguably significantly smaller than the effects of the railway, steamship and telegraph in the first half of the19th century. The extent of change brought about by electronic funds transfers, for example, can be put into perspective with a simple comparison. On the one side, calculate the time required to send a bill of exchange or purse of silver coin by sailing ship across the Atlantic in the period up to the early 1800s, and compare it to the time required to make a telegraphic transfer once the first trans-oceanic line was laid by the mid-1800s.

Then calculate the relative time saving from the switch from telegraphic (electrical) funds transfer to electronic funds transfer in the latter half of the 1900s. In the first case the difference was truly revolutionary; it is not in the second. It is important to distinguish new crime from new methods. To take one common case, frequently "computer crime" is singled out as a prime new area of concern. But it really boils down to a series of traditional criminal acts (e.g. extortion, counterfeiting or fraud) that happen today to be assisted by the use of computers. The crimes remain the same. The only difference is the technique used to commit them, and the ability to do them from much further away than was commonly the case.

Furthermore, even these electronic changes in technique noticeable today can be exaggerated compared to the effects of their analogues a century and a half back. The advent of the telegraph not only permitted the creation of a genuine world market in which all traders had access to the same price information at almost the same time, therefore transcending the constraints of location, but it also gave criminals a fancy new tool. Brokers lost little time in using the fast access to data to trade on privileged and insider information; scam artists and commodity traders alike used it to rig markets. From the start, too, telegraph companies worried about hackers and about the security for telegraphic funds transfers in a manner little different in its essentials than the concerns about Internet commerce and finance today. This is not to say the techniques are without importance.

Clearly, devices like callforwarding can be used to confuse potential targets in fraud operations. New electronic technologies, too, permit multiple iterations of certain acts that, in the past would have been extremely time consuming, perhaps, impossible. Electronic technologies have certainly been important recently in counterfeiting of cheques, credit cards, securities and currency. But all they represent is the latest stage in an ongoing struggle between issuers of financial instruments and would-be fraudsters that dates way back to the onset of modern credit instruments. Furthermore, three other factors must be taken into account.

One is that the bulk of criminals are scarcely techno-wizards. Most crimes are committed using old-fashioned techniques. Even with money laundering, not a single case of the use of e-money for laundering has been unearthed, while there is ample evidence criminals still cart large amounts of currency notes across borders.

Second, on the other side, there seems not nearly so much hesitation by the state to use the new technologies for information exchange and surveillance. Therefore, it is arguable that the new technologies contribute more to detection and resolution than to commission of crimes.

Third, and ironically, while the alarmist scenario speaks of technology increasing the opportunities for traditional crime groups by moving into white-collar offences, the truth has seemed to be the opposite - technological changes have had a greater tendency to render larger organizations uncompetitive and unnecessary. Incidentally, this democratization of criminal opportunities argues further for moving the locus of attention away from the offender to the offence.

Profit-Driven Crime

Traditionally, understanding profit-driven crime has been hampered by weaknesses in the existing paradigms. Not only has the primary concern of criminology always been who offenders are, but the criminal justice system obviously focuses on prosecution of the person deemed responsible for an act, not on the act per se, the growing popularity of in rem forfeitures notwithstanding. Since offenders are all treated under a common criminal code, there is little incentive to investigate what, in terms of economic organization and economic consequences, differentiates contract killing from smuggling cigarettes, purse snatching from peddling child pornography, cracking a safe from pulling off a telemarketing scam. From this perspective, the main distinction between, for example, breaking-and-entry and insider trading is the social class and, presumably, the potential for rehabilitation, of the offender. Yet it is possible to classify profit-motivated crimes into several distinct economic categories without getting bogged down into disputations about the social origins of the offender.

Predatory Offences

First are crimes of a predatory nature - everything from purse snatching to ransom kidnapping to extortion. Though there may be many complexities (derived, for example, from technological change) in how predatory offences are conducted, their essence is simple and direct.

A predatory crime:

- involves redistribution of existing wealth from one party to another;
- leads to bilateral transfers involving victim and perpetrator. Though others may be involved in subsequent actions involving the target property, the basic act remains a bilateral transfer;
- implies transfers that are also involuntary, generally using force or its threat, though guile may sometimes suffice;

— creates readily identifiable victims (individuals, institutions or corporations);

— generates losses by victims which are simple to determine - the robbed or defrauded person or institution or corporation can point to specific money and property;

— invokes an unambiguous morality - someone has been wronged by someone else; and,

— calls for simple policy responses - over and above direct punishment of the guilty, restitution should be made to the victim of his or her property.

Historically, the justice system and law enforcement apparatus were designed to deal primarily with the predatory form of profit-driven crime, where there was a clear victim, readily identifiable property that had been misappropriated, and a straightforward resolution based on simple moral principles that enjoyed a broad social consensus. Law enforcement remains heavily biased toward seeing crime as essentially a predatory phenomenon (simply put, a "cops and robbers" worldview). Yet other forms of profit-driven crimes are quite different in nature and in their social and economic impact. In these other categories, the harm is harder to assess, the identity or even the existence of victims more problematic, and the borderline between the responsibilities of economic regulator and police no longer so clear.

Market-based Offences

The second category consists of market-based (or enterprise) crimes. Although there are isolated incidents of bans on trafficking in occasional goods and services dating back centuries, for the most part these are relatively new. Most of what are today regarded as market-based offences date from decisions (if they really merit the term) in the early part of the 20th century to criminalize personal vice - the consumption of drugs or alcohol, gambling, prostitution, etc. A market-based crime:

— involves the production and/or distribution of new goods and services that happen to be illegal by their very nature;

— leads to exchanges that are multilateral involving (among others) producers, distributors, retailers and money managers on the supply side and consumers on the demand side, much like legitimate market transactions;

— generates transfers that are voluntary;

— makes it difficult to define a "victim", unless it is some abstract construct like "society as a whole";

— generates income earned by the supplier and expenditure by the consumer rather than losses;

— invokes an ambiguous morality that can also be subject to sudden and radical change; and,

— creates socially divisive debate as to what the appropriate policy response should be.

This last constitutes a very important distinction between predatory and market-based offences. There is not now, nor in the foreseeable future is there likely to be, a credible lobby, including veteran police officers, that calls for the legalization of armed robbery. Nor should it ever be presumed that because of the lack of formal record keeping or simplicity of institutional arrangements, markets in illegal goods and services are radically different from legal ones, or unsophisticated.

There are complex arms-length commercial interactions between various levels on the supply side, and different types of debit and credit relations between suppliers and customers all along the chain. Drugs, arms, gold and a host of other commodities reveal those characteristics. Market-based offences can be further subdivided into three subsets:

1. those encouraged by regulatory restrictions;
2. those driven by taxation;
3. those that result from prohibition.

In the first case, restrictions on total amount permitted, or administrative rules dictating allocation, cause the emergence of a parallel market in which the "regulated commodity" is available at a higher price than on the legal-but-controlled market. That is the case, for example, with black market steroids diverted from the legal pharmaceutical distribution system, and, to some degree, with the illegal trade in such things as wildlife or ivory.

In the second case, goods subject to excise, sin or luxury taxes may be available on the parallel market at a lower price than on the legal one, the difference being largely (though not exclusively) a function of evaded tax. These can be termed "relative contraband".

In the third case, where the goods or services are "absolute contraband", there is no corresponding legal price - the illegal market stands alone. There are also certain services that could fall into any of the three subcategories, depending on the legal context. Underground gambling, for example, is absolute contraband in areas that ban it completely. It is, however, relative contraband where placing bets is permitted in outlets that pay heavy taxes. And it is a regulated service subject to diversion into a parallel market if the law permits only state-owned or statelicensed establishments to offer citizens the right to ruin themselves financially in the long run in exchange for an adrenaline rush in the short.

Market-based Offences: A Typology

Type	Created by	Price Relationship
Regulated commodity	Restriction	Illegal higher than legal
Relative contraband	Taxation	Illegal lower than legal
Absolute contraband	Prohibition	No legal reference point

These differences are important, both for the kinds of policy options that might be called for, and for methods of evaluating success or failure of such policies. For example, a policy that is successful against the first type of good or service will work by restricting the flow onto the parallel market and thereby increase the spread between legal and illegal prices. A policy successful against the second will increase the supply on the legal market relative to the illegal and therefore reduce the spread. A policy successful against the third cannot be evaluated by reference to price alone. With no legal source or substitute, price hikes as a result of increased enforcement may do more to increase the amount of income spent on the banned item than to reduce the quantity consumed.

Nonetheless, all three types fall into the general category of market-based crimes, and are therefore fundamentally different from profit-driven crimes of a predatory nature. To be sure, in practice the contrast between predatory and market-based offences at times seems murky. Some predatory crimes, for example, require market-based ones to dispose of the merchandise or launder the proceeds. Nevertheless, complex though such transactions might be, they are secondary. The primary act generating the money is unambiguously predatory since it involves an involuntary transfer of existing wealth.

Similarly, some market-based offences are committed in an environment punctuated by force or fraud. Occasionally, drug dealers settle accounts at gunpoint and adulterate their merchandise before sale to final customers.

The basic act, however, is usually a consensual contract between the supplier of and customer for new goods and services. And therein lies the problem. It takes two to commit a market-based offence - there can be no market unless there is a supply side and a demand side. Why, then, should suppliers be singled out for special treatment? That is the usual approach taken today, but it has no basis in morality and logic. With predatory offences, the "supplier", so to speak, takes the initiative against an unwilling victim. However, an illegal market is almost always demand driven. The customer is, in that sense, more guilty than the supplier - though the criminal justice system works on precisely the opposite assumption.

Commercial Offences

A third, somewhat messier category might be called commercial crimes (with a more restricted meaning than that usually ascribed to the term by police forces with "commercial crime" divisions). These crimes are committed by otherwise legitimate entrepreneurs, investors and corporations. Commercial crimes, too, can be subdivided, into crimes of production and crimes of distribution. In the first, an entrepreneur or executive might engage in illegal dumping of toxic waste to avoid the costs of proper disposal, or violate safety standards to save money on equipment. These are crimes whose basic intent is to reduce costs. In the second, the responsible party might falsify data on a contract to pad the bill, or con customers with worthless product guarantees. These are crimes whose basic intent is to increase revenues. Although the range is wide, commercial crimes have certain common characteristics.

A commercial crime:

— involves the production of goods and services which are inherently legal, but whose methods of production and/or distribution are illegal;

- — creates exchanges within a normal business setting that are multilateral;
- — produces exchanges that are also superficially voluntary with an involuntary hidden aspect;
- — leads to clear victims by virtue of involving fraud against workers, suppliers, customers or, in such things as environmental offences, against the public as a whole;
- — generates income earned but unmerited by virtue of the illegal methods;
- — invokes, in principle, unambiguous morality, since fraud is involved; and,
- — calls for punishment that logically should involve restitution for misappropriated or damaged property.

Once again, what is clear in theory is not necessarily so in practice. In many cases, it is difficult to be sure where sharp business practice ends and fraud begins. At what point does a high-pressure sales tactic become a confidence trick? At what point does effective advertising become deliberately deceptive? Once the border between pure information and advertising is crossed, the distinction between legitimate advertising and marketing fraud becomes quite problematic.

The result of such ambiguities is that, although some commercial offences may be clear cut enough for traditional criminal prosecution, others may not. The civil courts often seem the most logical way to resolve many disputes that fall into this category. Yet the tendency has been toward criminalization of actions formerly regarded as regulatory problems or issues to be settled by civil litigation. This is particularly evident with some kinds of securities offences. If a case involves falsifying a prospectus with completed fabricated sales figures or seeding an ore sample prior to announcing an issue of junior gold mine shares, there is clear fraud involved. However, in securities dealing, things are rarely so clear. Most prospectuses are designed to titillate rather than inform. Furthermore, one other major type of security offence, that of insider trading, criminalized in many Western countries following US lead in the 1980s, raises some particularly serious questions.

Insider trading was first conceived as an offence involving officers of corporations about to merge who took advantage of that knowledge to speculate to their own profit. It was then extended beyond its original mandate to embrace employees of law firms planning mergers and acquisitions, merchant banks involved in financing them, reporters for financial newspapers who got leaks, and even janitors who picked up discarded memos in the trash. If any of them used such information to anticipate stock price movements for their own gain, they were guilty of insider trading. It thus became unclear just where the frontiers between "inside information" and the normal search by potential investors for data on which to base a stock purchase really fell. Simultaneously, the core issue ceased to be breach-of-fiduciary-duty, and became simply obtaining profit that other people thought should rightfully be theirs, from correctly guessing stock price movements.

This tendency to seek an ever-expanding mandate while blurring the central moral issues seems a danger inherent in all attempts to use the Criminal Code for purposes of economic regulation. However, even if the offence of insider trading were redefined to accord better with its original mandate, its logic could still be open to question. Insider trading is not a predatory crime - it does not involve the forced transfer of property. It is not a marketbased crime - the object of the exchange, securities, is perfectly legal. It is not even clearly a commercial crime - to trade on privileged information to capture the profits from market movements that take place for independent reasons is quite different from rigging the market to make it move in a particular direction. With insider trading there is no victim in the classical sense. What is at issue is a quarrel between two sets of investors over distribution of profit.

In the past (and in the bulk of instances also in the present) most such disputes were (are) left to the civil courts. With stock markets as with race tracks, it should never be forgotten that insider tips can provide an advantage but, unless combined with painting the tape or doping the horse, can never guarantee the results. Thus, the three types of profit-motivated crimes vary enormously in terms not just of their economic nature and impact, but also in terms of their legal implications. With predatory crimes, the basic act and the method are both illegal. With market-based ones, the basic act is illegal while the method per se (free market exchange for fair value) is not. With commercial, the basic act is legal, while the method is not.

Social Offences

It is possible to define a fourth, more nebulous category that might be called social crime. Here the offence is the indirect consequence of otherwise legitimate action. The goods and services are inherently legal and the method of production and distribution conforms to established rules and regulations. But accidental or unpredictable "externalities" (the impact of otherwise legal acts on the broader society or environment) lead to powerful anti-social consequences.

In this category, actions have to be judged against a higher standard than that defined in the Criminal Code, and against those actions there is often no well-defined institutionalized recourse. It is a major problem determining just who the responsible party may be - corporate executives and managers in their individual capacity, or the corporation itself as a distinct entity. And if the second, just how can corporations be presumed to have a mens rea without which the application of criminal law becomes hard to justify? Furthermore, the problem of balancing, for example, the loss of employment, income and tax revenues from clamping down on cigarettes against the costs to public health from their consumption is not one with which the criminal justice system is or ever will be equipped to deal.

Crime and Economic Welfare

Some insist it is a pure negative, entailing losses to legitimate citizens plus the cost of operating the criminal justice and corrections system. Indeed, the standard procedure is to trot out reams of crime statistics lumping all offences together into some grand crime "rate" along with an estimated aggregate "loss" to society. Others argue that aggregate crime statistics are meaningless, given how widely the sub-components vary in nature and social consequence, and that certain types of crimes, judged in strictly economic terms, constitute a net benefit by generating new incomes to some citizens. The reality is that both sides are right, for they are talking about two quite different things.

Predatory crimes are crimes purely of redistribution of existing wealth. They do not generate new goods and services and therefore do not increase total income flows. Therefore, barring indirect consequences like the costs of increased security (which could be argued either way), their net effect on Gross National Product (GNP) is zero. By contrast, market-based crimes involve the production and distribution of new goods and services. Judged in strictly economic terms, they should have a positive impact on GNP. Indeed, it is now standard procedure in many countries to try to estimate the value of underground transactions in both legal and illegal goods and services, provided they are based on consensual exchanges, and to add that value to their existing national income data to get a better picture of just how "well" their economies are doing.

Commercial crimes are more complex to judge. The essence of a commercial crime is to apply illegal methods to the production and distribution of legal goods and services that would otherwise be produced by someone else using legal methods. The supplier, for example, using illegal methods to reduce costs, does not gain at the expense of other suppliers or its own workers; it is a matter purely of redistribution. There is no net effect on the economy's total production of goods and services. The gains made by the supplier at the expense of customers by cutting quality or engaging in deceptive marketing, arguably the supply of goods and services conforming to what the customer thinks he or she is getting, are actually reduced. GNP, adjusted for the quality of goods, should fall in this case.

On the other hand, it is remotely possible that, on occasion, the commission of a commercial offence helps expand the supply of goods and services. If, for example, the fraud takes the form of something like illegal disposal of hazardous wastes, with the result that costs to consumers are reduced at the expense of environmental degradation, depending on how the economic impact of the environmental damage is reckoned, the result could be an actual increase in GNP - even though sensible environmental accounting would dispel any notion this represents a net gain in economic welfare.

Similarly, with social crime, the net effect depends entirely on how the measurement is done. If national income is estimated in the normal way, by examining total value of market transactions, then any production of new goods and services unambiguously increases society's total

GNP and, with it, supposedly, economic welfare. This is all the more true because in this case, unlike that of market-based crime, the new goods and services, being legal, can be directly measured. But if national income is measured in a broader way to take account of potential depreciation of human and ecological capital, there are unintended costs which should be subtracted. It is impossible to say a priori what the net effect will be.

In all cases, when assessing the overall economic effects of criminal acts, it is necessary to distinguish between the immediate impact of the act at the micro level, and the consequences of increased expenditure for policing, prosecution and correction at the macro level. If an economy is at full employment, arguably the diversion of resources into economically unproductive activity associated with crime control is a net loss. But if the economy has unemployed resources, increased expenditure on police, prosecution and imprisonment operates just like any other net injection of funds to produce a positive multiplier effect. Indeed, one of the reasons the US economy did not stumble badly in the post-Cold War period may be that increased expenditure for the prison-industrial complex more than offset reductions in what previously went to the military-industrial complex.

Over the last decade, the military budget has fallen about US$50 billion, while the crime-control budget has risen by about $100 billion. Furthermore, that the US employs so many people in construction and maintenance of prisons, and jails such a large percentage of its economically active population, may itself account for the fact that the US unemployment rate is lower than that of other wealthy Western countries.

Secondary Crimes

The existence of such distinctions which are clear in theory, though in practice less so, has important further implications in terms of just what secondary criminal acts are involved in their commission. Take as examples violence, money laundering, tax evasion and corruption. Violence (actual or implied) plays a radically different role depending on the specific type of crime. In predatory acts, violence is a central instrument without which, in many cases, the principal act could not take place. Therefore, legitimate society is directly and deliberately threatened. By contrast, in market-based acts violence per se is not required - the transfers of money and goods are voluntary.

Violence occurs mainly in an ancillary phase, in struggles between rival suppliers over the resulting profits. It is therefore a consequence of the fact that certain goods and services are illegal rather than being inherent in the act of serving the market per se. With money laundering, there is also a difference. With all three types of crimes, it may be necessary for the criminal to, first, hide and, later, launder the money to evade detection and enjoy the proceeds. But, in the event the perpetrator is caught, the ultimate fate of the money is quite different.

With predatory offences, there are no "proceeds" in the normal sense, and therefore no presumption of forfeiture of the proceeds. Rather, there is property which must be restored to the victim. In market-based offences, there clearly are illicitly earned proceeds, with no victim to whom restitution is due. This is precisely the rationale for forfeiture laws. In commercial offences, there might be a mixture of both - there may be both fraudulently obtained property and illicit profits. Logically, they should be treated distinctly. The major types of economically motivated crime also differ according to their fiscal implications.

With predatory offences where both the basic act (misappropriation of resources) and the method by which it is carried out (force or fraud) are illegal, there are no fiscal implications. Income taxes are levied on net new income flows, not on redistribution of existing ones. Criminals who commit predatory offences should repay victims and perhaps incur fines in addition to, or instead of, prison terms. But logically they should not be expected to pay taxes on their ill-gotten gains, since the victim, to whom full restitution should be made, would end up being the one who bears the burden of the tax in the form of reduced funds available for restitution. With market-based offences, where the basic act (the sale of explicitly banned goods or services) is illegal, but the method by which it is carried out (voluntary market exchange) is not, the fiscal implications are also unambiguous.

Income taxes are legally due on the proceeds of the sale of any good or service, legal or illegal in nature. Failure to render such taxes to the fiscal authorities adds an additional layer of criminality over and above the basic offence. If the commodity sold is one that is taxed in legal markets, there may be yet another layer of fiscal offence from the failure to pay excise, sales and value-added taxes. This, of course, does not apply in the case of prohibited goods. And with regulated goods, it may or may not apply, depending on whether the goods were diverted to the black market directly from the supplier or after passing through the formal marketing chain.

With commercial offences, the situation is more complicated. Whether or not the offence has any fiscal implications depends on the precise instance and the precise type of tax. If a commodity is subject to special excise taxes, evasion in itself constitutes the market-based offence. The commodity becomes contraband, which can be seized and destroyed. However, if a commodity is subject, not to excise, but only to sales or valueadded taxes, evasion of those taxes constitutes a commercial offence. What is involved is the sale of a legal good or service by illegal means. The commodity is not in itself contraband.

Thus, three distinct fiscal offences are committed. The first, evasion of excise and other special taxes applicable to a particular commodity involves the conversion of that commodity into contraband. The fiscal offence and the market-based crime become synonymous. The second, the evasion of sales tax, involves a crime with respect to methods of production or distribution, and therefore converts a legal act into a commercial crime. The third, evasion of income tax, involves a crime with respect to the financial proceeds of acts of production or distribution. It applies mainly to market-based offences, though could be present in a commercial one as well. These considerations indicate that the three types of crime imply three different types of responsibilities for the criminal justice system with respect to the resulting proceeds.

With predatory offences, the role of the justice system is to find and restore to the proper owner misappropriated property, and nothing more. In enterprise offences, that role may consist of both finding and taxing hidden revenues, or of finding and forfeiting illegal profits - it would be illogical to attempt both. In commercial offences, that role may include all three - restoring misappropriated (fraudulently obtained) property, finding and taxing hidden revenues and/or finding and forfeiting misbegotten profits. In all cases, fines can be used as a form of punishment for the guilty party - they are quite distinct in logic and purpose from restitution, tax collection or forfeiture.

Finally comes corruption. Here, too, there is a big difference in the categories. With the possible exception of drug trafficking, no criminal act has achieved greater notoriety of late than corruption. The struggle is led by transnational corporations worried not about the morality, but about the possibility their competitors might steal the edge, or that they might have to shell out, in bribes, the money they save from evading taxes. Politicians routinely rail against it in public, though how many continue to practice it in private is anyone's guess. New governments see the fight against corruption as an excellent means of discrediting the predecessor regime and purging the public service of old regime loyalists, therefore clearing the space for patronage appointments of their own supporters.

The battle has been recently joined by international lending institutions whose main concern is that leakage of foreign exchange into the offshore retirement accounts of Third World officials will threaten the capacity of their countries to repay their foreign debts. Thus, for a variety of reasons, a powerful anti-corruption coalition has formed - albeit with corruption defined, implicitly or explicitly, as nothing more than the direct payment of bribes, likely its least insidious form. Despite the fervour, in profit-driven crime, corruption (in the limited sense of cash payment for economic advantage) is usually not a primary offence.

Predatory acts do not involve corruption per se. Nor, strictly speaking, do market-based offences, to the extent the market exchanges involve fair value and free transfer. However, corruption can occur as a secondary consequence of both when perpetrators attempt to subvert the law enforcement system to cover up their actions. Corruption may occur in certain types of commercial offences, when those seeking commercial advantage use it to bypass normal mechanisms for getting access to contracts or resources. Even then it is not likely to be the norm. Where corruption is pervasive is in social crimes, where it also takes a form particularly difficult to root out. It is no mystery why in some countries economic regulations are so spottily enforced.

Regulatory agencies quickly become captive of the industries they supposedly regulate. They become dependent on them for the primary information necessary to enforce the rules. Moreover, between regulator and regulated, there is usually a revolving door through which top personnel routinely come and go. (Perhaps the most notorious instance in recent years involved U.S. military contractors and the Pentagon.) But even more important, corporations subject to regulation are almost always heavy political donors. They, therefore, influence directly, through campaign contributions and lobbying of politicians, and indirectly, through information designed to mould public opinion, both the shape of regulatory legislation and the degree of enthusiasm with which it is enforced.

Indeed, one of the major reasons why corporations do not face more criminal sanctions is not that they respect the need for workers' safety and the integrity of the environment so scrupulously, but because of their capacity to shape the regulatory context through a form of legalized influence peddling.

Major Complications

Once profit-driven crime is viewed more through an economic than a legal lens, and the distinctions brought into sharper relief, difficulties faced by the traditional justice system in coping with it also become clearer. These are both moral and practical.

Pioneer or Profiteer

Far from the existence of absolute standards for judging deportment, what constitutes a profit-driven crime depends very much on the historical and political context. Opium trafficking, slave trading and privateering (piracy under a national flag against ships of designated enemies) were, until quite recent times, much more likely to secure for their perpetrator a knighthood than a noose. In Medieval Europe usury (which meant simply lending at interest, regardless of the rate) was more than a crime, it was a sin. Indeed, it is still is in countries where Islamic law prevails. In the old Soviet Union, two of the most serious economic crimes were "exploitation" and "speculation", hiring labour outside the household and buying with intent to resell at a profit, things that are the essence of a capitalist economy.

Today, prominent in the list of economic crimes are violations of intellectual property laws. The US pushes particularly hard for serious action by host countries to curb piracy of patents, trade marks and industrial designs - apparently forgetting the degree to which its own industrial supremacy was built in the 19th and early 20th centuries on deliberate copying of other countries' technology without accreditation or compensation. Thus, it is misleading to assume that economic activities currently seen as criminal will always be so regarded. Someone viewed as a profiteering criminal by one set of people at one point in time might be viewed by others, or even by the original set at another point in time, as a pioneering entrepreneur.

While a counter-argument can be made that civil society across the world by now has a fairly common set of standards to judge what constitutes a predatory crime, by no stretch of the imagination can the same be said for market-based and commercial ones. Take for example, one activity, a crime in some jurisdictions and legal in others, that promises to become increasingly important, and increasingly contentious, in the new century. During the last two decades, the development of immunosuppressive drugs, combined with, on the one side, an affluent and aging population in the North, and, on the other, an increased number of impoverished young people in the South, has led to an international traffic in organs for transplant.

In the North, it is strictly forbidden to buy or sell human spare parts, a position endorsed by the World Health Organization. In much of the South, even where the traffic is illegal, the law is rarely enforced. Although various bodily parts are sold - everything from bits of skin to ovaries and sperm - the most controversial involve organs from living donors that do not regenerate, particularly kidneys and corneas. Horror stories abound of hijackings of organs from drugged patients in hospitals, or the kidnapping of people by organ theft rings, but the most important source is actually voluntary.

Although there have been some recent efforts to suppress the trade, to this day in India organ brokers tour the slums to find people willing to sell vital parts to rich patients jetting in from the Gulf states, Europe or North America to private hospitals. A similar traffic exists in parts of North Africa, South East Asia and South America. There was even in Germany an entrepreneurial individual who set up an international kidney exchange; and there have been proposals for the traffic to be legalized even to the point of creating a futures market - people would be able to sell their organs now for delivery on their death to hospitals specializing in transplant surgery.

Clearly once beyond the realm of predatory crimes involving involuntary redistribution of existing wealth, rights and wrongs become fuzzy. With market-based offences that position is rendered especially awkward by the apparently willing participation of so many members of legitimate society, and by the fact that so much police activity involves interfering in decisions about personal moral choices. This, in fact, can be gauged from the internal logic of the offences. With a predatory crime, both the act and the method are illegal, and the public has a clear understanding of the nature of the offence and the harm done.

With market-based crimes, the act is illegal, though whether it should be is subject to contention, while the method is not, making the morality doubly debatable. With commercial crimes, while fraud is always deplored in principle, it is often hard to define in practice. The goods and services being transacted are inherently legal. And there is the additional complication that often the general public, not to mention juries and perhaps some law enforcement officers and judges, do not understand just what the offence really is. Moreover, with a predatory offence, the victim takes the initiative in counteraction and the victim, along with most other citizens, can be expected to cooperate fully with the police.

In a market-based offence, the police take the initiative, and the public response might be indifferent or even hostile. There is an expectation that each and every predatory offence will be investigated. In market-based crimes, since those who buy are really as guilty as those who sell, there are so many "guilty" parties that the police are necessarily selective about whom to target. Police actions may catch only the most visible and vulnerable who are also the most easily replaced component of the trafficking networks, leaving the illicit market operating largely unscathed.

Indeed, there is a sense in which police action is actually counterproductive. With a predatory crime, a police crackdown can be expected to reduce the number of perpetrators and the number of instances of the offence. With a market-based crime, the opposite is true. The response of illegal markets to intensified police action is to increase, not decrease, the number of participants and the number of transactions - there are more intermediaries, each dealing in smaller amounts of merchandise. Therefore, ironically, what would be taken in predatory offences as a sign of a law enforcement crisis, more offenders and more illegal actions, in market-based offences can be taken as a sign of success. By virtue of confounding and compounding the two, crime data become easy to misinterpret. That can lead to serious mistakes in policy and in resource allocation.

Modern Market-based Offences

Even within North America, the creation of modern market-based offences was scarcely a matter free of controversy. During the 19th century, most governments accepted the sensible notion that personal vice was the business only of the person with the vice, thereby excluding from the criminal code a whole host of offences that would later be incubators of modern "organized" crime. Then, in the early 20th century, North America was swept by a wave of Puritanism made up of several components: the temperance movement; a resurgence of smalltown "decent" values against big-city cosmopolitan decadence; Anglo-Saxon racism (blacks were associated with cocaine, Mexicans and "Hindoos" with cannabis, Orientals with opiates and the Irish with alcohol); and a movement to disenfranchise immigrant voters by closing the saloons which functioned as working men's political clubs.

These political currents were compounded by another. The US Constitution seemed to drastically curtail federal law enforcement powers. Policing serious predatory crime was the preserve of the states. Hence, to assert its presence, the federal authority took the form of regulation, taxation and prohibition of certain goods and services - in effect, the very creation of the category of market-based crime. Recreational drugs, prostitution, gambling and even alcohol were criminalized and federalized. Canada and much of the Western world followed the American lead, albeit usually with less intensity. There were several consequences. One was the extinction of the old red light districts - henceforth, the business of supplying and demanding personal vice ceased to respect intra-urban frontiers.

Indeed, the criminalization of supply meant that criminal entrepreneurs had to deliberately mix with polite society to lower their profile. A second was the creation of a class of wealthy criminals who could use the profits resulting from criminalization of personal vice to penetrate legitimate parts of the economy. A third was the emergence of the view that "organized crime" in the vice trade was the result of an alien conspiracy, a view that continues to misinform debate to this day. Although the distinction between predatory, market-based and commercial crime should be offender-neutral, there is a stereotype with respect to the nature of the offender population associated with each type. With predatory crime, the popular presumption is that most offences are the work of individuals or gangs which are regarded, and treated under law, as merely aggregations of individuals.

However the rise of market-based offences is inevitably associated in the public (and police) mind with "organized crime". This involves applying to a group the notion that the whole is larger than the sum of the parts, and that it should be so treated in law. This view is used to argue for harsher punishments for members of an "organized crime" group and treating membership in proscribed organizations an offence per se. At that point, association rather than action becomes the crime. Most predatory crimes are the work of individuals or ad hoc groups. Debate often confounds two quite distinct things - a criminal association and an association of criminals. Serious research has shown that, to the extent "organized crime" groups actually exist, they are not economic but political and social in nature. They form a kind of underground government to adjudicate disputes and allocate property rights. But once the rules are set, each individual member operates alone or in partnership with others, who may or not be members of the group. In the same vein, criminal markets are not based on hierarchical administrative structures operating on command to monopolize a market, but loose and ad hoc networks engaged in armslength commercial transactions.

The concept of "corporate crime" is also problematic. Is it even possible for a corporate crime to exist independently of the actions of managers and executives? How can the When it comes to actually meting out punishment, there are even more problems. For an individual, apart from fines, the criminal justice system can mete out punishment in the form of loss of liberty or, in some places, loss of life. If a corporation is deprived of loss of liberty, its charter is suspended and it is almost inevitably driven to bankruptcy, a punishment that seems to fall as much on shareholders and creditors as on the executives whose decisions were responsible.

If a corporation is deprived of life, in the sense of having its right to operate permanently repudiated, the same results clearly follow. Therefore, almost all corporate punishment takes the form of fines. But they, too, fall on the general shareholders who are powerless, and the executives who made the decisions that led to the charges are almost always indemnified.

Corporation Cooperate with Career Criminals

There is another form of crime associated with corporations that seems, on the surface, easier to handle: the case where a corporation cooperates with career criminals to advance their joint interests. Take, for example, the case of hazardous wastes. For many decades, hazardous wastes were handled just like ordinary garbage. But after major scandals in the 1970s, governments began to toughen up. For key sectors of the US economy like oil, chemicals and pharmaceuticals, this seemed like a major new regulatory burden. In fact, the regulatory structure was shaped largely to the demands of the chemical industries which were intent on two things - to make sure there would be no interruption of production, and to guarantee that their liability would be kept under control. They had help.

The trick was to turn the wastes over to licensed disposal companies which would pick up the hazardous material, charging the producing corporations much more than the fee for ordinary garbage but less than the cost of proper disposal. Then they would haul it to a landfill site where the owner would sign off on the manifest. Ultimately, the hazardous waste might be buried with regular garbage, dumped in rivers or municipal sewer systems or stacked on vacant lots or buildings. At that point, the companies producing the waste were in the clear. If the material is ever discovered it may be very difficult if not impossible to trace it back to the company of origin and the disposal company could well have gone bankrupt and the principals vanished.

Not only are the borders between crime and aggressive commerce often blurred, in some cases explicitly criminal acts and inherently legal ones are embedded together in a matrix of economic activity to such a degree that the two, while theoretically distinct, are mutually interdependent. Consider, for example, the situation in the garment trade in many urban centres in North America. Conditions reminiscent of sweatshops, long regarded as extinct in North America, reappeared in the 1980s. Typically they drew their labour from a number of sources: first time entrants into the labour force whose lack of documentary history facilitated income tax and social security charge evasion; moonlighters cheating unemployment insurance agencies; welfare recipients working for cash on the side; and illegal aliens in a state of debt-bondage to the gangs that brought them over.

Since they often lacked collateral, they could not get working funds from the formal capital market. So some turned to loan sharks recycling money from drugs, gambling or other criminal sources. If New York experience is a general guide, these small shops might also have to pay extortion money to mob-run trucking firms which signed sweetheart contracts with the owners at the truckers' expense. Thus taxes were evaded, social security charges unpaid, wages reduced, and regulations regarding working conditions brazenly ignored. What the workers lost in wages and benefits and the public sector in revenue turned up on the other side of the ledger as increased profit.

Mobsters took their share in the form of usurious interest charges, payoffs from trucking companies, kickbacks from suppliers, extortion payments from manufacturers and the occasional extra like the privilege of putting the odd associate or relative on the payroll or the profits from alien smuggling operations. Meanwhile the output (strictly legal) was sold to respectable fashion companies and big department stores which had subcontracted to the sweatshops. These legitimate firms took their share in the form of increased corporate net income as a consequence of reduced supply costs. Without their active participation, none of the explicitly illegal earnings would have been possible.

Subcontracting Responsibility

When such interrelations occur, it is often difficult for the justice system to allocate responsibility fairly. Seemingly respectable businesses maintain sufficient distance from the explicitly illegal acts from which they are clearly and consciously beneficiaries, so that they cannot be judged legally culpable. This problem has been highlighted recently by attention paid to tobacco smuggling. Canada, it appears, was shocked to discover that its major tobacco producers deliberately set up subsidiaries abroad to link up with career smugglers who would bring cigarettes back into Canada to be sold on the black market and therefore expand total tobacco sales in the face of steadily rising taxes.

Yet, since World War II cigarettes have been the most widely smuggled commodity on the planet. To this day one cigarette out of every three entering world trade disappears from sight. In total about 300 billion cigarettes per year are sold illegally. Tobacco companies ship en masse to what are euphemistically called "free-trade" centres and sell the cigarettes, often on credit, to wholesalers. They in turn hire or sell to career smugglers who move the merchandise into the target country, along with loads of whiskey, weapons, electronics and American brand-name jeans. In the countries of destination, the tobacco companies arrange for local advertising and marketing companies to handle the arrival of the merchandise in order to create an extra layer of insulation. Since any sensible smuggler wants a two-way flow of cargo, on the return leg the small boats or planes typically carry everything from cocaine to illegal immigrants. Yet to this day it is difficult to make a criminal case against the companies because they are not the ones who do the actual smuggling.

Consequences of Crime-fighting

Where a particular criminal activity can be isolated, law enforcement action may produce unexpected and costly feedbacks that might generate more crimes than they solve. These can be especially difficult to handle when they manifest themselves on an international scale as with international trade in Jamaican ganga in the 1980s. If ganga farmers were driven out of business. They would move en masse into the urban slums, swelling an already enormous problem of urban crime that threatened Jamaica's social stability as well as tourism, the most important source of legal foreign exchange. Banks and the country's exchange reserves could be depleted sufficiently to drastically reduce imports of capital equipment necessary for economic growth. Consequently, loans extended to Jamaica by both Western commercial banks and international development agencies might have gone into default, and exports from other countries to Jamaica might drop precipitously. In this not-purely-hypothetical example, what started as a resolution of a straightforward criminal justice problem developed into a full-fledged international social and economic crisis.

Diverting Attention

Not least of the problems associated with these more complex forms of profit-driven crime is the fact that treating them essentially as criminal justice issues may give a false impression of the real nature of a problem. Take the example of the recent savings and loan (S&L) bank crisis in the US where attention paid to a handful of crooks diverted attention away from the real issues - a combination of serious structural malaise and profound weaknesses in the regulatory apparatus. Historically created to use local savings to finance local housing development particularly in small-town America, during the mid-to-late 1970s the S&L associations got into trouble.

Population growth slowed, industrial depression blighted many small communities in the northeast, and interest rates began to shoot up. As other institutions began offering high and rising interest rates, the S&Ls were drained of deposits to which they had to respond by bidding up the deposit rate, while their loans, almost all in the form of long-term residential mortgages, yielded very low returns. Then came "deregulation" to complete the disaster. The US federal government decided that the solution lay in freeing the S&Ls to speculate in stocks, play the junk bond market and pump money into commercial real estate areas in the South and West.

Simultaneously, it opened the door to the takeover of the industry by individuals who turned out to include corporate raiders, real estate sharks and bank fraud artists plus a smattering of gun-runners. Every species of bank job figured in the action. There were bust-outs in which insiders would siphon the money off into phony loans to confederates, and then vanish. There were cash-for-dirt deals, land flips, linked financing schemes, nominee loans and more. These all became standard operating techniques in which turned into the most expensive financial debacle in history. The cost to the taxpayer for bailing out the system was US$325 billion.

In the wake of the collapse, public attention was riveted on high-profile prosecutions of a few individual crooked financiers and developers. It was claimed that fraud figured in nearly 75% of the hundreds of S&Ls that had failed. But the crooks who were prosecuted accounted directly for only a few tens of millions of the hundreds of billions "missing". It would have been extremely difficult to recover the rest since it was not criminality but regulatory failure which permitted the uncontrolled lending and wild speculation and the beneficiaries included legitimate borrowers, mainly real estate developers and construction tycoons, who were operating within fuzzy and selectively enforced laws. In environmental crime as well, a weak regulatory environment was the critical factor. The failure of the regulatory apparatus to keep activities under surveillance led previously legitimate business people to, first, cut the occasional corner, then, once their confidence and their greed grew, to make violations the norm rather than the exception.

Law and Order

Ideally, criminal justice should punish the perpetrator and give aid and comfort to the victim. The problem with dealing with complex profit-driven crimes is that law can be easily captured by one side in a commercial dispute and used, not for economic redress but for economic advancement. History is full of examples. In the late 20th Century intellectual property has become a critical battleground. An example is the controversy over the Napster, the program, widely diffused over the Internet, that permitted easy downloading of music or videos onto a writeable CD? On the one hand, corporations insisted this was "piracy" that would ruin their business. On the other hand, certain artists and writers used this and similar technology to bypass the usual commercial channels and deal directly with their audiences. Is the Napster an instrument of property crime against corporate intermediaries or a commercial innovation that will aid communication between artists and audiences? Is that the kind of decision the criminal justice system should be called upon to make?

Alternatives

Profit-driven crime is a serious problem but not always or solely a serious criminal justice problem. There may be other alternative approaches to increase compliance. When a profit-driven crime like armed robbery, involving redistribution of existing wealth through force (actual or implied) or deceit, takes place, the act, the cost and the victim are easy to define; and standard methods of crime control will continue to take centre stage. But when a profit-driven crime (like trafficking in some restricted good or service or manipulation of the terms and conditions under which normal goods and services are produced and sold) takes place, it usually does so as part of a complex of other, legitimate business transactions.

When a corporation peddles goods with deceptive product guarantees there may be difficult to distinguish between aggressive marketing and an explicit con-job. When criminal activity and legitimate commerce act in mutually complementary ways, it is not always easy to bring the more guilty parties to justice. When an attempt is made to "solve" such crime problems, there is danger of setting off a host of unexpected social and economic consequences that may end up being more of a problem than the designated crime. When crimes involve apparently legitimate institutions used in an apparently illegitimate way, proceeding with traditional criminal justice methods that focus on bad individuals presents the additional danger of distracting attention from deeper causes, like the need for profound structural and regulatory reform.

Because so many crimes of a market-based or commercial nature involve complex interrelations with the legitimate economy and can have profound, unintended and unexpected consequences, that it may be unwise to rely on the criminal justice system alone (or in some cases at all) for their resolution. There is serious need to consider alternative instruments. There are three distinct levels at which alternative instruments can be directed. These instruments can try to broadly prevent, by creating an environment that is not conducive to crime. In this case, they should aim to improve operating standards, levels of transparency and information flows among various institutions of the legitimate economy.

This is one of the primary roles of the regulatory system. They can try to narrowly deter by protecting a particular institution from actual incidents. In this case, they should aim to enhance operational security in the actual conduct of affairs. It is widely believed (though by no means proven) that one of the best techniques is to work with and through the private financial system. The theory is that it is easier to monitor the financial flows that result from crime than to watch out for forbidden transactions in goods and services that generate the flows. Or they can try to detect and to deal with particular offences once they have been committed. In this case, the tax system has a powerful, often underutilized, role to play.

Regulatory System

Clearly, the distinctions between these three are not absolute. Although the main function of the regulatory system, for example, will be to upgrade the overall environment by improving information flows, increasing transparency of transactions, assuring high standards of staff training, etc., it is sometimes called upon to help in the detection and prosecution of specific offences. However, expectations have to be tailored to the type of offence. With a predatory crime, there is usually little the regulatory system has to offer. Prevention is almost entirely in the hands of private-sector institutions and individuals, while solving and prosecuting such crimes is mainly the preserve of the traditional law enforcement apparatus.

With a market-based crime, for the most part the regulatory system also has little to offer. Banned goods and services are traded on markets that run parallel to, but are institutionally distinct from, those that handle the products of the legal economy. With a commercial crime, there is clear scope for the regulatory system to be of considerable use, since a commercial crime involves the provision of legal goods and services in illegal ways, at least some of which should be picked up routinely by the oversight apparatus of the regulatory system. But how that happens can be a matter of some concern. In the US case, regulatory institutions function as deputies in the detection and prosecution of specific offences and offenders.

Regulatory bodies ranging from the Securities Exchange Commission to the Post Office routinely initiate criminal investigations and bring criminal charges. Ludicrous though it seems, among the branches of the US government which have recently initiated money-laundering cases are the Departments of Agriculture and Education! But this is role for which the competence of the regulatory system is subject to much doubt. And there is a realistic fear that the more energy regulatory bodies put into attempts to enforce criminal law, the less they will have for their proper roles. This deputization process involves more than simply using criminal law enforcement for regulatory enforcement, something that is in itself of debatable merit. It involves subordinating the regulatory framework to the demands of criminal law enforcement. In that regard, working with economic regulators can scarcely be described as a bona fide alternative to the criminal justice process.

Role of the Private Financial System

Today, it is becoming increasingly popular across the world to attempt to recruit financial system employees as "front-line troops" in the "war" on money laundering. When banks and similar institutions hesitate to volunteer, requiring governments to conscript them, there are allegations that the banks are not merely "soft on crime", but actively complicit with the "enemy". They do not wish, so the accusation goes, to scare off such prime customers as criminals dripping filthy lucre. Not only is this characterization wrong - bankers generally are extremely frightened about the possibility of being caught in some big money-laundering scandal - it reflects, once more, the confusion generated by the failure to appreciate the fundamental differences between various forms of profit-driven crime.

Bank employees are expected, and are trained, to be on the alert for various forms of theft or fraud against an institution - bum checks, forged letters of credit, bogus collateral, diverted loans or counterfeit currency offered on deposit or in exchange. They also have to be on guard against insider abuse - theft or electronic-funds transfer fraud. This means that bank employees will be on the lookout for transactions resulting from predatory or commercial crimes in the normal course of business. In these cases, crime control and the financial institution's self-interest coincide.

However, with enterprise crimes, the bank is involved in quite a different way, as a depository or transferor of perfectly sound, if illegally earned, monetary instruments. Anti-money-laundering rules put the bank in a position of conflict of interest between its role as a profit-seeking institution and its new law enforcement obligations. Furthermore, unlike predatory crime directed against the financial institution, where a bad cheque or phony collateral can be subjected to appropriate scrutiny under standard banking practices, there is nothing to physically and objectively differentiate the deposits of drug dealer or used-car dealer.

On what basis can banking personnel make the required judgements as to "suspiciousness" and balance this against rights to privacy? The problem lies not just in the information requirements, and the way they have progressively escalated, but also in the very nature of the information and the bankers' role in providing it. These requirements began, first in the US and then elsewhere, with the Currency Transaction Report, a form that had to be filled out by financial institutions and their clients in the event of a large cash deposit. Although one type of information requirement seems to flow logically into the next, in fact each represents a qualitative change in the relations between "banker" and client, and between financial institutions and the law enforcement apparatus. Furthermore, these rules fly squarely in the face of modern banking trends - where more and more transactions are initiated and conducted by the client, where tabulation of deposit records is centralized, and where as much business as possible is being impersonalized. Once again, the profit-seeking (cost-reducing) interests of the financial institution put it at loggerheads with any desire to draft the financial sector into the front lines of the "war" on crime.

Not least, this is one area where technology clearly acts to facilitate criminal transactions. The advent of electronic purses with peer-to-peer transfer capacity, and the propensity for people to enter and leave countries, not with cash or travellers' cheques, but with debit cards, threatens to soon make the reporting apparatus now being carefully put in place, largely irrelevant. As well, there are serious doubts whether the crime control approaches involving the financial sector in the war against crime are worth the cost. We lack the fact-based research on how much of a threat profit-driven crimes really pose.

Role of the Fiscal System

Although also a part of the government regulatory apparatus, the fiscal system has an importance that is quite distinct. While the main role of the regulatory system is to change the general environment in which business takes place, the tax system can be used much more aggressively on a case-by-case basis. Still, there is a limit to the range of crimes against which the tax system is effective. Most commercial crimes take place in a way that embeds them in a matrix of legal economic activity, and the flows of illegally earned income will, as a rule, be subject to taxation. Tax evasion may take place, but it will be a secondary offence, and the tax code then acts to complement normal law enforcement measures.

The real power of the tax system comes in dealing with enterprise crime. All incomes earned, whether legally or illegally, are taxable. Both failure to pay and providing false information are potentially criminal offences. No peddler of child pornography is likely to either accurately report his chosen profession or declare the income from it. But it has been proven by practical experience that using the tax code is by far the most efficacious way to strip criminals of illegal income. It is better than the various provisions for criminal asset forfeiture; and it can accomplish most of what civil forfeiture procedures do without the same adverse effects on due process and civil liberties.

Civil forfeitures are particularly popular in the US, and there is talk of introducing them in Britain as well as in Ontario. That should not occur without considerable debate. Civil forfeitures involve in rem procedures and, as the US Supreme Court has ruled repeatedly, property has no civil rights. However, it is impossible to label someone's car or home or bank account the proceeds of cocaine trafficking without at the same time tainting the owner with the same accusation. Even worse, this happens routinely in procedures where the burden of proof is reversed. And in the US, there is no obligation to file criminal charges in order to seize property deemed the "proceeds-of-crime". With tax law these kinds of dangers do not exist, for there is no need to stipulate the origin of the money. Everyone must pay their income taxes, or be subject to heavy penalties and back interest, and potentially jail terms.

Most procedures, though, are civil; there is also no inherent problem of reversing the onus. The existence of unaccounted money is sufficient proof of failure to pay taxes. Furthermore, attacking illegal income through the tax code sends out an important message - everyone must pay their taxes, and if they fail to do so voluntarily, the state had tough means at its disposal to collect what is due. There have been three main objections to reliance on the tax code for such purposes. One is that it legitimizes criminal activity. This is false. The law is clear - income taxes must be paid regardless of whether the source of the funds is legal or illegal.

Furthermore, market-based crimes are driven, at least partially, by the search for profit. If the theory behind proceeds-of-crime approaches is correct, it does not matter who takes away the proceeds. The loss will remove both the motive (profit) and the means (working capital) for further crimes. Another objection is that using tax proceeds will take away only a percentage of the net income, depending on the tax bracket. This objection, too, is easy to dismiss. Add in the penalties, back interest and fines, and a great deal more than just the amount given by the tax bracket disappears.

Finally, it is argued that by using tax instead of asset-forfeiture procedures, criminals would have the right to write off expenses. To this the response is, not only is that perfectly legitimate, but it is actually an advantage. It is legitimate because the income of enterprise criminals does not come from theft or fraud. As market-based entrepreneurs enterprise criminals do have costs; and it is net income or profit that they earn which motivates them, not what they have to spend as costs. On the one hand, failure to let them deduct costs subjects them to double punishment - they would have had to lay out money to cover costs and then pay taxes on that sum to the government. On the other hand, there are major advantages to crime control from letting market-based criminal entrepreneurs write off their costs.

To do so, they must present details of their expenses - identifying the purposes for which it was spent and the beneficiaries. In effect, the criminal's profit-seeking instincts can be put to work to actually improve information on criminal markets and to map out criminal networks. These advantages, it must be stressed, derive from the use of the tax code as a tax code. There is, unfortunately, another model that is much less worthy of emulation. When the movement to ban alcohol and narcotics began in the US, it faced a Constitutional problem. Regulating such matters seemed, at first glance, beyond the powers of the federal government. Yet state-by-state variations in prohibition laws would have rendered them unworkable. However, the Supreme Court ruled that the federal government had the right to regulate anything that it had the right to tax. Hence, both early drug law and the alcohol regulations were written as revenue statutes. That meant primary responsibility for enforcement went to Treasury agents.

Unlike practice in any other country deriving its institutions from British practice where the two functions are kept firmly apart, in the US the Internal Revenue Service (IRS) became at once a police force and a tax collection agency. This blurring of the distinction between tax and criminal code enforcement took another big step forward in the 1930s when the US government used charges of income tax evasion against Chicago kingpin Al Capone. The objective in this and similar future cases was not to grab the assets of mobsters and so deter them from further sins, or to cripple their "organizations" by taking away their working capital. Rather, it was simply to find something for which they could be tossed in jail. By so doing, the IRS put matters squarely in reverse.

Instead of the threat of criminal sanction being used to enforce tax regulations, tax law was (and in the US continues to be) used to enforce the criminal code in proceedings in which the objective is to get the individual rather than his or her overdue taxes. Not only has that meant the IRS ties up resources in high-profile criminal cases instead of using them to generate tax revenues for general government purposes, it also means that using tax law to prosecute criminals indirectly for other offences sends out to the public the message that it is all right to cheat on taxes provided the money originates from legitimate sources.

Role of the Civil Courts

All of these alternatives - the regulatory system to raise operating standards, the private financial system to generate information, and the tax system to engage in search and destroy missions against the profits of crime - seem to have a role, albeit a highly qualified one, to play in enforcing criminal justice. But not only is that not their primary job, it also begs the question of whether or not many of the things against which they are to be deployed should even be considered crimes. It may be time to consider seriously decriminalization of a whole range of actions, and to therefore throw back onto the civil court system the job of dealing with any damage these actions might have done. The most obvious are securities cases where what is at issue is a quarrel between sets of investors over distribution of profit. But there are many more.

Today, for example, not only have most anti-trust procedures abandoned the criminal route, but courts are hearing more and more cases of civil torts for damages in antitrust cases. Indeed, the history of anti-trust is instructive. In the US the first anti-trust legislation, the Sherman Act, introduced a legal innovation, the implications of which are perhaps still not fully appreciated. It permitted the government to choose to proceed against corporations that engaged in conspiracies to fix prices on either civil or criminal grounds. It also permitted "victim" firms to attempt private law enforcement through civil suits. Indeed, it strongly encouraged them to do so by introducing the concept of "triple damages" that a plaintiff could obtain This not only muddied the distinction between civil and criminal proceedings, not only subcontracted law enforcement to private actors, but made the implicit judgement that bounty hunting was a stronger motive than civic responsibility in motivating people to assist in maintaining the law.

The result over the next century was a series of court cases in which contests between economic competitors were transferred from the marketplace (where, in theory, they would be conducive to increasing efficiency) to the courts (where, in practice, the main objective was not to rectify a wrong but to see what they could grab at the other party's expense). Thus, there is a right and a wrong path to returning functions to the civil courts. In the US, use of civil procedures has too often become simply a backdoor way of reducing the burden of proof in criminal cases. Apart from the litany of outrages under civil asset forfeiture, there is also the misuse of things like RICO. The very name - Racketeer Influenced and Corrupt Organizations Act - means that defendants are labelled criminals, while in the event of civil RICO cases, their prosecutors (mislabelled plaintiffs) are required to meet only a civil standard of proof.

The civil-criminal distinction is further muddied by the device, uncritically picked up from anti-trust procedures, of "triple damages". Indeed, the very term is absurd. There are either damages, used for compensation in civil suits, or there are fines, used as punishment for criminal conduct. What happens in RICO cases, as in anti-trust, is that punishment takes the form of fines disguised as damages which are then paid to the plaintiff rather than the government, unless, as so often is the case, it is the government itself that is bringing a civil suit against the plaintiffs in response to their allegedly criminal conduct! In strict theory, civil actions are supposed to involve:

1. actions by one private citizen against another;
2. seeking damages that correspond to actual acts; and
3. procedures that require only a slim margin of proof (balance of probabilities).

On the other hand, in strict theory, criminal actions are supposed to involve:

1. actions by the state or its agencies against a private citizen;
2. seeking punishment that can involve loss of life and liberty; and
3. procedures that, because of the gross imbalance of resources between the two parties and the heavy consequences, require a high standard of proof (beyond reasonable doubt).

Therefore, there is something fundamentally at variance with notions of natural justice when the state or its agencies, with the overwhelming preponderance of resources, proceed against a private citizen in actions that have punitive effects, while being required to meet only a civil standard of proof. This is particularly the case when it is realized that criminal laws are mainly legislative acts, while civil is largely judge-made. Granted, these instances are mostly in the regulatory field where punishment usually takes the form of monetary losses. But they nonetheless are punishment, not compensation.

On the other hand, it could be argued that it makes little sense to proceed with a criminal process if the potential result is not loss of life and liberty, but merely money. That is precisely why, for decades, there have been calls for the definition of a type of offence, mid-way between that which gives rise to a civil damage suit and that which can bring about a criminal prosecution with punitive consequences.

Civil Compensation and Criminal Prosecution

Two factors seem to make such a middle-ground approach desirable. One is the need to restore clarity and meaning to the distinction between civil and criminal procedures. The second is the inappropriateness of the criminal sanction in dealing with many profit-driven offences that fall into the market-based or commercial category. Traditionally, the criminal sanction worked because it targeted a special subset of actions which the public at large regarded as particularly odious. Not only was the harm clear, but the acts themselves were readily comprehensible. Hence, labelling someone a criminal was by itself the most important part of the sanction - fines or imprisonment were secondary, as much atonement as punishment. But the more the criminal sanction is used to regulate personal moral choices, the more it loses its bite.

The public at large may cease to view the "criminal" act with opprobrium. Therefore, to maintain any capacity to deter, the secondary part of the sanction must be escalated, perhaps out of all proportion to the public's perception of the severity of the actual offence. As US experience shows, sentences lengthen, the proportion of the population incarcerated grows, and prisons become less places of penance than training schools in criminal skills for a disgruntled population, disproportionately from ethnic and social minorities. If a middle ground between civil compensation and criminal prosecution is to be found in which, as in a criminal case, the state or its regulatory agencies proceed against a citizen, it requires rethinking the standard of proof.

Since the state or its agencies are seeking something beyond compensation and restitution typical in a normal civil case, it should require a higher than civil standard of proof. Since the action carries no threat of loss of life or liberty, and carries less of a stigma than a criminal process, it should not require a criminal standard of proof. Recently in the US there has been considerable debate about the consequences of civil asset forfeiture - the fact that it involves criminal accusation and criminal punishment without criminal trial.

It has often been suggested that a procedure in which a citizen could face heavy losses of property to the government on the ground that his or her property was the proceeds of crime, even though the actual property owner was not subject to criminal prosecution, demanded something better than the standard of proof used in civil suits. The suggested alternative was called "clear and convincing" proof. Thus, if the civil standard was about a 51% probability, the criminal perhaps 90%, clear and convincing proof stood at somewhere between two-thirds and three-quarters.

Furthermore, there actually are precedents. In the US, it requires something that falls between civil and criminal standards, for example, to put people in a mental institution against their will. This is precisely the kind of legal middle ground that would make sense in dealing with profit-driven offences that involve either citizens exercising moral choices of which the majority of other citizens disapprove, with no obvious damage to anyone but the person exercising the choice, or which involve complex economic relations that are beyond simply regulatory matters but are not clearly criminal. It is a standard of law, incidentally, that could be applied either to individuals or to corporations. And it would therefore also sidestep the legal and moral morass produced by the unwieldy, almost indefinable concept of "corporate crime".

3

Economic Offences in India

Since the early 90's India has witnessed a spate of major economic scams in different sectors of the economy. While millions of small investors have lost thousands of crores of rupees, the economic crimes have also caused havoc in the government managed institutions like Banks, Public Sector Under-takings, Telecom Department, Insurance Companies, etc. The magnitude and the new methods of committing economic crimes have been a cause of serious concern to the Government as well as to the people.

Economic Crimes are not a new phenom-enon in our country. Even one and a half cen-tury ago, when the Indian Penal Code was enacted, punishment was provided for Cheat-ing (Sec.420), Criminal Breach of Trust (Sec-409), Counterfeiting of Coins (Sec-232), Mak-ing and Selling of Adulterated Drugs (Sec.274 & 275), Fraudulent use of Weights and Mea-sures (Sec.265), Counterfeiting Govt. Stamps and their Sale (Sec,255 and 258), Making and Selling of Fake Goods (Sec. 481 to 489), Soon after the introduction of currency notes in our country, counterfeiting of the currency led to addition of Section 489-A and B in the Indian Penal Code in the year 1955. But what has changed in the past few decades is the magnitude and enormity of economic crimes owing to the development in technology and improved means of transport and com-munication and their use by the perpetrators of these crimes.

Magnitude of the problem Economic offenders have exploited weaknesses in almost all areas of economic activity and siphoned off thousands of crores. Their depredations will continue till the law makers plug loopholes in the affected system. But the economic offenders, as they have the knack of exploiting weaknesses in any system either traverse a new territory or subvert the system which is their specialized field. In the recent past alone, scams have cost the exchequer and millions of Indians, astronomical sums of money. Some major scams/ economic offences, which have adversely affected our national economy in the recent past are:

i) *Primary Market Frauds*: The Stock Market Scams of 90's affected millions of small investors across the country. Fly-by-night operators entered the primary markets and through Initial Public Offers (IPOs), collected hundreds of crores and vanished! The irony is that the whereabouts of over 100 companies are still not known either to SEBI or to the other investigating agencies. Even those companies, which did not vanish, used the people's money for purposes other than for which it was collected. As a result, the value of their shares plummeted resulting in heavy losses to the investors.

ii) *Secondary Market Frauds*: Insider trading has the dangerous potential of market manipulation and misuse of unpublished price sensitive information by a privileged few insiders who are in possession of such information. This kind of malpractice defeats the very principle of fair and ethical business practices, besides spelling a doom for the common and small investors. The Capital Markets in India have been victims of this malady for years and more particularly when liberalization attracted small investors to the markets. Instances of artificially jacking up prices of shares and thereby inducing gullible people to buy them are also common. People have lost heavily on account of frauds of this nature committed by unscrupulous market players.

iii) *Bank Frauds*: Economic offenders have targeted nationalized and cooperative banks and siphoned off thousands of crores by having criminal nexus with the managements of the banks. The big borrowers alone are responsible for the huge non-performing assets (Rs. 55,000 Crores in 2003) the nationalized banks are saddled with. In the 90's, unscrupulous economic offenders set up large number of UCBs (Urban Cooperative Banks) in the States of Andhra Pradesh, Maharashtra, Gujarat and collected thousands of crores by offering unsustainable high rate of interest and later siphoned off hundreds of crores either by sanctioning loans to themselves, or to the borrowers with whom they had criminal nexus. Naturally, such banks collapsed, which caused havoc to the millions of small investors.

iv) *Import /Export Frauds*: Money laundering operations by under- invoicing imports and over-invoicing of exports have been resorted to by unscrupulous traders in a big way and thereby converted their black money into white and at the same time, obtained liberal incentives given by the Government in the form of exemption of income tax on the earnings, etc. This is in addition to import/export frauds being committed based on forged and fictitious documents.

v) *Insurance Frauds*: Insurance companies have been victims of frauds perpetrated by unscrupulous claimants with or without the active connivance of insurance officials. Instances of deliberately setting fire to the insured goods, go-down, factory, making more than one claim on the basis of same accident, inflated claims supported by corrupt surveyors, are quite common.

vi) *Intellectual Property Crime/ Theft*: The Federal Bureau of Investigation (FBI) of USA has estimated that in 2003 alone, $3 billion (Rs. 13,500 Crores) worth money was lost world wide as a result of criminals swiping copyright protected digital copies of music, movies, software and games and distributing them through websites, chat rooms, mass e-mails.

According to a music and film market survey, the Indian Music and Film industry is losing around Rs. 1800 crores because of piracy, since some unscrupulous people are making copies of DVD movies and MP 3 songs illegally without obtaining permission and paying royalty to the concerned producers. Some internet sites are offering free of cost latest music from hit movies by uploading to the internet which can then be downloaded by people anywhere in the world without paying anything to the original producers of the music. Thus, the original producers of movies and songs as well as exchequer lose heavily on account of this new type of economic crime committed with the help of technology.

vii) *Non -Banking Finance Companies (NBFCs) Frauds*: NBFCs engaged in wide range of activities like hire-purchase finance, hiring finance, equipment leasing finance, loans and investments have been performing an important role in our financial sector. However, unscrupulous market players targeted NBFCs in a big way in the early 90's . As a result, the number of NBFCs which were 24,009 in 1990,rose to 55,995 in 1995 with deposits of Rs. 45,000 crores. By offering very high rate of interests and commissions, which were commercially unviable in the long run, thousands of crores of rupees were collected from investors across the country. However, the bubble burst sooner than later, when the scamster C.R. Bhansali, who alone floated over 130 companies, was arrested for the frauds committed by him, in which the investors and the nationalized banks lost a staggering amount of Rs. 1200 crores.

In the wake of CRB scam, the Reserve Bank of India introduced compulsory registration of NBFCs with the RBI. It is interesting to know that of the 37,880 applications received by the RBI as on 31st March, 1994 for registration, only 9000 were found eligible. As many as 28,500 NBFCs did not have the required net owned funds of Rs. 25.00 lakhs, but they were collecting crores of rupees from the investors. Consequently, many of the NBFCs failed to repay the amounts to the depositors and finally they collapsed. And hundreds of NBFCs vanished, leaving investors in financial crisis. Unfortunately, till date, non-repayment by NBFCs is still a non-cognizable crime. The Financial Companies Regulations Bill 2000, which seeks to protect the interest of investors, introduced in the Parliament on 13th December, 2000, has not yet received the attention it deserves.

viii) *Fake Currency*: Large scale circulation of fake currency can undermine the economy, as well as national security of any country. In India, the problem is age old, but with the development in technology, high quality fake currency notes have been recovered from terrorists, who had come from across the border. Fake currency printed abroad is generally channelised into India through Nepal and Dubai. Besides high quality fake currency notes being pumped into the country from across the border, criminal gangs and individuals within the country are making use of computers and sophisticated printers in making fake currency notes. Since the problem has national as well as international dimensions, it needs to be tackled effectively by the RBI, CBI and State Police Forces.

ix) *Fake Stamps Scam*: A multi crore fake stamps racket operated by Abdul Karim Telgi throughout the length and breadth of the country for many years with the active collusion of Police, Security Press and officials of banks and insurance companies exposed vulnerability of the system. The extent of the revenue loss caused to the exchequer by this gang alone is being estimated to the tune of Rs. 25,000 crores. Since there are many other gangs also engaged in different parts of the country, the problem needs to be dealt with in a pro-active and holistic manner.

Measures in Economic Offences

Despite a slew of measures taken by the Governments there is neither decline in overall volume of economic crimes, nor reduction in the number of major scams that are occurring with regular frequency in the country. In fact, the menace of economic crimes has assumed serious proportion, which needs to be addressed with a holistic approach. The following measures are recommended:

i) Revamping of Laws Governing Economic Offences: The Laws governing economic offences are soft as compared to the laws enacted to deal with violent crimes like murders, dacoities, etc. Moreover, the laws have not kept pace with the time, as a result, they have lost their efficacy. In fact, many of the laws seen in the present context have become absurd. For instance, frauds in telecom sectors are costing exchequers hundreds of crores of rupees annually, but the action against the culprits has to be taken under the Indian Telegraph Act, 1885 .

The highest punishment provided under the Act is three years imprisonment with a maximum fine of rupees one thousand only! Imagine a culprit sentenced to a fine of one thousand rupees for causing loss of a few hundred crores! The Drugs & Cosmetics Act too has become anachronistic. The fine provided for selling spurious drugs (Section 275 IPC) is a meager one thousand rupees, even when the offender would have made crores of rupees by making and selling fake and spurious drugs. Therefore, all the laws relating to economic offences need to be reviewed and revamped to create necessary deterrence as has been done for dealing with the menace of terrorism, smuggling of psychotropic substances, etc.

ii) *Deprive Economic Offenders of the Proceeds of Crime*: Though thousands of crores of rupees are siphoned off by economic offenders every year, they continue to enjoy a luxurious life, since the proceeds of crime in most of the cases continue to remain with them. Therefore, enforcement agencies dealing with the economic crime should make all out efforts to ensure that the fruits of crime are taken away from the economic offenders. Unless this is done, economic crimes will be a paying proposition to criminals.

iii) *Tightening of Bail Provisions*: Economic offenders are able to engage the best legal brains to defend them and obtain bail, though they would have duped lakhs of investors causing unimaginable agony to the investors. The State should also engage prosecutors with sound knowledge of law and impeccable integrity, to ensure that the economic offenders are not released on bail and thereafter secure strong conviction. The Ruling of the Supreme Court of India in Narenderjeet Singh Sahni v/s Union of India, needs to be followed by the courts in dealing with economic offenders.

"The White Collar Crimes are akin to *economic genocide* and considering for bail of such accused, would be misplaced sympathy of the Court because accused have deceived millions of countrymen who had invested their entire life's saving in fictitious and frivolous companies."

iv) *Creation of Exclusive Courts*: For a variety of reasons, the courts in India are not able to dispense justice promptly. One of the principal reasons is heavy backlog of cases. Therefore, there is need to create exclusive courts to bring offenders to book quickly.

v) *Need to Simplify Court Procedure*: Economic offenders with their huge ill-gotten wealth are known to have taken the criminal justice system in India for a ride. Either they corrupt it or derail it by procrastination of trial. The end-result is that hardly any economic offender is punished in a reasonable time frame. For instance, the cases against late Harshad Mehta the biggest scamster of 90's and his associates, are still pending trial for more than a decade, whereas in the case of Lesson, who committed a similar type of crime in Singapore at the same time, was convicted swiftly within a year. Hence, there is need to simplify Court procedure and ensure that economic offenders are not allowed to subvert the system. They need to be nailed within a year or two, which will definitely create necessary deterrence among their fraternity.

vi) *Notify Economic Offenders on the Internet*: Economic offenders target different financial institutions like banks, etc., and also people at different places in the country and abroad. Therefore, the known economic offenders along with their photographs need to be notified on the internet, which will help financial institutions and the public to take note of their modus operandi so as not to fall prey to their designs.

vii) *Need for Coordinated Action*: There are a number of Indian enforcement agencies / departments dealing with economic offenders, viz., Police, Income Tax, Customs, DRI, Serious Fraud Investigation Office, Enforcement Department, Commercial Taxes Department, SEBI, etc., but there is hardly any coordination among them. Every economic offence of significance needs to be examined by all the agencies dealing with economic offences.

viii) *Make Diversion of funds / loans a Specific Offence*: The financial institutions including banks are saddled with non-performing assets (NPAs) of over Rs. 1,00,000/- crores. Many of the big borrowers use them for the purpose other than for which the loans were sanctioned. Therefore, there is need to make diversion of funds a specific offence, with a punishment of over 10 years or more. It is also suggested that the loanees should submit an end-use certificate to the financial institutions.

Detection and Prevention of Economic Crimes

Crime is much wider than corruption. Crime prevention agencies have to look after prevention of Criminal offences (both physical and white-collar crimes) and Economic offences. The Government of India is determined to fight all economic crimes. For this purpose, the Government of India has setup the following Investigating Agencies which function under the Department of Revenue in Union Ministry of Finance:-

Agencies To Fight Economic Offences

— The Central Economic Intelligence Bureau (Apex Intelligence & Co-ordination body)

— Directorate General of Revenue Intelligence (for Customs related offences)

— Directorate of Enforcement (for Foreign Exchange related offences)

— Directorate General of Anti-Evasion (for Central Excise related offences)

— Directorate General of Income Tax (Investigation) [for Income Tax related offences)

— Narcotics Control Bureau (for Drugs related offences)

In pursuance of its commitment to fight economic crime, the Government of India has been implementing an attractive Reward Scheme for persons (irrespective of their nationality) providing useful information to the Government of India. Interested persons may access Internet site http://www.nic.in/ceib/ and send useful information to the Government of India by providing an Information Submission Form on this site. Information on the reward scheme and a copy of the reward form maybe obtained from the site.

Central Economic Intelligence Bureau

It is well recognised that the evasion of one tax usually entails evasion of other taxes as well. For the purpose of effective information gathering, collation and dissemination, a close co-ordination between the Agencies enforcing different tax laws is essential. Hence, the Central Economic Intelligence Bureau was set up with the intention of creating a body, which would coordinate and strengthen the intelligence gathering activities as well as investigative efforts of all the Agencies, which enforce economic laws. Accordingly, the following functions have been entrusted to the Central Economic Intelligence Bureau:-

1. To collect intelligence and information regarding aspects of the black economy which require close watch and investigation. Also, keeping in view the

scene of economic offences, the Bureau is required to collect information and provide periodical and special reports to the concerned authorities;

2. To keep a watch on different aspects of economic offences and the emergence of new types of such offences. The Bureau was made responsible for evolving counter -measures required for effectively dealing with existing and new types of economic offences;
3. To act as the nodal agency for cooperation and coordination at the international level with other customs, drugs, law enforcement and other agencies in the area of economic offences....
4. To implementation of the COFEPOSA(i.e. Conservation of Foreign Exchange & Prevention of Smuggling Activities Act, 1971 which provides for preventive detention of persons involved in smuggling and foreign exchange rackets under certain specified circumstances
5. To act as a Secretariat of the Economic Intelligence Council which acts as the apex body to ensure full co-ordination among the various Agencies including Central Bureau of Investigation, Reserve Bank of India, Intelligence Bureau etc.

Directorate of Revenue Intelligence

a. Collection of intelligence about smuggling of contraband goods, narcotics, under-invoicing, over-invoicing etc. through sources of India and abroad, including secret sources;
b. Analysis and dissemination of such intelligence to the field formations for action;
c. Working out intelligence directly, where necessary;

d. Keeping watch over important seizures and investigation cases;

e. Associating or taking over the investigations which warrant specialised handling by the Directorate;

f. Guiding important investigations/prosecution cases;

g. Functioning as the liaison authority for exchange of information among ESCAP countries for combating international smuggling and customs frauds in terms of the recommendations of the ESCAP conference;

h. Keeping liaison with foreign countries, Indian Missions and enforcement agencies abroad on anti-smuggling matters

i. Keeping liaison with the CBI and through them with the INTERPOL;

j. Coordinating, directing and controlling anti-smuggling operations on the Indo-Nepal border;

k. Referring cases registered under the Customs Act to the Income Tax Department for action under the Income Tax Act;

l. Keeping statistics of seizures and prices/rates etc. for watching trends of smuggling and supplying required material to the Ministry of Finance and other Ministries; and

m. Studying and suggesting remedies for loopholes in law and procedures to combat smuggling.

Directorate Of Enforcement

Foreign Exchange Management Act, 1999 [42 Of 1999]

The Parliament has enacted the Foreign Exchange Management Act, 1999 to replace the Foreign Exchange

Regulation Act, 1973. This Act came into force on the 1st day of June, 2000. To investigate provisions of the Act, the Central Govt. have established the Directorate of Enforcement with Director and other officers as officers of the Enforcement.

The object of the Act is to consolidate and amend the law relating to foreign exchange with objective of facilitating external trade and payments and for promoting the orderly development and maintenance of foreign exchange market in India.

This Act extends to the whole of India and will also apply to all branches, offices and agencies outside India owned or controlled by a person resident in India. It will also be applicable to any contravention committed outside India by any person to whom this Act is applicable.

The Directorate of Enforcement is mainly concerned with the enforcement of the provisions of the Foreign Exchange Management Act to prevent leakage of foreign exchange which generally occurs through the following malpractice

1. Remittances of Indians abroad otherwise than through normal banking channels, i.e. through compensatory payments.
2. Acquisition of foreign currency illegally by person in India.
3. Non-repatriation of the proceeds of the exported goods.
4. Unauthorised maintenance of accounts in foreign countries.
5. Under-invoicing of exports and over-invoicing of imports and any other type of invoice manipulation.
6. siphoning off of foreign exchange against fictitious and bogus imports land by

7. Illegal acquisition of foreign exchange through Hawala.

8. Secreting of commission abroad.

Directorate has to detect cases of violation and also perform substantial adjudicatory functions to curb such malpractice.

Directorate General of Central Excise Intelligence

The growth of the Central Excise revenue and extension of its coverage to nearly all manufactured products brought home the need for a specialised intelligence agency to target prevention of Central Excise duty evasion. The Directorate of Anti Evasion was created for this purpose with the following functions:(the agency has since been re-named as Directrate General of Central Excise)

a. Collection, collation and dissemination of intelligence relating to evasion of central excise duties on an all India basis;

b. Studying the modus operandi of evasion peculiar to excisable commodities and to alert the Collectorates of their possible use;

c. Studying the price structures, marketing patterns and classification of commodities in respect of which possibilities of evasion are likely with a view to advising the Collectorates for plugging loopholes;

d. Supplementing and co-ordinating the efforts of the field formations in investigation in cases of evasion of duty of Rs.10,000/- and above, wherever necessary;

e. Co-ordinating action with Enforcement agencies like Income-tax, Sales-tax etc. In respect of cases in which central excise evasion has come to notice;

f. Investigation of offences involving evasion of central excise duties having ramification in more than one

Collectorate, including investigation of complicated cases selected by the Directorate or entrusted by the Ministry to it;

g. Having at all times, a complete, detailed and up-to-date study of the taxation laws and implementation machinery and to have proper appreciation and assessment of possibilities for evasion;

h. Assisting in an advisory capacity in proper deployment of the Central Excise Preventive Staff in the Central Excise Collectorates for effective anti-evasion measures;

i. Examining and studying the effect and implementation of various tax concessions, exemptions and relaxation's in controls; and to make recommendations to the Government from time to time to see whether they are sources of evasion;

j. Maintaining liaison with other Central and State agencies in all matters pertaining to tax evasion"

Directorate General(s) of Income Tax (Investigation)

The Directorate Generals of Income Tax Investigation deal with all matters connected with investigations under the Income Tax Act of the Central Government. Some of the more specific functions entrusted to the Directorate Generals of Income Tax Investigation include :

a. Head the investigation wing of the Income Tax Department at the Regional Level;

b. Collection of intelligence pertaining to evasion of Direct Taxes;

c. Organise search action to unearth black money- from time to time;

d. Dissemination of information and intelligence collected- by passing on the same to the concerned authorities including assessing authorities;

e. Keep liaison and hold meetings with other organisations in the region to ensure co-ordination and smooth flow of information;

f. Take appropriate steps to ensure that information and other persons having information about tax evaders come forward with the same to the Department. Disbursement of rewards would be one of the measures.

Narcotics Control Bureau

Basic Objectives And Functions

National Policy on Narcotic Drugs and Psychotropic Substances is based on the directive principles contained in Article 47 of the Indian Constitution which directs that the State shall endeavour to bring about prohibition of the consumption, except for medicinal purposes, of intoxicating drugs injurious to health. The government's policy on the subject, which flows from the above said constitutional provision, is also guided by the international conventions on the subject. India is a signatory to :

— Single Convention on Narcotic Drugs 1961 as amended by the 1972 Protocol.

— Conventions on Psychotropic Substances 1971.

— United Nations Convention against Illicit Traffic in Narcotic Drugs and Psychotropic Substances, 1988.

The broad legislative policy in the matter is contained in the three Central Acts, viz. Drugs and Cosmetics Act, 1940, The Narcotic Drugs and Psychotropic Substances Act, 1985, and The Prevention of Illicit Traffic in Narcotic Drugs and

Psychotropic Substances Act, 1988. The responsibility of drug abuse control, which is a central function, is carried out through a number of Ministries, Departments and Organisations. These include Ministry of Finance, Department of Revenue which is having the nodal co-ordination role as administrator of the Narcotic Drugs and Psychotropic Substances Act, 1985 and the Prevention of Illicit Traffic in Narcotic Drugs and Psychotropic Substances Act, 1988.

Laws to Regulate Economic Offences in India

India has on its statute book a number of enactments providing for seizure and forfeiture or confiscation of illegally acquired property.The Smugglers and Foreign Exchange Manipulators (Forfeiture of Property) Act, 1976, provides for forfeiture of both movable and immovable property illegally acquired by smugglers and foreign exchange manipulators and their relatives and associates.

The Conservation of Foreign Exchange and Prevention of Smuggling Activities Act, 1974, contains provisions for the detention of certain persons to prevent them from undertakingcertainprejudicialactivities. The normal maximum period of detention under the Act is one year, but in respect of certain activities and in specified areas highly vulnerable to smuggling, it may be extended to two years.

The Customs Act, 1962, provides for penal sanctions against infringement of its provisions, including departmental adjudication in respect of smuggled goods, imposition of penalties and prosecution by a court of law, which in certain cases may impose a sentence of imprisonment of up to seven years. The Foreign Exchange Regulation Act, 1973, provides for confiscation of securities, moneys and properties arising from such offences as the unauthorized export or import of currency and non banking foreign exchange transactions. The existing central laws on narcotics - the Opium Acts, 1857 and 1878, and the Dangerous Drugs Act, 1930 -contain provisions for confiscation of narcotics and related goods under certain circumstances.

Since stringent measures generally lead to greater ingenuity and sophistication in methods of drug trafficking, India has evolved legislation that enables law enforcement authorities to take penal action notonly against mere carriers and minor links in drugtrafficking chains, but also against the organizers and financiers of such trafficking, including international drug traffickers.All the laws provide for suitable appellate and other remedies in comformity with the constitutional requirements.

Provisions on forfeiture of property contained in the Act of 1976

The Smugglers and Foreign Exchange Manipulators (Forfeiture of Property) Act, 1976, provides for forfeiture of the illegally acquired property of smugglers and foreign exchange manipulators and their relatives and associates.

The Act makes it unlawful for any person to hold any illegally acquired property, both movable and immovable. It is unlawful to hold such property not only in the names of smugglers and traffickers, but on their behalf under the name of other persons as well. In accordance with the provisions of the Act, the illegally acquired property is liable to be forfeited to the Central Government.

The Act provides that a competent authority shall make the forfeiture order and in so doing shall be required to follow the procedure established by the Act. A competent authority studies and examines income tax and related records and makes inquiries into the activities of various persons associated with an infringement of the Act. If a competent authority has reason to believe that all or any of the properties being investigated are illegally acquired, it may give a "show-cattse" notice to a person possessing such property.

The authority calls upon such a person to indicate the sources of his or her income, earnings and assets, out of which or by means of which he or she has acquired such property. The suspected person is also called upon to exhibit the evidence on which he or she relies and other relevant information and particulars, and to show cause why all or any of such properties, as the case may be, should not be declared to be illegally acquired and forfeited under the Act. After receiving an explanation of the showcause notice, the per.son is given an opportunity to be heard. ln a case where the person involved holds, through another person, any property specified in the notice, the other person is also given an opportunity to be heard.

lt is only after consideration of the evidence and allowing the persons concerned to be heard that a competent authority can conclude whether all or any of the properties under investigation have been illegally acquired. lf a competent authority concludes on the basis of the evidence that any of the investigated property has been illegally acquired, it declares that such property shall, subject to the provisions of the Act, be forfeited to the Central Government free from all encumbrances. ln certain cases, a competent authority gives the person an option to pay a fine in lieu of forfeiture.

The Act provides for the right of appeal to the Appellate Tribunal for Forfeited Property appointed by the Central Government.

Up to the end of June 1984. the competent authorities had issued notices for investigation of property suspected of being derived from illegal sources in approximately 2.420 cases.

Extracts highlighting the main features of the Act are summarized below.

Extracts from the Smugglers and Foreign Exchange Manipulators (Forfeiture of Property) Act, 1976

The preamble of the Act includes the following:

> ". . . for the effective prevention of smuggling activities and foreign exchange manipulations, which are having a deleterious effect on the national economy, it is necessary to deprive persons engaged in such activities and manipulations of their ill-gotten gains;
>
> "And whereas such persons have been augmenting such gains by violations of wealth tax, income tax or other laws or by other means and have thereby been increasing their resources for operating in clandestine manner;
>
> "And whereas such persons have in many cases been holding the properties acquired by them through such gains in the names of their relatives, associates and confidants;
>
> "Be it enacted by Parliament in the Twenty-sixth Year of the Republic of India . . ."

The provisions of the Act apply to the persons specified below:

1. A person convicted under the Customs Act of 1878 or 1962 of an offence in relation to goods of a value exceeding R.s 100,000, if convicted for the first time. For a second or subsequent conviction. the value of the goods is not relevant;
2. A person convicted under the Foreign Exchange Regulation Acts of 1947 or 1973 of an offence involving an amount or value exceeding Rs 100,000. if it is a case of first conviction. For a second or subsequent conviction the amount or value is not relevant;
3. A detainee under the Conservation of Foreign Exchange and Prevention of Smuggling Activities Act

who is not released by the detaining authority before the expiry of the period during which his case has to be placed before an advisory board, or whose detention is not revoked by the advisory board, or whose detention order is not set aside by a court of competent jurisdiction ;

4. Any person who is a relative of a person referred to in paragraphs (a), (b) or (c)above;
5. Every associate of a convicted person or detainee;
6. Any holder of property which was at any time previously held by a convicted person or detainee unless the holder was a transferee in good faith for a consideration.

Under the Customs Acts or the Foreign Exchange Regulation Acts, the term "conviction" means a conviction by a court of law where the convicted person is sentenced to imprisonment or payment of a fine or both. A penalty levied by the departmental authorities in adjudication proceedings does not amount to a conviction.

The term "relatives", in relation to persons convicted under the Smugglers and Foreign Exchange Manipulators (Forfeiture of Property) Act, 1976, means the following:

1. (a) Spouses;
2. (b) Brothers or sisters;
3. (c) Brothers or sisters of spouses;
4. (d) Any lineal ascendants or descendants;
5. (e) Any lineal ascendants or descendants of spouses;
6. (f) (Spouses of persons referred to in clauses (b), (c), (d) or (e);
7. (g) Any lineal descendants of persons referred to in clause (b)or (c).

The term "relatives" under this Act covers a much wider number of individuals than under the Income-tax Act, in which the term relatives mean spouses, brothers, sisters or any lineal ascendants or descendants of those individuals.

The term "associates", in relation to persons convicted under this Act, means:

1. (a)Any individuals who were or are residing in the residential premises of such persons;
2. (b)Any individuals who were or are managing the affairs or keeping the accounts of such persons;
3. (c)Any association of persons, body of individuals, partnership firms, or private companies, of which such convicted persons were or are members, partners, or directors;
4. (d)Any individuals who were or are members, partners, or directors of an association of persons. body of individuals, partnership firm or private company referred to in clause (c)at any time when such convicted persons were or are members, partners or directors of such associations, bodies, partnership firms or private companies;
5. (e)Any persons who were or are managing the affairs or keeping the accounts of any association of persons, body of individuals, partnership firm or private company referred to in clause (c);
6. (f)The trustees of any trusts, where:
7. The trust has been created by such persons; or
8. The value of the assets contributed by such persons to the trust samounts to not less than 25 per cent of the value of the assets of the trust on the date of contribution ;

1. (g)Where a competent authority, for reasons to be recorded in writing, considers that any properties of such persons are held on their behalf by any other persons.

The term "associates" includes a private limited company. The private company would be liable to investigation in respect of its property, though the individual action may be taken in respect of one of its directors.

Illegally acquired property

Broadly, the property that is liable to forfeiture under the Smugglers and Foreign Exchange Manipulators (Forfeiture of Property) Act, 1976, includes any property acquired by a person to whom the Act applies, either before or after its entry into force:

1. (a)Wholly or partly out of or by means of income, earnings or assets derived or obtained from or attributable to any activity prohibited by laws relating to any matter in respect of which Parliament has power to make laws; or
2. (b)Wholly or partly out of or by means of income, earnings or assets in respect of which any such law has been contravened; or
3. (c)Wholly or partly out of or by means of income, earnings or assets, the source of which cannot be proved and which cannot be attributable to any act or thing done in connection with any matter in respect of which Parliament has no power to make laws; or
4. (d)For consideration or by any means wholly or partly traceable to any property referred to in clauses (a), (b) or (c)above or the income or earnings from such property.

Burden of proof

The Act explicitly places the burden of proof on the persons involved who must prove that their property and assets indicated in the show-cause notice have not been illegally acquired. This requirement is based on the principle that the source of acquisition of a property is within the knowledge of the property holder. The person involved must, by production of the necessary evidence, explain the source and nature of the property under investigation.

Certain transfers to be null and void

If, after the issue of a show-cause notice, any property referred to in that notice is transferred by any mode whatsoever, such transfer shall for the purposes of the proceedings under the Act be ignored. If such property is subsequently forfeited by order of the competent authority, the transfer of such property shall be deemed to be null and void. A bank or a debtor who has received an intimation from the competent authority should not pay monies to the person involved without obtaining a clearance from the competent authority.

Powers to take possession

Where any property is forfeited under the Act the competent authority may order the person involved or any other persons who may be in possession of the property to surrender or deliver possession thereof to a person duly authorized by the competent authority within 30 days of the order. If the person involved refuses or fails to surrender or deliver the property within the stipulated period, the competent authority may take possession of the property and use such force as may be necessary for that purpose.

Appeals

The Appellate Tribunal for Forfeited Property hears appeals against orders passed by the competent authority. The appeal must be filed within 45 days from the date of service of the order, subject to an extension of 15 days for sufficient cause to the satisfaction of the Tribunal. The Tribunal is the last forum of appeal. The only remedy is a writ petition either to the Supreme Court of India, under article 32 of the Constitution, or to a High Court under article 226.

Extracts from the Conservation of Foreign Exchange and Prevention of Smuggling Activities Act, 1974

The preamble of the Act includes the following:

> "An Act to provide for preventive detention in certain cases for the purposes of conservation and augmentation of foreign exchange and prevention of smuggling activities and for matters connected therewith.
>
> "Whereas violations of foreign exchange regulations and smuggling activities are having an increasingly deleterious effect on the national economy and thereby a serious adverse effect on the security of the State;
>
> "And whereas having regard to the persons by whom and the manner in which such activities or violations are organized and carried on, and having regard to the fact that in certain areas which are highly vulnerable to smuggling, smuggling activities of a considerable magnitude are clandestinely organized and carried on, it is necessary for the effective prevention of such activities and violations to provide for detention of persons concerned in any manner therewith."

With regard to the power to make orders to detain certain persons, the Act includes the following provisions:

> "3 (l) The Central Government or the State Government or any officer of the Central Government, not below the rank of a Joint

Secretary to that Government, specially empowered for the purposes of this section by that Government or any officer of a State Government, not below the rank of a Secretary to that Government, specially empowered for the purposes of this section by that Government, may, if satisfied, with respect to any person (including a foreigner), that, with a view to preventing him from acting in any manner prejudicial to the conservation or augmentation of foreign exchange or with a view to preventing him from

> "(i) smuggling goods, or
>
> "(ii) abetting the smuggling of goods, or
>
> "(iii) engaging in transporting or concealing or keeping smuggled goods, or
>
> "(iv) dealing in smuggled goods otherwise than by engaging in trans porting or concealing or keeping smuggled goods, or
>
> "(v) harbouring persons engaged in smuggling goods or in abetting the smuggling of goods,
>
> "it is necessary so to do, make an order directing that such persons be detained."

Under the provisions of this Act, the maximum period of detention varies according to the category of detainees, but does not exceed two years.

Confiscation of goods under the Customs Act, 1962

The penal action against smuggling offences comprises a departmental adjudication and in certain cases prosecution by a court of law. The departmental adjudication is carried out by appropriate officers and leads to action against the smuggled goods and to imposition of a penalty, which may in certain cases be five times the value of the goods. The court of law may punish a smuggler by a sentence to imprisonment that may in certain cases extend to seven years.

If adjudication provides evidence that the goods have been imported or that attempts have been made to export them in contravention of the Customs Act, 1962, or any other law in force, the goods may be confiscated. In order to make the penal provisions more effective and to deter accomplices, the Act provides for confiscation of such goods as vessels, vehicles and aircraft used by the owner or any person in command who knows or is in a position to know that the goods carried out are smuggled.

In addition, goods that are used for concealing smuggled goods are also liable to confiscation as well as those that are mixed with smuggled goods in such a manner that the latter cannot be separated. Smuggled goods, even after they are changed in their form, are liable to confiscation. The proceeds of the sale of smuggled goods are also in given circumstances liable to confiscation.

Goods Suspected of having been smuggled are first seized by authorized officers for further investigation and enquiry, and if these show that such goods have been smuggled, a formal order is issued for their confiscation. The confiscated goods are taken over and kept in custody by the Government. According to the magnitude and extent of the offence, the adjudicating authority is empowered to release the goods on payment of an appropriate fine. The adjudicating authority is required to give such an option to the owner in all cases, except in respect of goods Subject to import or export prohibition.

It should be noted that prior to the issuance of the confiscation order the owner of the goods must be given an explanation of the ground upon which the proposal for confiscation is made and also an opportunity to file objections in his defence or be heard personally, if so desired. If adjudication results in an order of confiscation, the owner has the right to appeal before an appellate body and for revision before a tribunal. The owner of the goods has also the right to approach the higher judiciary if he can make a prima facieCase of miscarriage of justice.

When all the proceedings are completed the confiscation order is executed. The Government becomes the owner of the goods and disposes of them to the best advantage of the State, such as selling or destroying them, as the case may be.

Confiscation of goods under the Foreign Exchange Regulation Act, 1973

This Act is closely related to the Customs Act, 1962. Its objectives are, inter alia, to prevent the following: any non-banking transactions in foreign exchange; unauthorized export or import of currency; and underinvoicing or overinvoicing for imports or exports, or fictitious payment for non receipt of goods. Unauthorized foreign exchange is liable to confiscation not only at the time of import or attempted export at the frontier, but also if it is found in the possession of any person at any place in the country. The Act provides for confiscation of securities, monies or properties in respect of which the Act has been contravened.

The penal provisions and procedures relating to adjudication, appeals, revisions and recourse to the higher judiciary are similar to those described above under the Customs Act.

Confiscation provisions under the existing central laws on narcotics
The Opium Act, 1857

This Act, in addition to providing for control of legal cultivation of opium poppy and for preventing and dealing with cases of illicit poppy cultivation and related offences, contains provisions relating to confiscation.

Forfeiture of Properties

Under these provisions, if opium tendered by a cultivator

is found to be adulterated, it will be liable to confiscation on the order of the opium agent and Such orders are not open to question by any court. If any cultivator of poppy under licence of the Central Government embezzles or otherwise disposes of any part of his opium production, he will be liable to penalties, and the opium, if found, will be confiscated. Apart from the penalty to which a person is liable for illegal purchase of opium from a cultivator and for illegal connivance or embezzlement, the opium, if found, is liable to confiscation. Opium obtained from unlicensed cultivation is subject to seizure and Confiscation and a person responsible for such cultivation is liable to penalties.

Opium Act, 1878

This Act deals with the power of the State Government to make rules to regulate possession, transport, inter-state import and export, and sale of opium. Opium involved in the contravention of this Act is liable to confiscation. The vessels, packages and Coverings in which opium liable to confiscation is found and other contents, if any, in which opium may be concealed, as well as animals and Conveyances used in carrying it, shall likewise be liable to confiscation. Unclaimed opium is also subject to confiscation. Confiscation in all such cases is ordered by a magistrate. The State Government has the power to make rules to regulate the disposal of all things confiscated under this Act.

The Dangerous Drug Act, 1930

This Act, which deals with the entire range of narcotic drugs, contains a number of provisions regarding confiscation of smuggled narcotic drugs and related goods. It provides, interalia, that dangerous drugs, materials, apparatus and utensils in respect of which or by means of which an offence punishable under the Act has been committed shall be liable to confiscation.

In addition, the Act provides that the receptacles, packages and coverings in which dangerous drugs, materials, apparatus or utensils liable to confiscation are found and the other contents, if any, and the animals, vehicles, vessels and other conveyances knowingly used in carrying the same shall be liable to confiscation. There is also a provision for confiscation of unclaimed narcotic drugs. The order of confiscation in such cases is issued by the court trying the offence. The Central Government is empowered to make rules to regulate the disposal of all articles confiscated under this Act.

4

Private Corporate Sector

The private sector has a special role to play in the maintenance of a country's national integrity - not only where corporations are based, but also in the markets where they choose to operate. Corporations exist to make profits, and if they fail, their employees and those of associated enterprises, surffer along with their shareholders. To make those profits, corporations have to live in the world the way it actually is - and not the world as many of us would like it to be.

Fortunately, the traditional view that corporations exist solely to make profits for their shareholders - all that matters is a profitable bottom line - is giving way to a new sense of a wider corporate responsibility, not only to customers and clients, but also to the communities and societies in which they operate. It also recognises that "people seem happier working for organisations they regard as ethical and that in a booming jobs market, that can become a powerful incentive to do the right thing". Given the increasing role of the private sector in providing essential goods and services, many of which for generations have been the preserve of government agencies, improved corporate responsibility is a powerful tool in fighting corruption. With the passing of control to the private sector, accountability through Parliaments and

Legislatures is, of course, effectively diminished, if not completely lost.

In this process, the private sector is coming to see itself more as a part of civil society than it has in the past. In the pursuit of profit, private sector players are simply self-serving; however, when they address community and society objectives and enter into coalitions with others to pursue a wider public benefit, they are acting as a civil society member. Corporations are increasingly seeking partnerships with relevant non-governmental organisations, and in par-ticular with Transparency International. The views of major corporations are increasingly farsighted and, in many parts of the world, there are arguably the highest standards of ethical leadership being demonstrated by business leaders. There is also a challenge here for legal systems. Courts in a growing number of countries have seen themselves as having an oversight role - through judicial review - of the legality of public actions.

As noted elsewhere, a whole body of law has been developed to act as a check on the abuse of public power. Similar jurisprudence is likely to become increasingly relevant for governing at least some of the activities of the private sector, where these impact on the public interest to a major degree. Social Accounting is being increasingly recognised as a necessity, not just a desirable activity. Standards of corporate governance are being developed to provide greater protection, not only for corporations and their shareholders, but for all those who have a stake in the success of the private sector, which includes just about everyone. Legitimising "whistle-blowers" is also being recognised as important in protecting the public interest.

Employees who raise matters of public concern that arise in the course of their employment, but which their employers may be trying to hide, must be protected.

Examples include the health risks of company products, the presence of unsafe signals on railway lines, not to mention the abuse and misuse of public funds. In parallel, regulatory structures are being developed in many countries, simply to impose standards and ensure that ordinary people are not being exploited by monopolies and near monopolies.

The United States has been the leader in this area. Critics of the market economy should reflect on the fact that in the USA, the Bell Telephone Corporation was broken up on the insistence of regulators, simply because it had been so successful as to be unduly dominant. It is a myth that under 'capitalism', the market is everything and 'capitalists' are free to do what they wish. For a system of competition to work, it is crucial that dominant positions are not abused.

If the market-place is to serve the needs of all, then it must be effective, efficient and fair - and above all, it cannot be corrupt without negatively impacting on everyone. As well, actions within the private sector, for better or for worse, impact on others within the sector. For example, when banks give neutral references for staff who they are dismissing for reasons of dishonesty, they are taking an easy way out. However, it is one which can lead to other employers hiring staff who they believe to be honest, but who are, in fact, the very reverse.

The activities of the private sector take place in two quite separate arena: transactions with the public sector and transactions that lie wholly within the private sector. What in the past have been traditionally seen as "public sector" activities are now increasingly passing into private hands. As privatisation proceeds apace in many countries, the importance of checking corruption in the private sector grows ever more urgent. Activities in both arena need to be purposefully addressed.

Public Sector Corruption

Corruption of public officials is explicitly or implicitly illegal in every country which has a legal system, therefore it should not be an option for any private sector company. There is no difference in principle between a large bribe given to a minister or top official ("grand corruption") and a small bribe given to a junior official ("petty corruption"). However, the practicalities of working in certain countries may cause some companies to justify the distinction, describing "petty corruption" as being a "facilitation payment" to obtain what they are entitled to, for example, clearance of goods by customs or the connection of a telephone line. However, the directors of a company have a specific responsibility for ensuring that the company obeys all relevant laws.

Private Sector Corruption

Corruption in the private sector is far from being as clear-cut as public sector corruption. While some countries have laws explicitly criminalising the acceptance by employees of "secret commissions" or "kick-backs", many do not. Yet it is increasingly recognised that such activities are criminal. The recipients of kick-backs within the private sector, or who exploit their positions to sell their employers' goods at a premium when in short supply, are effectively stealing from their employers. As formerly publicly-owned utilities pass into the private sector, frequently in monopoly or near-monopoly situations, the need for individual countries to ensure that any loopholes in this area are closed, becomes ever more compelling.

Private sector bribery is pervasive in all parts of the world and in numerous industry sectors. Given our global economy, it is as international in scope as public sector bribery. Foreign bank accounts are widely used as repositories for private bribes. The Board of Certified Fraud

Examiners asserts that trust, and abuse of it, is the cornerstone of occupational fraud, and it recommends striking a balance between trusting employees too much and trusting them too little.

It argues for:

— the ethical tone being set by top management;

— a written code of ethics (something many small firms do not have and who are at highest risk);

— the checking of employee references;

— the designation of a responsible person, unconnected to bank reconciliations, as the one who receives the company's unopened bank statements and who looks for unusual patterns or disbursements;

— maintaining a "hotline" that facilitates employees reporting malpractices;

— and for creating a positive work environment where employees will not feel an urge to strike back at their employer because they believe it is treating them unfairly.

The Board predicts a continuing rise in occupational fraud and abuse, arguing that the expansion of the use of computers has drastically changed the speed of transactions and that they do not necessarily create the documents needed to detect fraud and abuse - although computers can, in some circumstances, also be tools for detection. Among the major areas where private sector bribery occurs are the following:

— *Procurement*: Bribery of purchasing agents for private sector projects is just as common as bribery for government projects. Efforts made to bribe buyers for large chains, such as Wal Mart and K-Mart are very common, particularly in connection with Asian suppliers. This is also true in the procurement of high-tech electronic components. There were well-publicised scandals in the USA involving payments made by paint manufacturers to purchasing agents for major automobile companies. Closely allied, and also common, is bribery to obtain sub-contracts on major projects.

— *Distributorships, Licences and Franchises*: The German "Opelgate" scandal, where company officials accepted bribes to award lucrative distributorships, is an example of widespread corruption in the granting of distributorships.

— *Retail Display Space*: Sales representatives of consumer goods manufacturers commonly bribe store managers to provide favourable display space for their products. Likewise there is the bribery of radio disk jockeys by record companies to play their records.

— *Proprietary Technical and Commercial Data*: There are numerous cases of competitors paying a company's technical and marketing employees to obtain copies of proprietary information such as manufacturing drawings, customer lists, and pricing information.

— *Financial Industry*: Bribery of bank officials to obtain loans or better interest rates have been common, as disclosed in investigations following bank scandals in Japan, Indonesia, as well as the USA's Savings & Loans crisis. In the securities industry there have been cases of bribes paid by brokers to obtain special allocations of shares in attractive IPOs (initial public offerings).

— *Scrap Disposal*: This is a common area for bribery, often involving organised crime. There are several variations, including bribery of quality control inspectors to reject good products, which can then be purchased as scrap and resold as quality products.

— *Sports*: Recent examples include leading members of the International Olympic Committee accepting "inappropriate gifts"; a boxing organisation that accepted bribes from managers of fighters to grant higher rankings, which then qualify fighters for more lucrative matches; bookmakers who have bribed cricketers to under-perform; and football players rigging results.

Internal concealment of bribes can lead to false accounting, false tax declarations and kick-backs to company staff. Furthermore, one of the main principles of competitive tendering is that contracts should be won by those companies offering the best combination of price and quality, with other factors such as delivery or financing terms sometimes being taken into consideration. Corruption is an unacceptable factor which destroys such free and fair competition. It is also the case that corruption in the market-place retards private sector development. New players are effectively excluded, and inefficiencies are rewarded, rather than redressed.

Fraud, particularly in the area of financial management, is, of course, a long-standing problem for the private sector no less than for the public one. An example is the accountant who warned her superiors that a book-keeper was fiddling the books by raking money from the payments system. The book-keeper was prosecuted and sacked, but the company did nothing to improve its management scrutiny. As a result the very same accountant started running identical scams, but for even larger amounts, writing cheques to suppliers who were, in fact, supplying herself. In another instance, a company secretary started paying his bills with company cheques drawn on the directors' current accounts.

Being careful to use the same wine merchant, travel agent and garage as the board, the swindle went undetected for a long time. Such malpractices are hard to spot, and even harder to stop. Controls are not breached, they are simply circumvented. However, bribery to obtain contracts is still the most frequent form of fraud in the private sector, and probably more widespread than employers realise. Simply having tenders evaluated by different people at different stages is no real safeguard unless the procedures also prevent people from:

— Carefully selecting who is to tender;

— Drawing up specifications which favour one supplier over another; and

— Sending different specifications to other suppliers.

As procurement moves onto the Internet, so does fraud. However, the Internet's electronic systems record all the traffic meticulously and there are "datamining" programmes which can unearth and expose suspicious patterns. E-trade customer checks recommended in a recent report include:

— Checking the company name, incorporation and registration

— Looking at the last three years' accounts to check solvency

— Finding out the names and addresses of directors and shareholders

— Checking other positions for conflicts of interest

— Looking for records of court judgments or bankruptcy orders

— Verifying the trading address and registered office

— Checking that the e-mail, billing and delivery addresses match

— Checking that the mailing address is not a service bureau or a post office box

— Locating the customer's internet service provider.

Procurement frauds range from creating cartels to faking invoices, but the most frequent is the kickback in exchange for a contract. As this is effectively a "refund" on the price (but paid to the employee, not the employer) it drives up the costs of business.

Private sector companies feel the pressure to bribe, on the grand corruption scale, in three main areas. The first concerns certain countries, particularly in the developing world, where it can be very difficult for anyone to win a major government or parastatal contract without paying a large bribe. This is normally done through a representative who receives a percentage commission when the business is secured. The commission is a generous one, and well able to withstand the payment of the necessary bribe.

A company may justify its action not only on the ground of 'business necessity', but also that it is merely conforming to local practice. If the local representative is not 'playing straight' with the principals, there have been suggestions that they may inflate the amounts claimed as needed to "buy" a Minister or a head of government, and then either keep the surplus for themselves or split it with corrupt elements within the sales staff of the company on whose behalf the bribing is being done. The second point of vulnerability is that off-shore bribery is generally condoned 'because everybody does it'. It may even be morally defended on the grounds that the resulting business is saving jobs, regardless of the fact that it may be costing jobs elsewhere. The third factor comes into play when companies, seek to create work by offering very attractive bribes to decision-makers to approve unneeded purchases or projects.

The first two points discussed above have a sufficient element of truth in them to satisfy the conscience of the company which is hungry for business and does not consider itself legally bound to reject grand corruption as a tool, particularly when used indirectly through a representative. Many company directors also feel entitled to shelter behind their ignorance of the company's operations, particularly its foreign operations. While this position is not supported legally, it is a widespread phenomenon and can lead a director to feel no responsibility to question the level of an overseas representative's commission, even if it seems excessive.

If a company resident in Country A bribes an official in Country A, it is committing a crime. If the same company bribes an official in Country B, it is committing a crime in Country B. Is it also committing a crime in Country A? If the company is American and therefore subject to the Foreign Corrupt Practices Act (FCPA), there is no doubt about its criminality. But until recently, if the company was not American and the entire transaction took place outside its own country and through a third party, it had generally not committed a crime in its own country. This situation is now changing, and changing radically. Action at the Organization for Economic Co-operation and Development (OECD) led to the signing of the OECD Convention on Combating Bribery of Foreign Public Officials in International Business Transactions.

As described elsewhere, the Convention requires signatories to criminalise bribery of foreign public officials. It is accompanied by a raft of "soft law" requirements which parallel the "hard law" of the Convention, including a requirement to end the tax deductibility of bribes as being a "legitimate business expense". The Convention and its "soft law" recommendations are not being left on the shelves of justice ministries' law libraries. Rather they are being closely and vigorously monitored to see that each country's laws and practices are adequate and effective.

Arms control treaties apart, never before has there been an international convention which has involved peer reviews, and teams of signatories entering the territory of others to examine their practices and procedures. Much is at stake, and the forceful, authoritative forms of peer review provide reason to hope that the Convention will succeed. Certainly, anything less would have failed. In the meantime, the private sector has to continue to go about its business in an environment in which the rules are in a state of flux.

Directors should understand and accept their responsibility for keeping their companies within the laws of all countries where they operate, and play an active and probing role in ensuring, wherever possible, that the spirit and the letter of the law are observed. It appears that grand corruption in international transactions, which distorts competition and has a restrictive impact on trade, will also offend the rules of the World Trade Organization. While there is no difference, in principle, between grand and petty corruption, companies may be excused for believing that the difference is more than merely a matter of scale.

Grand corruption is intended to influence decision-makers in favour of one company against another, or to favour one project or purchase over the alternatives. By contrast, "grease" or "facilitation" payments to minor officials (to do the work which they are already being paid to do, and to provide services to which the company is legally entitled) are highly undesirable; but it is recognised that, in the real world, companies cannot always be expected to adhere to the strictest principles on very small matters. For example, the American FCPA does not apply to "grease payments", although it certainly does not condone them.

Huge shipments of vitally-needed equipment may be stranded at the dockside, with customs officials demanding small payments before they will release them. This is a complex and contradictory area, and the dilemma will subsist until there are reliable enforcement procedures in the countries concerned. In the meantime, where companies accept, however reluctantly, that on occasions they may be victims of extortion and have little option but to pay, clear rules are needed to guide their staff. All such payments should be recorded, and any payment which is more than a very small one should require authorisation at a senior level to ensure that "grease payments" do not become a gateway for grand corruption.

Above all, the companies should make it clear to all staff that these practices are not condoned. As long as the position of bribes paid in international transactions remains unclear in criminal and civil law, companies' voluntary codes of conduct will be important to set the tone for all employees and to indicate to third parties the standards to be expected from the company. Company codes vary greatly in strength. The least useful are those which are limited to wellintentioned, but vague expressions of principle. The most effective are those which are specific in their descriptions of what employees are not allowed to do on behalf of the company.

The best are those which are not only specific, but also require an annual or six-monthly signature from the chief executive to confirm that they have been observed in every respect. However, it must be recognised that the best voluntary code is only as effective as the company's board of directors is determined to make it. Directors should take responsibility for monitoring the application and observance of company codes, recognising that they can be an effective means of discharging their liability for maintaining the company's legal and moral standards.

Large companies should ensure that there are ethics programmes to breathe life and meaning into what are otherwise decorative documents: and these should not be lectures on what to do and what not to do, but involve real life situations and dilemmas, and active discussion among employees as to how these should be resolved. In the present situation of widespread grand corruption and legal uncertainties, many companies seeking international contracts are reluctant to risk losing business to those who continue to pay bribes. All companies, however, can welcome the Anti-Bribery Pacts (or Integrity Pacts) increasingly imposed by certain countries on tenderers for major public contracts.

In such Pacts, all the players start on a level playing-field so that the risk of a bribe is greatly reduced. There also appears to be considerable scope for international professional associations and federations to include a mandatory anti-corruption clause in their ethics codes, with expulsion from its membership as the sanction for non-observance. When such an association is strong in terms of world-wide membership, its members have relatively little to fear from non-members gaining an unfair advantage from bribery.

For example, financial institutions could be expected to support members of an appropriate professional body against non-members. Finally, private sector companies should recognise that grand corruption is the enemy of high standards and efficiency. When the decision-maker is influenced by a bribe, opportunities are created for sub-standard performers to gain a contract at the expense of those whose product, reputation or skills would make them the likely winners of a fair competition.

One of the most compelling reasons for companies to review their ethical behaviour is likely to be that of self-interest. There is a growing body of evidence which appears to indicate that companies which tolerate corruption abroad by their employees are placing themselves at risk. "Off the books" accounts, secret bank accounts, payment of staff serving prison terms and use of former senior staff as "middlemen" all cultivate an atmosphere in which the bottom-line justifies criminal activity. This is inherently dangerous, and it may be only a matter of time before the company itself finds that it is the victim of similar conduct on the part of its employees. In some countries the legal system does not yet permit the prosecution of corporate bodies for criminal actions, based on the premise that only living human beings are capable of forming the necessary intention to commit a crime.

The effect of such a prohibition can be to greatly reduce the penalties that can be imposed, and to significantly increase the problems of gaining the necessary proof of guilt: it may be obvious that a company has broken the law, but to successfully prosecute, a prosecutor will have to name specific individuals and prove that they were personally responsible. Even if these can be identified, they may have left the company's employ, or even the country. In any event, any financial penalties would have to be related to the individual's ability to pay - not to the company's, or to the profit that may have flowed to the company as a consequence of the illegal actions. Where a prosecution is successful, a company may be left paying legal costs for an employee, and continuing their salaries while they serve prison terms, but in reality these penalties may be insignificant when set against the profits being made.

If the company finds itself in court in countries that do prosecute corporate bodies, how best can it defend itself when some of its employees have been violating the law? If the company has kept information about illicit payments to a small number of officials and away from the Board of Directors, whether the Board is aware of it or not, no judicial officer is likely to be impressed by the company management's claims of innocence. Legal systems increasingly demand that companies have internal compliance procedures in place. In doing so, they are following the lead set by more enlightened corporations. The USA is assisting in this process. It has developed an excellent model for other countries to consider following - the Federal Sentencing Guidelines of 1991.

The Commission which developed these Guidelines was originally established to examine the sentencing of individuals, but its greatest contribution to criminal jurisprudence came when it examined the position of corporations. Responding to research that showed that the median fine for a corporation averaged only about 20 per cent of the losses that the offences had caused, the Commission decided that sentences should be governed by the kind of company that was involved; in other words, the 'good corporate citizenship' of the company should be assessed. This decision is not intended to penalise companies for bad corporate behaviour, but rather to reward the good. If a company is convicted of an offence, a fine would normally be about three times the size of the loss caused. However, where a company can prove that it has an effective ethics program in place, the fine can be reduced by as much as 95 per cent.

US Federal Sentencing Guidelines of 1991

The (US) Federal Sentencing Guidelines state that:

The hallmark of an effective program to prevent and detect violations of law is that the organisation exercised due diligence in seeking to prevent and detect criminal conduct by its employees and other agents. The concept of due diligence comprises seven steps:

(1) There must be compliance standards and procedures to be followed by employees, etc. that are reasonably capable of reducing the prospect of criminal conduct;

(2) There must be a specific individual or individuals assigned with overall responsibility to ensure compliance with (1);

(3) The corporation must have taken due care in not delegating substantial discretionary authority to individuals known (or who should have been known) to have a propensity to engage in illicit activities;

(4) The corporation must have communications and training programs in place;

(5) It must also have taken reasonable steps to achieve compliance with its standards (perhaps including advice lines and protection for whistle-blowers);

(6) The standards must have been enforced consistently through appropriate disciplinary mechanisms, including instances where individuals are responsible for a failure to detect an offence; and

(7) After an offence has been detected, the corporation must have taken all reasonable steps to modify its systems to obviate repetition.

There is considerable interest in these Guidelines and the ways in which they are fostering ethical behaviour and self-policing in the corporate sector in the United States. There is every likelihood that they will also find favour elsewhere, especially since the criminal responsibility of companies is a difficult question in most systems of jurisprudence and the trend is increasingly towards self-regulation. It has also been suggested that businesses should undertake an audit of how ethical problems are currently being dealt with, to test its behaviour both against external standards and against its own declared values. The European Institute of Business Ethics has developed a "Dilemma Training Device" which helps organisations to address ethical issues, to discuss them and to find ways of using them to attain the objectives of the organisation.

In general terms, a business can be ethically justified in working in a culture which has certain unethical features when:

- the features are unavoidable, at least for the time being;
- one is operating for good business and social reasons; and
- one is working to change those unethical features.

This argument points to instances where official complaints by groups of companies have changed the practice of bribery in some countries and proved to be more effective than efforts by individual firms. The experience of responsible US corporations also suggests that, even in unethical marketplaces, the fact that a government is dealing with a company known to be ethical can, in itself, be a selling-point. "Deal with us, the corporation is saying, and your own people will know of your integrity." US sales staff also claim that being able to quote the existence of the USA's Foreign Corrupt Practices Act, and their company's policy of compliance, can be enough to sweep any talk of kickbacks and sweeteners from the agenda.

However, it would be simplistic to suggest that, in business, profits go only to those who are ethical. The evidence is plain: large volumes of business are being won by companies through unethical behaviour which, in some sectors, has transformed competition from being one of competitive advantage to one of competitive bribery. It would, therefore, be unrealistic to ignore the impact of the FCPA on responsible American corporations, or their wish to see the same restraint applied to their competitors. It is also the case that large corporations can be in a much better position to be able to walk away from a deal once corruption becomes manifest, than a small company which has invested heavily in the project and has, comparatively, much more to lose.

Best practice dictates that private sector companies should:

— obey the law in all countries in which they operate;

— ensure that directors are fully aware of their legal liabilities;

— press for clarification or strengthening of the law, if current law places the company at a disadvantage relative to its competitors;

— introduce specific anti-bribery clauses into corporate codes of conduct and ensure that all employees know that these must be observed;

— encourage directors to actively monitor the application and effectiveness of corporate codes of conduct;

— encourage any international professional body to which the directors belong to include a mandatory anti-bribery clause in its code of conduct;

— support a national Anti-Bribery Pact in relation to any major offshore tender where this is offered by a government; and

— press relevant governments, directly or through the company's relevant commercial or professional body, to support the OECD anti-corruption initiative and to encourage the World Trade Organization to recognise grand corruption as a barrier to fair trade.

Personal contacts in business, as in other walks of life, frequently find expression in exchanges of gifts and hospitality. However, in business, when potential buyers and potential sellers come together, this can become a question of something rather more meaningful. The question can quickly arise as to whether a gift is appropriate, and perhaps, whether it should be described more bluntly as a bribe. For example, when a sales person works for a performance bonus, or needs to land an order to preserve his or her job, the temptations to use all means available (including presenting "gifts" to clients) can be considerable. It is therefore desirable for companies to have internal policies and rules governing the giving and receiving of gifts.

The International Chamber of Commerce's Rules of Conduct to Combat Extortion were first adopted as long ago as 1977. They were revised and brought up to date in 1996 and again, in 1999. The ICC Rules go further than the minimum legal requirements of many countries. If followed, the Rules would induce a sea change in international business behaviour. However, the Rules are still intended "as a method of self-regulation", and in the hope that "their voluntary acceptance by business enterprises will not only promote high standards of integrity in business transactions, but will also form a valuable defensive protection to those enterprises which are subjected to attempts at extortion."

Firms have been happy to sign up, but none have actually felt obliged to obey the Rules because the voluntary nature of the ICC reduces its ability to police its members and to establish effective monitoring mechanisms. However, the ICC has been responding to criticisms by revisiting its Rules and looking for ways in which they can be made effective. Understandably, the ICC (as an organisation with a voluntary membership and dependent on subscriptions) remains cautious about the external monitoring of corporations' conduct. At present Transparency International is undertaking a feasibility study on the development of a private sector "internal integrity management standard", an exercise in which the ICC has participated. This is being undertaken with a number of interested corporations, and NGOs from a variety of regions.

The study is exploring the possibility of a standard which can, if particular companies wish, be independently verified. With a sharp focus on integrity, rather than a broad focus on corporate governance, and an intention that the standard be verifiable, the initiative is very different from the exercises underway in other for a dealing with areas of corporate governance and business accountability.

There is substantial debate over the extent to which corporate codes actually alter corporate conduct.

Although codes have become increasingly popular with companies in industrialised countries, they have by no means always been embedded within those organisations. The codes have often been seen as ends in themselves, not as a means to an end. There have been various studies relating to corporate codes, but many simply undertake broad surveys of existing codes, rather than analysing the essence of what makes a code effective. In addition, much research relates to slightly different questions, such as whether general corporate ethics programmes promote social accountability. Nonetheless, some studies do point to possible factors which may contribute to the effectiveness of codes of conduct.

One report, Ethical Concerns and Reputation Risk Management, focuses on the means chosen to implement business ethical norms, including the types of training they provide, which individuals play the greatest organisational role in promoting business ethics, and whether stakeholders are involved, rather than assessing the effectiveness of such efforts. The report found that Values and Mission Statements and Codes of Conduct remain the most widely used business ethics practices, with about 80 per cent of companies implementing such programmes. These results represent substantial increases over surveys conducted three years ago when less than 60 per cent reported having codes. Perhaps the most interesting finding of the report relates to the lack of management systems used to implement codes:

— In 20% of the companies surveyed, the codes were not made available to all employees;

— In 65% of the companies, codes were developed by legal/compliance and corporate secretariats; and

— Human resource personnel were involved in developing codes in only 43% of companies surveyed.

In other words, firms' senior management have tended to supervise the development of codes, and the codes have had a legal, rather than a behavioral focus. Some 40 per cent of companies provided training only to selected employees. Of these, less than half related the training to practical application of their codes in realistic situations; and fewer still involved a sharing of participants' experiences. Not surprisingly, the survey concluded that the average employee in most companies was not nearly as aware of the existence of the code as were senior personnel.

The study also found that fewer than half of the companies surveyed had helplines for raising concerns or hotlines for reporting suspected misconduct - and 60 per cent of those with these facilities, reported no use being made of them. This is hardly surprising when significant numbers of companies provided no protection for callers or for alleged offenders alike. The report concluded that many business ethics programmes fail to reflect important principles, and that many organisations still grapple with how to make their employees actually "live" their values and codes. A different report, prepared by KPMG, on fraud among companies in Southern Africa, provides a different perspective on the most effective means of combating fraud.

Of the 540 companies which responded to the survey, 83% indicated that they had experienced an incident of fraud in the prior year. To reduce the possibility of fraud, the majority of companies surveyed indicated that they would review and improve controls (83%) and either establish a corporate code of conduct (46%) or implement a comprehensive ethics program (32%). The relatively low level of interest in implementing corporate codes or ethics programmes suggests that at the very least, such measures are perceived as not being particularly effective when compared to bolstering internal controls. In a paper prepared for the 9th International Anti-Corruption Conference in Durban, South Africa, Ronald Berenbeim argued that while codes have become widely instituted in corporations, but they have not had the impact which they should have had.

Surveys undertaken by his organisation revealed that in nearly 80 per cent of corporations, the board of directors is involved in the drafting of the codes - so they do not "belong" to staff as a whole. He notes that many corporate codes contain virtually identical provisions prohibiting corrupt practices, and argues that internal corporate procedures, which require disclosure and accountability (including whistleblower protections and other means of reporting of violations), are essential to an effective code. Another somewhat different study prepared for the Business & Society Journal in 1999 concludes that their analysis did not demonstrate that good social performance "leads to" poor financial performance.

The OECD, now highly active in the field of corporate governance, conducted a survey of 233 corporate codes of conduct in 1998. The survey was limited to documenting the provision of the codes rather than analysing the accomplishments or effectiveness of the codes. The results of the survey indicated that the majority (82%) of codes covered the conduct of the corporation itself, while comparatively few were codes extended to include the conduct of contractors and sub-contractors (50% and 22%

respectively). In terms of the norms articulated in the corporate codes, only 18% referred to international standards explicitly. Only one of the 233 referred to the OECD Guidelines for Multinational Enterprises, and just two cited the OECD Recommendation on Combating Bribery in International Business Transactions (the precursor to the Convention on Combating Bribery of Public Officials in International Business Transactions).

Other codes merely referred to "international human rights" or "universal" norms. In the companies surveyed, the monitoring of codes received relatively little attention. The majority provided for internal corporate monitoring, and some 40 per cent did not mention monitoring at all. Only a quarter provided for corrective action, and very few stated that noncompliance could or would result in termination of a contract or business relationship. Also in 1998, the London-based Institute of Business Ethics carried out its second survey of the use of codes of business ethics. From the responses, the Institute estimated that 57% of the largest UK companies had codes of conduct, compared with only 18% in 1987. There was wide divergence in approach between communicating codes internally and externally.

Nearly all companies (93%) gave their codes some internal communications support. Only one third publicised their codes externally. Fewer than half of the companies with a code provided training of any kind as to the meaning and use of codes, and some 30% did not even furnish copies of the code to their staff. The results confirmed the impression that for many companies, the drafting and introduction of a code are seen as being an end in itself. In addition, the report found that in many firms, management perceived staff as sufficiently steeped in the ethos of the company that little or no instruction on the practical use of the code was needed.

Generally speaking, research on corporate codes of conduct is incomplete. The research sug-gests that codes have, indeed, had some positive influence, but such a broad conclusion still lacks a firm empirical base. The research indicates that the degree to which the code of conduct becomes "embedded", or a part of the corporate culture, will have some positive effects on employee behaviour. However, determining precisely what "embeddedness" means in terms of organisational structures and managerial leadership, remains elusive. The key determinant in achieving organisational adherence to a code appears to be training, monitoring and enforcement activities - another conclusion still more intuitive than scientific.

5

Concept of White Collar Crime

The meaning of white collar crime, like that of other abstract terms in legal, social science, and philosophical discourse (think, for example, of "coercion," "violence," "victim"), is deeply contested. Definitions vary both across and within disciplines and linguistic practices. White collar crime scholars have sometimes sought to find an agreed-upon meaning of the term; other times, they have looked for substitutes. But none of these efforts has been successful: Whatever definitions have been offered have failed to find general acceptance; whatever alternatives have been suggested have proved inadequate.

Despite its fundamental awkwardness, the term "white collar crime" is now so deeply embedded within our legal, moral, and social science vocabularies that it could hardly be abandoned. The term persists and proliferates not so much in spite of its lack of definitional precision, but because of it. Speakers attribute to it those meanings that correspond to their own particular analytical or ideological concerns.

One interesting difference between white collar crime and many other contested concepts in law, the humanities, and the social sciences is that its origins are so easily known and so widely acknowledged. The term was first used only sixty-five years ago by Edwin Sutherland, the most influential American criminologist of his day, in a presidential address to the American Sociological Association. Sutherland was famously vague and inconsistent in saying exactly what the term should mean. But even if he had been precise and consistent in his usage, it seems likely that the term would still have generated uncertainty and misunderstanding among other users of the term. The concept that Sutherland was the first to put a label on is one that is so inherently complex and multifaceted that it seems unlikely that one single definition could ever prevail. The story of how the social sciences have used the term "white collar crime" has been told on many occasions.

To lawyers, the term "crime" denotes a legal category. It refers to particular kinds of conduct that our legal institutions recognize as "criminal." Such conduct must be defined in a particular manner, employing certain characteristic concepts such as actus reus and mens rea; it must have a certain "public" character in the sense that a wrong is committed against the public as a whole and charges are brought in the name of the government or the people; the question whether a crime has been committed must be adjudicated in a particular manner, with various actors playing distinctive roles, employing distinctive procedures and burdens of proof, and recognizing distinctive procedural rights; and it must entail certain characteristic forms of punishment.

To lawyers, therefore, it seems obvious that when one talks about "white collar crime," one should be talking about some subcategory of conduct that reflects such criminal law-like characteristics. To social scientists, this point is less clear. Sociologists and criminologists are concerned less with legal labels and categories than with describing patterns of behavior, its causes, and society's attitudes towards it. Thus, for Sutherland and many of his fellow sociologists, white collar crime is not "crime" in the legal sense of the term. At the time he was writing, much of the activity he was concerned with-such as restraint of trade, violation of patents, unfair labor practices, and adulteration or misbranding of food and drugs-either was not subject to criminal sanctions at all, or, if it was, was rarely prosecuted as such.

Indeed, this was precisely Sutherland's point: a good deal of conduct that is at least as, or even more, harmful or wrongful than what has traditionally been viewed as criminal is subject to a range of procedures and penalties that differ from those used for (and is largely excluded from official statistics on) traditional crime. This is not to say, however, that everyone has agreed with Sutherland's approach to defining white collar crime. Indeed, there have been two distinct responses to the confusion caused by including in the notion of white collar "crime" conduct that is not regarded as criminal by the law.

The first is simply to insist, as Paul Tappan and others have done, that only conduct regarded as criminal by the law should be included in the notion of white collar crime. The second is to set aside the term "white collar crime" and instead use terms such as "elite deviance" to refer not only to actual crimes committed by the elite but also to deviant activities of the elite that do not violate the criminal law. From a sociological perspective, this second alternative makes some sense. Much of the conduct we are dealing with here could be treated either as:

(1) a crime (whether a serious felony or a relatively minor misdemeanor);

(2) a non-criminal violation of law (e.g., a tort, breach of contract, or statutory violation); or

(3) a merely "deviant," aggressive, or anti-social act which is violative of some informal norm but is not contrary to either criminal or civil law.

For example, there is a great deal of conduct falling within the scope of the Securities Exchange Act of 1934, Sherman Act, Clean Water Act, Bankruptcy Code, Tax Code, Truth in Lending Act, False Claims Act, and Federal Food, Drug and Cosmetic Act in which precisely the same conduct can be treated either as a crime or as a civil violation. In light of such overlaps, one can easily imagine a sociological study in which the distinction between deviant activity that is criminal and that which is not would seem arbitrary.

Moreover, to the extent that one is concerned with reforming the criminal law-so that currently noncriminalized behavior is made criminal, or currently criminalized behavior is decriminalized-there is much to be said for a general term that refers to both kinds of conduct. Indeed, there is a significant polemical or reformist strain that runs through a good deal of the sociological literature on white collar crime. From the perspective of law and legal theory, however, the term "elite deviance" is highly problematic. The discipline of criminal law is defined by what is criminal. A wide range of critically important procedural questions turns on whether conduct alleged is violative of the criminal law. To replace the concept of white collar crime with the concept of deviant behavior is thus to blur a distinction that, at least in legal discourse, is foundational.

Moreover, not only is there deviant behavior that is not criminalized, there is also criminal activity that is not generally regarded as deviant. For example, a good deal of regulatory crime involves so-called malum prohibitum conduct, which is wrongful only, or primarily, in virtue of its being prohibited. And there are other forms of conduct that may well be regarded as deviant in one social setting (e.g., courtside at Wimbledon), but not in another (say, the trading floor of the Chicago Board of Trade).

A final problem with substituting the term "elite deviance" for "white collar crime" is that much white collar crime is not committed by elites at all. For example, many people would consider insider trading to be the quintessential white collar offense. Yet, as one scholar has noted, the Supreme Court first addressed the subject in a case in which the defendant was not a high-level corporate executive, but rather a "markup man" for a printing press. It thus seems obvious that many cases not only of insider trading, but also of perjury, obstruction of justice, mail fraud, bribery, extortion, and tax fraud involve defendants who cannot be said, in any meaningful sense of the term, to be elite.

To refer to a crime as "white collar" is to draw attention to the characteristics of the person (or entity) that committed it. Indeed, it was the qualities of the offender, rather than those of the offense, that were the main focus of Sutherland's critique. Sutherland sought to question the then-prevalent theory that associated crime with the activities of the lower classes and emphasized poverty as its principal cause. He argued that because there is a significant category of crimes that are committed by persons of wealth, "respectability," and social status, poverty cannot be viewed as the sole, or main, cause of crime. And, in fact, recent cases involving the likes of super-wealthy alleged white collar criminals such as Martha Stewart, Kenneth Lay, Bernard Ebbers, Richard Scrushy, and Dennis Kozlowski seem to demonstrate the truth of such an assertion.

From the perspective of the criminal law, however, such an approach is once again problematic. Deeply rooted equal protection-type norms forbid us from distinguishing among offenders on the basis of wealth, occupation, race, gender, ethnicity, or other personal characteristics. To be sure, there are special immunity rules that apply to certain kinds of governmental actors. But outside of such narrow exceptions, the law is not ordinarily permitted to take account of a defendant's social status in determining criminal liability. Nor, ordinarily, is legal theory. One alternative is to change the focus of the inquiry from social class to occupation. Thus, Marshall Clinard and Richard Quinney suggest that the term "white collar crime" be replaced with two constitutive terms: "corporate crime" and "occupational crime."

The first category is meant to include offenses committed by corporations and their officials for the benefit of the corporation. The second kind of crime is defined as that which is committed "in the course of activity in a legitimate occupation" and is meant to apply to offenses involving persons at all levels of the social structure. As such, occupational crimes can be committed by employees against employers (as in the case of embezzlement), employers against employees (as in the case of workplace safety violations), and by those who provide services and goods to the public (e.g., consumer fraud, health care fraud, procurement fraud, and environmental pollution). In somewhat more precise legal terminology, we might say that white collar crimes are those offenses that require, as an element, that the offender be (1) a corporate entity or officer of such entity, or (2) performing a particular job or serving in a particular position at the time she committed the offense. And, indeed, such an approach is not at all foreign to the criminal law.

For example, one cannot commit the offense of receiving a bribe unless one is performing an act as a member of Congress, a juror, a witness, or "an officer or employee or person acting on behalf of the United States, or any department, agency or branch of Government thereof." Such an approach would likely forestall the anomaly of having to include under the category of white collar crime cases in which a person of high social status and wealth commits a presumptively non-white collar crime such as murder, rape, or possession of a controlled substance. But it would at the same time create a host of other problems.

Much of what could presumably be included within the category of "occupational" crime-including theft of office equipment, workplace assaults, police brutality, and serial killings of patients by doctors and nurses-would not ordinarily be regarded as white collar crime. Even more problematic is the fact that a great many white collar crimes have nothing at all do with either corporations or a defendant's occupation. Indeed, perjury, obstruction of justice, the offering of bribes, extortion, false statements, criminal contempt, tax evasion, and most intellectual property offenses are only rarely committed by employees against employers, employers against employees, or by those who provide goods and services to the public; and only rarely involve corporations. In short, there is a vast range of presumptively white collar crime that falls outside the categories of both corporate and occupational crime.

Law Enforcement

Having looked broadly at the kinds of definitional issues that have revolved around the term "white collar crime," we can now focus more narrowly on how the term is used in a number of important, specifically law-related contexts which the definitional literature has, for the most part, ignored. Let us consider, first, the defense bar. Hundreds of law firms and thousands of private lawyers throughout the United States and, to a lesser extent, Great Britain, now hold themselves out as specialists in what they refer to as "white collar" criminal defense work.

One indication of the prominence of white collar crime as a criminal law subspecialty is the existence of the American Bar Association's Section on Criminal Justice

Committee on White Collar Crime. Another is the monthly column on white collar crime in the Champion, the magazine of the National Association of Criminal Defense Lawyers. Moreover, there is a growing industry in continuing legal education programs, newsletters, books, and other materials designed for the white collar criminal law practitioner. The emergence of white collar crime as a distinct practice area can also be seen among prosecutorial offices and law enforcement agencies.

Specialists in white collar crime can be found in numerous prosecutorial offices at the federal, state, and local level; at the FBI and in local police departments; and in the U.S. Department of Justice Criminal Division's Section on Fraud, which is "charged with directing the Federal law enforcement effort against fraud and white-collar crime." The National White Collar Crime Center, a federally funded, non-profit corporation whose membership comprises primarily law enforcement agencies, state regulatory bodies with criminal investigative authority, and state and local prosecution offices, has as its focus the assistance of state and local prosecutors in the battle against high tech and economic crime. And some agencies, including the Department of Justice, even have offices that deal specifically with the victims of fraud and other white collar offenses.

Not surprisingly, the definition of exactly what constitutes "white collar crime" tends to vary within and among these various constituencies, though to a lesser extent than in the case of the social scientists. Law enforcement officials, prosecutors, and defense attorneys are all more inclined than sociologists to use the term to refer to acts rather than actors, and to real crime rather than mere deviance. Some white collar criminal defense lawyers emphasize their experience in representing individual and corporate defendants in criminal cases. Others highlight their skill in establishing and administering corporate compliance programs and conducting internal investigations. Almost all claim expertise in dealing with the complex procedural and evidentiary contexts in which many white collar crime prosecutions occur.

Among the specific "white collar" areas in which expertise is frequently claimed are securities fraud and insider trading; health care fraud and False Claims Act cases; antitrust; banking, financial, and accounting fraud; environmental and health and safety violations; RICO; trade secret theft; and customs violations. A similar range of usage can be observed among prosecutors and law enforcement agencies. The White Collar Crime Reporter, perhaps the leading practice-oriented publication in the field, covers insider trading, forfeiture, fraud, money laundering, foreign corrupt practices, health care fraud, perjury, espionage, and trade secrets.

The U.S. Sentencing Commission, in its Sourcebook of Federal Sentencing Statistics, defines its "non-fraud white collar category" to "include the following offense types: embezzlement, forgery/counterfeiting, bribery, money laundering, and tax." And the Department of Justice speaks of its section on white collar crime as being concerned with various forms of fraud-corporate, financial institution, securities, insurance, telemarketing, government program, Internet, and banking; identity theft; and the bribery of foreign officials.

Legal Education

Within the last generation, white collar crime has developed into a standard subject in the curriculum of most American law schools. There are now at least four major casebooks, two hornbooks, an anthology, an annual student-edited law review survey, and scores of law school courses expressly devoted to the subject. Indeed, white collar, federal, business, and environmental crime are among the most rapidly proliferating subjects in the curricula of American law schools. Law professors are clearly less inclined than their social science counterparts to think of white collar crime in terms of either offender characteristics or mere deviance. Almost all law school courses and texts in white collar crime deal with the general principles of corporate criminality and with the specific offenses of mail and wire fraud, perjury, obstruction of justice, conspiracy, and RICO. But beyond that there is little consensus.

Many courses emphasize white collar crime as a body of substantive law, while others focus on the procedures associated with its prosecution, particularly in the federal courts. Some, but by no means all, of the courses emphasize constitutional issues raised by the supposedly increasing federalization of criminal law. Others cover grand jury and forfeiture proceedings. Still others deal with specific offenses such as insider trading and other forms of securities fraud, computer crimes, bribery, gratuities, money laundering, environmental and other regulatory crimes, extortion, false claims, bank fraud, and tax crimes. The almost universal inclusion of conspiracy and RICO in the law school white collar crime curriculum is, in some respects, surprising.

Both are essentially inchoate or procedural crimes, in which the predicate offense is often far removed from the domain of what would ordinarily be considered white collar crime. (Under RICO, for example, the definition of "racketeering activity" includes, among many other offenses, both sexual exploitation of children and the use of interstate commercial facilities in the commission of murder for hire -neither of which could even remotely be considered a white collar crime.) The reason for such inclusion seems to be simply that such law school courses are designed to prepare students for the complex procedural context in which white collar criminal law is practiced, regardless of the actual substance of offenses studied.

In any event, given the tortuous definitional history of white collar crime in the social sciences, it is somewhat surprising that legal academics have expended relatively little effort in defining white collar crime or explaining the criteria upon which specific offenses are included in a given curriculum. Most of the textbooks and law review literature deal with the definitional question only briefly, and some not at all. Rather, there seems to be an assumption that the subject matter of white collar criminal law can be defined simply by reference to the offenses that are actually covered in a given course or casebook.

Criminal Law

In 1992, the sociologist Gilbert Geis, perhaps the most influential scholar of white collar crime since Edwin Sutherland, wrote that "no such designation as 'white collar crime' is to be found in the statute books." By this, Geis presumably meant that "white collar crime" is not a category of offenses in substantive criminal law and has no specific doctrinal significance. But, in fact, Geis was only half right. Though its use as such is admittedly rare, there are at least five contexts in which "white collar crime" appears in substantive criminal law.

First, the term has been used to identify aggravating circumstances that are relevant to sentencing. California Penal Code section 186.11 imposes what it refers to as a "white collar crime enhancement" for "[a]ny person who commits two or more related felonies, a material element of which is fraud or embezzlement." The enhancement consists of potentially higher fines and other penalties than would otherwise apply. Second, the term has been used to define a class of victims who are entitled to certain rights. Florida Statutes section 775.0844 authorizes various remedies (including restitution) for victims of "white collar crime," defined as including computer-related crimes, fraudulent practices, issuing worthless checks, bribery and corruption, forgery and counterfeiting, abuse and exploitation of the elderly and disabled, and racketeering.

Third, the term has been used to define the jurisdiction of certain state prosecuting officials. Fourth, the term has been used in the creation of funding mechanisms for law enforcement programs and research facilities. Finally, the term has been used in the title or section heading of various substantive criminal law provisions.

Sarbanes-Oxley Act

The most significant piece of legislation ever to use the term "white collar crime" is undoubtedly the Sarbanes-Oxley Act. The Act was passed amidst a sense of urgency, one might even say panic, that surrounded a string of spectacular corporate crime scandals that came to light during 2001 and 2002, involving firms such as WorldCom, Adelphia, Tyco, Arthur Andersen, and, most infamously, Enron. The statute enacts a multi-pronged approach to the prevention and punishment of white collar criminality: It creates a variety of new offenses, imposes stiffer penalties for existing offenses, requires companies to have audit committees, creates a board to regulate auditors, imposes new duties on CEOs and CFOs, makes it easier to file class actions against corporations and directors, imposes new regulatory compliance requirements, and expands the authority of the SEC over corporate governance matters.

Title IX of the Act, which has five substantive sections, is entitled "White-Collar Crime Penalty Enhancements." Sections 902, 903, and 904 increase the penalties for attempt and conspiracy, mail and wire fraud, and violation of section 501 of ERISA, respectively. Section 906 makes it a crime for CEOs and CFOs to fail to submit certain financial statements required by the Securities Exchange Act of 1934. Section 905, entitled "Amendment to Sentencing Guidelines Relating to Certain White-Collar Offenses," is the provision that is of particular relevance here.

Section 905 directed the U.S. Sentencing Commission to "review and, as appropriate, amend the Federal Sentencing Guidelines and related policy statements to implement the provisions of this Act." In carrying out this mission, the Commission was specifically instructed to "ensure that the sentencing guidelines and policy statements reflect the serious nature of the offenses and the penalties set forth in this Act, the growing incidence of serious fraud offenses which are identified above, and the need to modify the sentencing guidelines and policy statements to deter, prevent, and punish such offenses." The legislative history to section 905, which was cosponsored by Senators Orrin Hatch and Joseph Biden, clearly reflects the view that there is a disparity in how white collar and street crimes are treated under federal law, and that such disparity should be reduced or eliminated.

Earlier, Senator Hatch had remarked: A person who steals, defrauds, or otherwise deprives unsuspecting Americans of their life savings-no less than any other criminal-should be held accountable under our system of justice for the full weight of the harm he or she has caused. Innocent lives have been devastated by the crook who cooks the books of a publicly traded company, the charlatan who sells phony bonds, and the confidence man who runs a Ponzi scheme out there. These sorts of whitecollar criminals should find no soft spots in our laws or in their ultimate sentences, but all too often have done so. Whether there really is a disparity in the way comparable street and white collar crimes are punished, and whether title IX and the Sentencing Guidelines that were promulgated in response to it are the right way to deal with such a disparity are surely matters that are open to debate.

As we have seen, the term "white collar crime" was invented and propagated primarily by American scholars in the social sciences. Given the serious definitional controversy it has spawned, however, it is surprising that the term has been used so broadly outside the United States as well. The idea that there is some distinct category of crimes that corresponds to one or another conception of white collar crime seems to have struck a chord in a remarkably wide range of legal, academic, and popular cultures.

The term "white collar crime" was vague and imprecise when first conceived, and seems even more so today. Frequently, it means exactly the opposite of what it says, as when it is used to refer to merely deviant, noncriminalized activity. Sometimes it has been used overinclusively, such as when it refers to RICO, conspiracy, and corporate homicide. At other times it has been used underinclusively, as when it excludes various regulatory crimes and non-business-related offenses such as perjury and obstruction of justice. It has been used to refer to characteristics of persons rather than of offenses in a manner that is unacceptable within the framework of equal protection norms.

Its ideological overtones are significant and, in the pursuit of objective scientific and legal analysis, unforgivable. And although it was coined only sixty years ago, the point at which all parties might agree on a definition has long since passed. In light of all these problems, is there any justification for continuing to talk about white collar crime? It would be presumptuous of me, an academic lawyer, to offer advice to social scientists, law enforcement officials, practicing attorneys, social activists, or journalists, among others, on whether and, if so, how, the term should be used.

We would do better to think of "white collar crime" as entailing a collection of what philosophers call "family resemblances," rather than as susceptible to definition through a precise set of necessary and sufficient conditions. According to linguist George Lakoff, under the traditional, Aristotelian, or classical approach to classification, categories are "assumed to be abstract containers, with things either inside or outside the category. Things are assumed to be in the same category if and only if they have certain properties in common. And the properties they have in common are taken as defining the category." Under the classical model, then, categories are thought to have clear boundaries and be defined by common properties.

Such an approach seems appropriate in the context of defining criminal offenses. We want to know, to the extent possible, precisely which acts will fall within the category of, say, "murder," "rape," or "theft," and which will not. But many concepts in the social sciences, the humanities, the arts, and in our daily lives are simply not susceptible to such precise in-or-out definition. Such concepts have "fuzzy" boundaries that do not fit into the classical model. Wittgenstein gives the example of the category "game": Some games involve competition and strategizing (like chess and capture the flag). Others involve merely amusement. With categories of this sort, it seems impossible to find any single collection of properties that all members (and only those members) share.

Instead, categories like "game" seem to consist of a collection of members who share what Wittgenstein called "family resemblances." Just as family members may resemble each other in a variety of different traits (say, hair or eye color, facial features, or physical stature), what defines the category of games is not some single well-defined collection of common properties, but rather a collection of different resemblances, a whole series of similarities and relationships shared by the class.

It seems obvious that, at least for purposes of legal theory, "white collar crime" is better approached as a family resemblance-, rather than classical-, type category. It is probably impossible to find consensus on any single, well-defined collection of properties that all members of the category (and only those members) share. Instead, the term "white collar crime" should be understood to refer to a loosely defined collection of criminal offenses, forms of deviance, kinds of offenders, and moral concepts that share a series of similarities and relationships.

Citizens and decision makers need to know, as precisely as can be made out, what it is that constitutes "murder," a "felony," or "self-defense," and what does not. We aspire to precision in defining mens rea and actus reus elements, defenses, jurisdictional elements, and procedural rights. The fuzzier the boundaries of such concepts, the weaker, it would seem, is the moral authority of our law. Following are the five ways in which the term "white collar crime" has been used in substantive criminal law legislation. The first is as a label for aggravating circumstances relevant to sentencing. As a matter of policy, we might well want to enhance punishments for crimes (such as certain thefts) when they are committed by white collar-like means such as deception or breaches of trust.

Without a specific provision defining which offenses are to be covered, however, reference to a prototypical category such as white collar crime is likely to lead to obvious problems of legality, as it surely did in the case of the Alaska provision referred to above, in which the court was forced to refer to a dictionary in determining whether to apply the white collar crime aggravator. A related problem would occur under statutes that use the term to define a class of victims entitled to compensation or other procedural rights. Although the doctrine of nulla poena sine lege would not directly be implicated, the vague quality of the term would nevertheless result in a serious problem of statutory ambiguity.

Likewise are those statutes in which an otherwise undefined group of white collar crimes delineates the prosecutor's jurisdiction. In each of these three cases, problems of statutory ambiguity and legality could be avoided only if the term "white collar crime" were defined explicitly, by referring to covered offenses either by name or, better yet, specific statutory provision. In cases in which the term is so defined, it would perform no real doctrinal function, however. Rather, it would be intended primarily to add rhetorical force to the statutes in which it appears.

One can easily imagine why a state or the federal government would want to provide special resources for the fight against some collection of complex business frauds, corruption, and the like. In such circumstances, a strict, classical category would be unnecessary, since no cognizable legal rights would likely be affected by the determination that a particular offense is or is not a white collar crime. Indeed, given the likelihood that some investigations will target persons suspected of committing both white collar and non-white collar crimes, a certain amount of fuzziness in defining an agency's responsibilities would probably be welcome.

As for statutes such as the Sarbanes-Oxley and District of Columbia Theft and White Collar Crimes Acts, it appears that the term "white collar crime" is serving what is essentially a signaling or symbolic function, rather than a definitional one. Once again, no specific legal rights are affected by how the term is defined. In each case, the legislature is doing nothing more than sending a message that it regards the offenses covered as part of a loosely defined moral or political, rather than legal, category.

6

Corruption, Governance and Security

Bribery abroad by transnationals headquartered in rich countries continues to be a serious issue in emerging markets. In order to assess the relative importance of legal and illegal forms of corruption, in which many in the corporate and public sectors in both rich and emerging countries appear to be involved, we have carried out an empirical analysis of the data emerging from this year's Executive Opinion Survey (EOS) of the World Economic Forum. In order to provide an initial framework of governance linkages that cut across national borders, we must bridge the traditionally separate issues of national governance and global and domestic security.

These security issues are not subject to measurement, and based on an analysis of the EOS data, empirically review the relative importance and links between global and domestic governance aspects of security, focusing on common crime, organized crime, money laundering, and the cost of terrorism threat. Number of countries in the rich world have serious domestic problems with undue influence-even capture-as concern key public policies, laws and regulations, in addition to the more recent onslaught of security threats. The mere fact of strong traditional rule-of-law institutions, as is the case in the G-7 and other rich countries, guarantees neither level playing fields-i. e. freedom from influence peddling-nor protection against terrorism.

Revisiting the long-term trend evidence from the most recent EOS, overall, this stagnating trend does not appear to have been reversed over the past year. While significant upward changes are unlikely in longer-term institutional issues, there appears to be some variation in trends across country groups. Notably, even if there is still a substantial governance gap between the two groups in many dimensions, there are some hopeful signs for emerging economies in certain governance aspects, in possible contrast with the wealthier OECD countries.

For example, in Figure 1, the EOS ratings given by firms on the control of judicial bribery since the late nineties, showing, somewhat surprisingly, that the perception of this phenomenon by executives in the rich countries has deteriorated, while improving somewhat in the new industrializing countries (NICs) of east Asia, as well as in emerging economies. The assessment of judicial bribery in Latin America is less dire than it was last year, although it remains very low, and still below the average for all emerging economies.

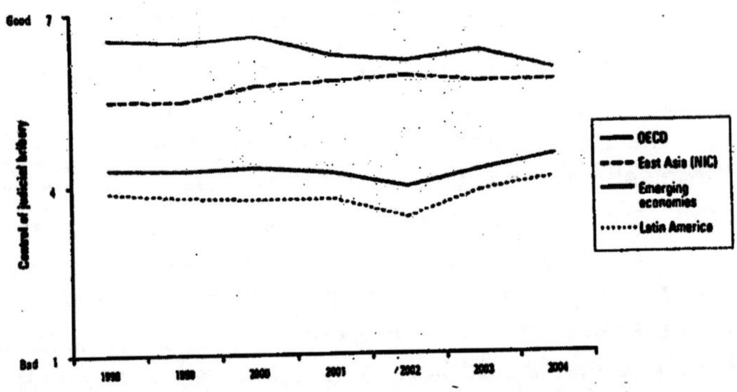

Figure 1. Control of judicial bribery over time: EOS 1998-2004

However, while this year's data suggest that there may be some early signs of potential convergence between the rich countries and emerging economies, the extent of the disparity in this and other traditional dimensions of corruption-particularly various forms of bribery-between OECD and emerging economies is large. Moreover, there is significant variation within regions and groups of countries. For example, Figure 1 also shows that the new tigers of east Asia (NICs) have approached the standards of the rich countries, while the middle-income Latin American countries rate well below the NICs, and even the emerging economy average.

Obstacles to Business Startup

A key insight that has emerged in the empirical study of governance in recent years, thanks in large measure to the analysis of the rich survey data from the EOS, is the importance of unbundling manifestations of corruption and governance. This implies that it is misguided to generalize, based on the assessment of one particular governance dimension, or of an average for the country. This is because there are large variations in governance quality and performance across different dimensions. By showing the trend over time in the ease of entry to enterprises, Figure 2 provides insight into a rather different challenge to businesses, related to the regulatory regime component of governance.

The evidence reveals that the striking gap is not between the rich countries of the OECD and the emerging economies overall-in fact, on average, the gap is not very large between both group averages-but between particular sub-regions. First, it should be noted that firms in the NICs of east Asia report fewer obstacles to business entry than those in rich OECD countries, reflecting the highly regulated nature of economies in some OECD countries.

The gap between the east Asian NICs, on the one hand, and Latin America-as well as the surveyed countries of the former Soviet Union, which also score poorly-on the other, is particularly acute, reflecting once again the magnitude of the institutional and investment climate challenges faced by many countries in Latin America.

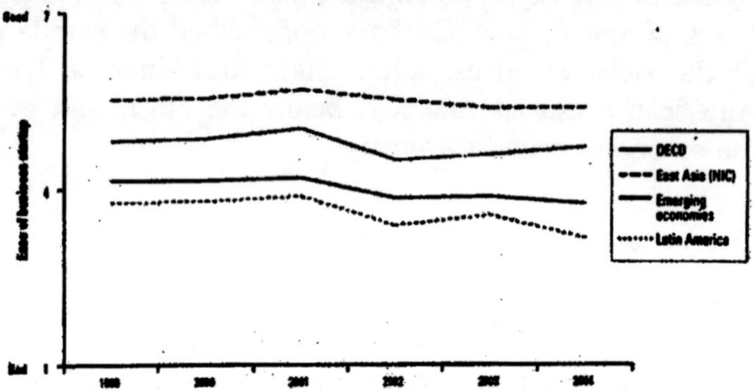

Figure 2. Ease of business startup over time: EOS 1999-2004

At the same time, there are also rather telling gaps among different subgroups of the rich countries of the OECD, challenging the traditional notion of bundling them as a uniform block. Although not shown in the figure, the data indicate that firms in the Nordic countries report exemplary ease of entry, in sharp contrast to the countries of southern Europe, which report greater restrictions on business startups than for Eastern Europe, even more restrictive than for developing countries.

The EOS survey data from firms themselves provide a window on what is taking place on the ground (de facto), to complement, and also challenge, assessments based on official statistics or information of an administrative or legal (de jure) nature. This microeconomic analysis of governance obstacles reveals particular challenges also afflicting countries in the OECD.

Some may react to Figure 2, showing firms' own reports on the ease of entry for enterprises in their country, by pointing out that such data are more telling about the conventional business climate than about governance. Furthermore, those who are keen to dismiss the sobering information provided by the EOS data tend to equate enterprise responses with unreliable perceptions, not mirroring what actually takes place in reality.

In fact, as both survey and statistical techniques have improved, it is increasingly possible to make cautious inferences from data emerging from a large number of enterprise responses. While an element of perception will undoubtedly remain, these perceptions are shown to be important, since firms' own assessments of the quality and characteristics of the surrounding business climate do shape their own business and investment decisions. A useful exercise to codify the regulations required to set up a firm was recently carried out by the "Doing Business" (DB) project at the World Bank, based on information provided by lawyers in many countries. This exercise, based on "objective" indicators, in contrast with what the EOS data suggests, revealed that an overall improvement in the regulatory environment faced by enterprises has recently taken place.

At the same time, as shown in Figure 2, we have the more subjective data from the firms themselves, on how they see the obstacles to business entry on the ground. This data, along with other variables from the EOS, constitutes what we could call the de facto data. How do the de jure and de facto data relate to each other? Table 1 explain the de facto perceptions of the firms emerging from the EOS data, taking into consideration the de jure information on administrative requirements. The de jure variable for minimum capital requirements has no explanatory power-a zero correlation, in fact-with the de facto variable.

The de jure variable, measuring the complexity of starting a business performs somewhat better than the others we reviewed, explaining, on its own, about one third of the variation on the "ease of entry" (de facto) variable reported by the firms. Yet even in this case most of the variance is left unexplained. Thus, an alternative one ought to consider is whether the de facto variable, based on the firm reports, is actually capturing a key dimension of the policy and regulatory "implementation on the ground", since the actual implementation outcomes are not measurable from the de jure information, based as it is on a priori information, on what is on the books, in legal statutes or official statistics.

Governance factors appear to be extremely important in explaining the firms' reported ease or difficulty in starting up a business; in fact, they appear to matter more than the particular number of official steps required. These results are operationally relevant, and are not merely a statistical or academic exercise. First, they suggest an important reason for systematically collecting and analyzing survey data such as the EOS, since these reported perceptions provide significant information on the quality of institutional implementation on the ground. Second, they caution against over-reliance on official, "objective" statistics on business/investment climate issues, which ignore key issues of implementation on the ground.

Thus, although objective measures can also be valuable, they should be supplemented by measures capturing the reality of how rules, regulations and policies are implemented on the ground. Finally, these results point to the fact that governance issues are critical for the business environment. Indeed, one of the key obstacles to ease of entry by firms, namely corruption, is, in itself, a core governance variable.

Investment climate and business development issues cannot be narrowly viewed, merely by counting the number of legal or regulatory steps, and without understanding the institutional context within which such regulations and policies are formulated-including the vested interests that shape them-and implemented. The nature and quality of institutional and policy formulation and implementation in this area is, in fact, strongly anchored in governance, and in many countries corruption may be a particular hindrance to enterprise development, the business climate, and competitiveness.

SIGNIFICANCE OF GOVERNANCE

Listening to the reports of firms can provide valuable information and insights. Figure 3, segmenting the sample between OECD and emerging economies, depicts the frequency of the leading constraints listed by each firm.

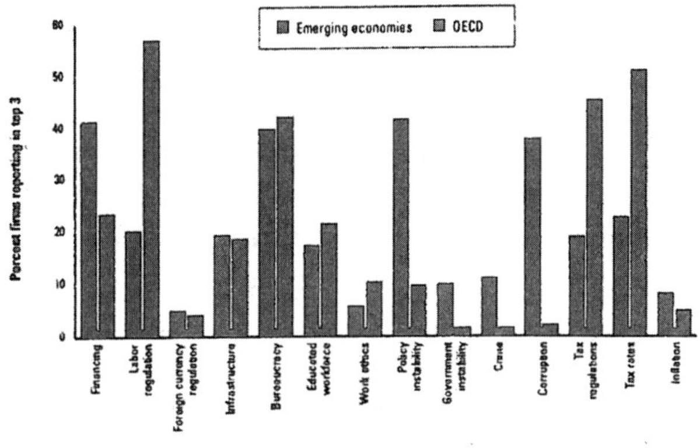

Figure 3. Key constraints to business: OECD vs. emerging economies: EOS 2004

For emerging countries, they were seen to be corruption, bureaucracy, policy instability and financing, while for the wealthy countries of the OECD, the leading obstacles were labor regulations, bureaucracy, and taxes. When organizing the fifteen listed constraints around seven key institutional and policy clusters, the governance cluster, comprising corruption and bureaucracy, emerges as the most binding constraint, on average, worldwide, and was named as one of the top three constraints by firms in 79 out of the 104 EOS sample countries. Although the clusters of finance, labor markets/human capital, tax regime and infrastructure also pose significant obstacles in many countries, they lag far behind the governance cluster.

Figure 3 also shows that at the other extreme of the spectrum, the macroeconomic policy cluster, represented by foreign exchange regulations and macro-economic instaility/inflation, no longer figures as a priority constraint to the enterprise sector. The World Economic Forum's Growth Competitiveness Index (GCI), which rates the relative competitiveness of all EOS countries, has been one of the key contributions of the GCR over the years. There are several ways to analyze the possible key determinants of country competitiveness, as measured by the GCI, but any viable analysis would have to account for the pitfalls of confusing simple association with clear causality, or of equating fundamental determinants of competitiveness with an observed empirical link between the GCI and current variables, which may simply reflect a quasi-tautology.

The latter is because the GCI is, in itself, a composite of many current EOS and external variables. For this simple empirical inquiry which has no input role in the construction of the GCI. We have seen that firms in many countries responded that some constraints, especially those have a direct bearing upon business. But does this necessarily imply the loss of a country's competitiveness edge? We probed statistically the link between the various constraints to business given by the firms, on the one hand, and the GCI for the country, on the other.

Sperformed simple correlations between the extent to which each potential constraint poses a significant obstacle to business and the GCI ranking. By far the highest correlation, at - 0. 76, was between the corruption constraint and the GCI. But this result does not control for other factors. In principle, it could be that in some countries there are many (more than five) significant obstacles to doing business, and corruption may be proxying for such omitted factors.

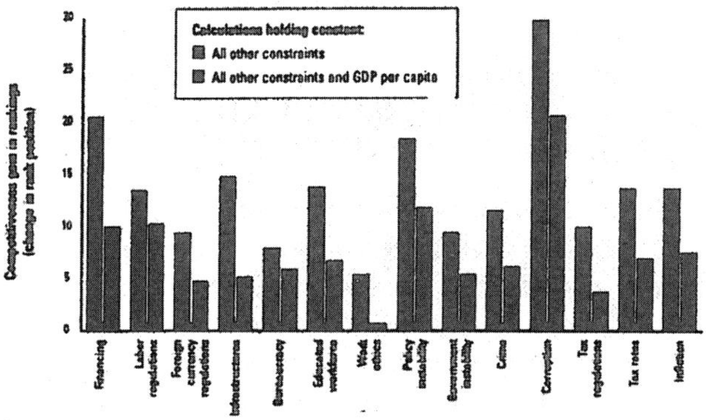

Figure 4. Impact on Growth Competitiveness Index: Rank of improvement in constraint to the firm

Under either scenario, the importance of tackling corruption in order to improve a country's competitiveness appears to be clear. A country that manages to reduce the extent of corruption as an obstacle to business by one standard deviation can expect on average, to move up about 30 rank positions-if income per capita is not maintained at a fixed level-or, more conservatively, about 20 rank positions if income per capita is held constant. The latter is indeed a conservative assumption, since it has already been empirically shown that improved governance results in higher incomes per capita. But even under this conservative scenario, the potential payoff for a country's competitiveness of addressing corruption as an obstacle to enterprise appears to be very large indeed.

In fact, based on the actual responses by firms worldwide to the list of 15 obstacles, removal of no single other obstacle would come close to offering such a large payoff for improving a country's GCI standing. But could this particularly striking finding be simply the outcome of the poor country-rich country global divide, capturing the "fact" that the poorer countries have a larger corruption problem than the richer ones? Indeed, even if one concentrates on only the top half of the EOS country sample, in terms of income per capita, the resulting magnitude and significance of the control of corruption constraint to its impact on the GCI is very similar to that of the full sample.

At the core of this finding is the fact that there is significant variation among middle- and higher-income countries as regards the quality of governance in general, and in the control of corruption in particular. While richer countries tend to exhibit less prevalence of blatant and illegal forms of corruption, the wealthier countries, including many in the OECD, do face challenges related to corruption and misgovernance.

Much recent study of governance and corruption has been based on the simple empirical observation, using available worldwide indices, that, on average, richer countries are perceived to be much less corrupt than poorer developing countries. The undisputed serious governance and corruption challenge faced by most emerging economies may have encouraged a sense of complacency in the richer world-and within it the OECD-regarding corruption and misgovernance. Moreover, such relative comparisons presumed a lack of interdependency, and thus ignored the potential role of OECD in setting standards of governance in emerging economies.

Using comparisons based on the analysis of the EOS data for 2004, some of the strengths and weaknesses of the richer world, with regard to issues of governance and corruption. Conventional wisdom points to low corruption within OECD countries. The first table in Kaufmann featured the average percentile ranks for each region, based on worldwide governance indicators. On average, OECD countries ranked at about the 90th percentile.

However, these are averages, within a relative ranking, and the measures included in these indices relate to the standard definition of corruption, namely the abuse of public office for private gain. Hence, the focus is on the illegal nature of acts such as bribery, in order to illicitly derive private gain at the expense of the public. Let us assess, however, whether even relatively satisfactory average rankings may mask problems within OECD countries, and whether some other non-traditional forms of corruption, may emerge as significant problems.

First, it is worth noting that, although this year's EOS provides some support for the notion that traditional corruption levels in OECD may not be very high-particularly as regards domestic bribery payments-even this relatively low bribery percentage can translate into sizeable absolute amounts. This is due to the sheer economic might of OECD countries, which account for about 80 percent of the world's output.

Second, while the average in relative terms is not high, there is substantial variation within OECD countries. The long-standing OECD members from southern Europe exhibit higher levels of bribery prevalence than the tigers of east Asia, or of some emerging countries in other regions, such as Chile, or Slovenia, other new EU members from Eastern Europe, and, in some dimensions, Botswana in Africa. The high variation within the OECD is illustrated by the fact that the gap in the prevalence of bribery between the exemplary Nordic countries, on the one hand, and southern Europe, on the other, is larger than the gap between southern Europe and the average for all emerging economies.

Third, there has historically been an epistemological and legalistic set of biases in the study of corruption, which, as hinted earlier, relies on a definition that, given today's realities and problems, begs an open challenge. Specifically, the traditional notion of "abuse of public office for private gain" has often been interpreted in a legal sense to mean committing an illegal act, and, more broadly, placing exclusive focus on the public sector. However, the reality of corruption is two-fold: first, it most often involves collusion between at least two parties, typically from the public and private sectors, for a corrupt act to take place; second, where the rules of the game, laws and institutions have been shaped, at least in part, to benefit certain vested interests, some forms of corruption may be legal in some countries.

For instance, soft forms of political funding are legally permitted in some countries, through the creative use of legal loopholes, and may exert enormous influence in shaping institutions and policies benefiting the contributing private interests, and at the expense of the broader public welfare. A similar problem is seen in favoritism in procurement, where, a transparent and level playing field may be absent, without necessarily involving illegal bribery. Consequently, it is timely to explore a less traditional definition of corruption, one that accounts more broadly for the undue benefits derived by the private few from their excessive influence in shaping the institutions, policies, laws and regulations of the state to their own ends.

Vested interests that remove public policy from the realm of democratic-i. e. contestable-decision-making should be an important component of this new definition. Undue influence by private vested interests on the state sector may, or may not, involve the exchange of a bribe or related form of illegal corruption. In other words, room is thus provided, in this more neutral definition of corruption, for so-called legal forms of corruption, which can by defined simply as the "privatization of public policy. " Such an alternative definition focuses on the key mediating institution or agent committing the abuse of power, namely the institution of (undue) influence, driven by vested interests.

It also provides for neutrality in terms of the legality, or lack thereof, of the corrupt act itself. Finally, it is neutral as regards the private or public nature of the sector players, implicitly recognizing the important and activist role of those in the private sector as well. In particular, it enables us to scrutinize the role of corporate ethics, in both its legal and illegal corruption dimensions, alongside the often-cited role of public sector ethics.

We posited that corruption can be more broadly construed as attempts to exert undue influence in order to "privatize" public policy, and/or appropriate the provision of public services for private purposes. To assess the empirical applicability and validity of this general notion, we carried out a data exercise with the EOS dataset, which contains a wealth of answers to questions on various dimensions of corporate and public sector ethics and governance.

To construct ehtic indices, each relevant individual governance question in the EOS was mapped to one index. Each set of input questions was averaged to create the respective ethics index. The theoretical range of each index is from 0 to 100, reflecting the average percentage of firms in each country reporting a satisfactory situation on the particular ethics-related EOS question. In brief, the main components and indices comprised the following:

i) the Corporate Illegal Corruption Component (CICC), measuring a) types of bribery, in which a private agent plays a key role (as in procurement, shaping regulations and policies), and b) the firm's own corporate ethics self-rating based on a question in the EOS);

ii) the Corporate Legal Corruption Component (CLCC), measuring legal dimensions of undue influence, such as legal political finance; the particular influence of powerful firms on politicians and policymaking, etc;

iii) the Corporate Ethics Index (CEI), which represents the simple average of both the legal and illegal corporate corruption components in items (i) and (ii);

iv) the Public Sector Ethics Index (PSEI), measuring the variables related to public integrity, bribery and favoritism in the public sector;

v) the Judicial/Legal Effectiveness Integrity Index (JLEI), focusing on questions of effectiveness and integrity of the legal and judicial system;

vi) the Corporate Governance Index (CGI), based on standard questions (internal to the firm) regarding corporate governance, such as the relationship between board and management, etc.

The last index, for Corporate Governance (CGI), which does not fall within the realm of ethics properly interpreted, was constructed as a comparator from a traditional corporate field. The five other indices all share a clear focus on ethics. What do these indices show? The indices for a number of selected sub-regions are presented in Figure 5, from which we can observe that, consistent with the earlier findings on traditional illegal forms of corruption, it is misleading to generalize about all rich countries, simply by focusing on the average of the rich countries in the OECD.

The first set of indices in Figure 5 focuses, in fact, on the illegal corruption component of corporate ethics (CICC). The gap between the Nordic and southern European countries is larger than that between the Nordic countries and the tigers of east Asia, or between southern Europe and the average for all non-OECD countries. As one moves to an analysis of the legalS corruption component of corporate ethics (CLCC, the second set of columns), the reality of OECD standards, on average, becomes even more disturbing.

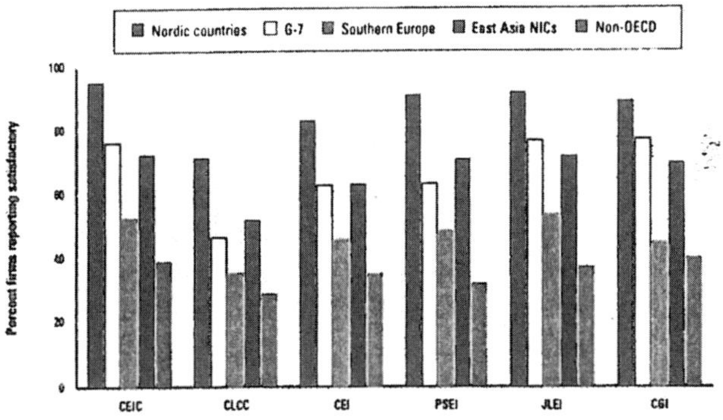

Figure 5. Corporate and public sector ethics indices for 2004

Again, that average masks large variations within the rich OECD countries: while the Nordic countries continue to excel, relatively speaking, the averages for the countries of the G-7 and southern Europe are rather low. On the better side of the corporate legal corruption ethical spectrum, countries such as Norway, the Netherlands, Finland and Singapore all score in the midto high 70s, indicating that the vast majority of the respondents regard their reality as satisfactory. On the legal corruption component of the corporate ethics index, the United States, in stark contrast, rates a mere 30, Italy 35, Spain, Portugal, France, and Canada about 40, and Japan 45-all below the emerging economies, such as Chile, Botswana, Colombia, and South Africa.

In short, the Nordics do well on this dimension of corporate ethics, but not so the G-7 and southern European countries. This points to the pitfalls of bundling the rich OECD countries as one homogeneous group. Indeed, it is telling that in this legal corruption component in particular, the tigers of east Asia perform better than the G-7 block. In fact, the OECD as a whole, and the G-7 in particular, perform much worse in this legal corruption dimension of corporate ethics than in its illegal counterpart. This evidence on the extent of the problem of legal corruption in the G-7 and southern Europe is noteworthy, because the focus of international comparisons has, until now, been on the illegal dimension of corruption.

This, in turn, has perpetuated the notion that there is a huge gap in ethical behavior between the first world-usually perceived as ethical across the board-and the third world, and has led to the neglect of the measurement and analysis of subtler forms of corruption. Clearly, in many of the heavyweight countries of the OECD, the powerful corporations exert extensive influence over policymaking. This recognition of the extent of undue influence by powerful elements in the corporate sector carries with it both domestic and global governance implications, as illustrated by the strong pressure to continue protecting trade in many rich countries. This, in turn, has been very costly to development of the emerging economies.

The third set of columns in Figure 5 presents the summary Corporate Ethics Index (CEI), as the simple average of the first two (illegal and legal) components. Not surprisingly, similar observations apply, indicating large discrepancies in corporate ethics performance within OECD countries and blocks, and the less-than-stellar performance on corporate ethics by firms in the G-7 and southern Europe. The fourth and fifth set of columns show the ethics index for the public (PSEI) and judicial/legal (JLEI) sectors, respectively. Here, it is noteworthy that the G-7 appears to rate relatively well in the Judicial/Legal Effectiveness and Integrity Index, but not as well for the executive side of the public sector. By contrast, the Nordics (at the top again), southern Europe, and the NICs of east

Asia all rate their executive and judicial/legal sectors similarly. It is also evident that the emerging economies still face major problems in public sector ethics, as indicated by their rather low standing in the PSEI index.

The final set of columns, as a comparator, refers to the measurement in a simple index, of traditional notions of corporate governance (CGI). In this area, the G-7 rates relatively well, in fact, closing in on the Nordic countries. This relatively good quality of corporate governance also contrasts with the undue influence (legal corruption) component of corporate ethics, where we observe that the G-7-as well as a number of others in OECD-rate rather low. Next we assess a particular dimension of global interdependence. Having analyzed the behavior of enterprises in their home countries, we now turn to the question of how enterprises from the same countries behave and operate abroad in a globalized world.

Bribing far from Home

A significant period of time has now elapsed, presumably permitting implementation to proceed on the OECD's Anti-Bribery Convention. The EOS collects information on whether firms operating in the surveyed country have headquarters abroad, and, if so, where they are located. Consistent with the OECD Convention, the focus of the brief inquiry reported here is on traditional forms of bribery, particularly, but not solely, on public procurement. From the analysis of the data on these transnational firms, comprising a significant portion of the sample, the following salient results emerged, summarized in Figures 6 and 7, measuring bribery at home and abroad, and procurement and administrative bribe fees, respectively.

The data show that transnationals (or multinationals, MNCs) operating abroad, within the OECD, exhibit behavior very similar to that of their domestic counterparts in the OECD home country. By contrast, those transnational firms headquartered in OECD countries, but operating in non-OECD countries, exhibit much lower (often illegal) corporate ethics standards, often more similar, in fact, to those of the recipient country. In Figure 6, the leftmost column (of the four representing each type of bribery) indicates the relatively low extent of bribery in the home OECD country, while the second column from left shows the relatively low incidence of bribery when operating in another OECD country. By contrast, the third column for each type of bribery presents the high prevalence of bribery by firms headquartered in a rich OECD country but operating outside the OECD.

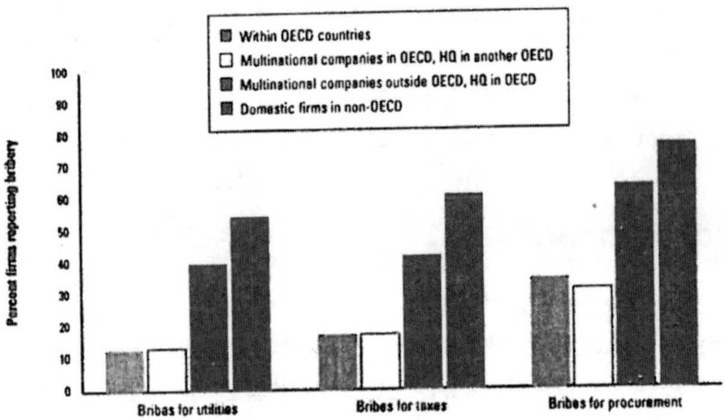

Figure 6. Frequency of bribery at home and abroad: EOS 2004

Rather than exhibiting practices consistent with many other (domestic) firms in the country of origin, in which they are headquartered, their behavior more closely resembles that of the domestic firms within the non-OECD destination country itself (fourth column of each bribery type). These differences in bribery practice, often determined more by the characteristics of the destination country than by the country of origin, or by international legal instruments, appear to be aimed at public procurement, an intended focus of the OECD transnational anti-bribery convention.

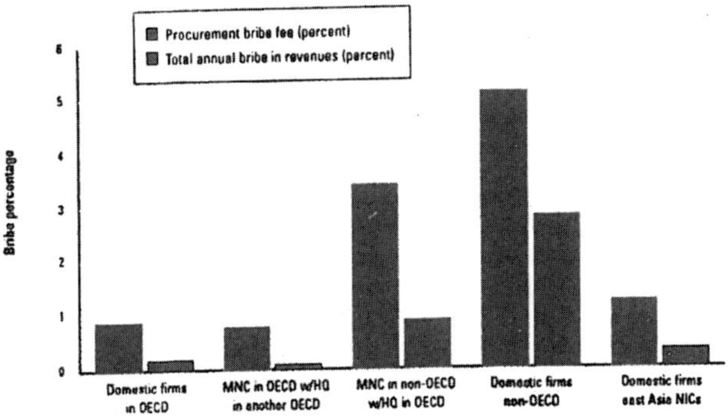

Figure 7. Procurement and administrative bribe fee and shares: EOS 2004

Figure 7 shows a similar pattern, if one focuses on a quantitative assessment of bribery, whether of the bribe fee percentage paid by firms in public procurement (left side of each paired column), or of the overall share of bribes in the firm's annual revenues (right side of each paired column). Again, the that firms headquartered in the OECD, operating outside of the OECD, are engaged in bribery to a larger extent than at home. In fact, their bribery levels may exceed those of the NIC firms at their home countries in east Asia. Thus, in spite of the years of implementation of the OECD Convention, it is apparent that there is an "adaptation" by many MNCs to the local bribery practices.

Corporations in countries having a much longer history of transnational anti-bribery legislation, such as the United States, also appear to exhibit a large gap between their corporate ethics standards at home, as compared with those operating in countries outside the OECD. Such a gap between corporate ethics standards at home and abroad is apparent across all the rich OECD countries, even for those settings where they have exemplary standards at home, such as the Nordic countries. Indeed, the significant gap between corporate ethics behavior at home and abroad suggests the extent to which incentives are important; hence, adaptation to local institutional arrangements takes place. Not all the evidence on transnational bribery points in the wrong direction, however.

While the levels remain high, so is the gap between practices at home and abroad. An initial comparison of the frequency of bribery this year, as compared with last year, suggests that the prevalence of bribery may not be as high as it was last year. It is obviously too early to tell whether this is the initiation of a trend of improvements over the coming years. Further, for such structural medium-term improvement to take place, it is worth pondering at this stage whether, in addition to exhortations, voluntary codes, and legal fiat, the incentives for improved corporate ethics practices abroad require fuller alignment. A focus on incentives, in turn, may require additional measures, to complement those already in place.

The rich countries of the OECD benefit significantly from trade, labor and human capital from the emerging economies. Similarly, the countries in emerging economies benefit from many economic linkages with their richer counterparts, and more generally from globalization. It goes without saying that there are areas where improvement is badly needed, such as those related to governance and to the corporate ethics of some MNCs abroad. Moreover, there are areas of close interdependence in today's world which entail particular costs and threats. One such area refers to security, where inter alia, data for empirical analysis has been lacking, impairing analysis and perpetuating misconceptions.

Security and Crime

Given the type of governance and security challenges facing many countries today, it is pertinent to ask whether metrics and data analysis can shed light on the global and domestic security concerns being faced presently by the rich world, and their implications for governance. Security has been an area notable for the paucity of internationally comparable and reliable empirical statistics. Preliminary empirical analysis of elements bridging the traditionally separate issues of national governance and global and domestic security. We also challenge the notion that these security issues are not subject to measurement. In order to do this, we performed a limited analysis of the EOS data on the report by firms of the costs to business of terrorism, common crime and organized crime, as well as their reports on the prevalence of money laundering through the banking and non-banking (informal financial) sectors. Some results of interest emerge, summarized in the following.

The global nature of the threats and costs of terrorism: In Figure 8, the costs of terrorism as reported by the enterprise sector appear to be similar, on average, for the key regions of the world. Each region reports a sizeable, if not extreme, cost of the terrorism threat. For instance, in Figure 8, it is interesting to note the contrast between the relative uniformity in regional averages of the perceived cost of the threat of terrorism, on the one hand, and the perceived cost of crime or state capture, which varies significantly from region to region, on the other. Terrorism is a globalized phenomenon.

The challenge for some rich countries: The reported threat of terrorism by firms in the rich countries is at least as high as the world average. Given the industrialized countries' generally high level of institutional development, this implies that the reported cost of the terrorist threat is high, as compared with other forms of crime. Thus, it is not surprising to observe, in Figure 8, that for the rich countries, on average, the terrorist threat exceeds the perceived cost of organized crime, of common crime, or of the impact on domestic competition of corrupt capture by powerful elite firms.

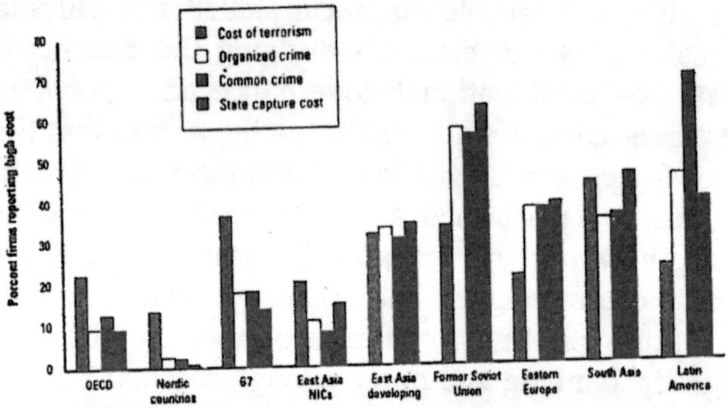

Figure 8. Global vs. domestic governance challenges: Firms reporting high cost of terrorism and crime: EOS 2004

In fact, there appear to be very significant differences within regions. Among the rich countries, as seen in Figure 8, there are sharp differences between the G-7 and the Nordic countries, between south Asia and the NICs of east Asia, and, among the former socialist countries, between the countries of the former Soviet Union included in the EOS and those of Eastern Europe.

Similarly, the differences in the perceived cost of terror across countries in a given region is striking. For instance, as shown in Figure 9, the cost of the terrorism threat as reported by the firms is significantly higher than the costs from organized crime in countries like the US, UK, Israel, Egypt, Spain, Sri Lanka, and Japan, while the contrary is the case in countries like Guatemala, Italy, Nigeria, Mexico, Ukraine and Venezuela. Countries such as Bangladesh, Colombia, and the Philippines face both problems acutely, according to the firms' reports; by contrast, neither of these security concerns seems to present itself in the reports from the Nordic countries.

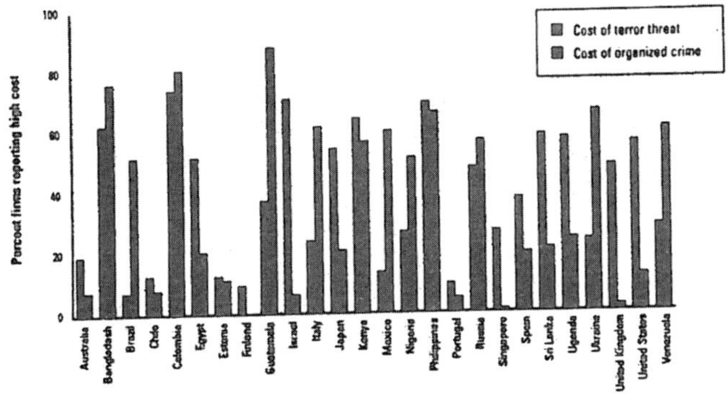

Figure 9. Firms reporting perceived cost of terrorism threat and organized crime: EOS 2004 (selected countries)

The level of development and quality of domestic institutions is weakly linked to terrorist threat, but strongly linked to other security challenges: The fact that terrorism has significant global aspects, in contrast to other problems, can be seen from the evidence summarized in Figure 10. First, to test whether the quality of domestic institutions may be a determining factor or not, there appears to be a very low correlation between an effective parliament in a country and the reported perceived cost of the terrorist threat to that country.

Even the correlation between the perceived cost of terrorism variable and the quality of the police in the threatened country is extremely low, as shown in the left half of the paired columns. This contrasts sharply with the close link between both organized and common crime, on the one hand, and the quality of domestic institutions, on the other.

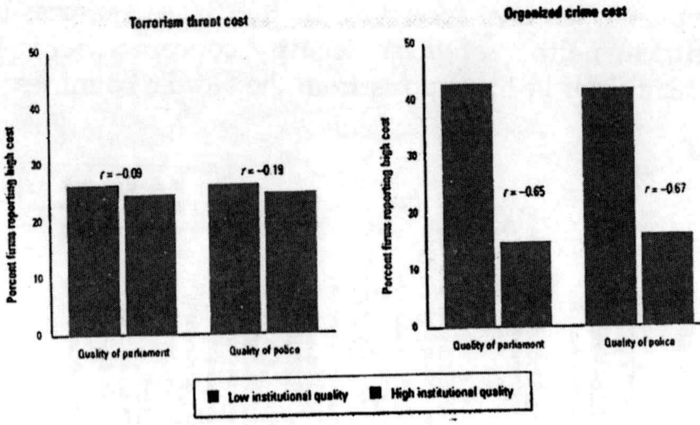

Figure 10. Relationship between threat of terrorism or organized crime and quality of domestic institutions

In the right half of Figure 10, the correlation coefficient between the quality of parliament or the police, on the one hand, and the cost of organized crime in the country is about 0. 7 (and similarly, although not shown, it correlates very closely with common crime) —a far cry from the negligible correlation between the costs of the threat of terrorism for the country's enterprise sector and the quality of their domestic institutions (in this case the parliament or the police). Indeed, the initial empirical analysis suggests that the cost of the terrorist threat for a country seems to be only marginally associated with its own levels of income per capita. In fact, there are countries under threat at every stage of development, ranging from poor countries such as Bangladesh, Nigeria, Indonesia and the Philippines, lowto middle- income countries such as Colombia and Russia, higher-income countries such as Israel and Spain, to the United States at the high end. Conversely, for each one of these stages of development there are examples of countries facing a low terrorist threat.

The complex link between domestic governance, money laundering, and terrorism: The evidence at hand suggests that the link between money laundering and terrorism is far less linear or straightforward than commonly thought, for a number of reasons. First, the financial requirements for terrorism can often be relatively modest; even though it is often linked to laundered money, the financing of terrorism does not necessarily depend on it; thus, for instance, financing can be state-sponsored, or be supported through legitimate businesses. Where the financing of terrorism depends on laundered funds, it does not follow that the culprit is money laundered through the banking sector.

To a significant extent, money laundering takes place through informal institutions. In fact, in response to the EOS question on the prevalence of different types of money laundering, the reports of firms from most countries indicate that money laundering through the non-banking sector is at least as prevalent, if not more, as that going through the banking sector. Terrorism may be construed, therefore, as an extreme global challenge, in that, in most settings, country-specific institutions and measures can have only a limited impact on diminishing the threat of terrorism in that country.

However, while it has global links, money laundering, as with organized crime, has a larger domestic component than terrorism, since the quality and strength of domestic governance and institutions are closely related to the prevalence of money laundering in a country. The empirical evidence at hand supports this contention. First, at a mere 0. 16, and contrary to conventional wisdom, the correlation between the extent of money laundering in a country and the threat of terrorism in that country is strikingly low. By contrast, in Figure 11, the correlation between corruption in the public budget and money laundering is much higher, at 0. 87.

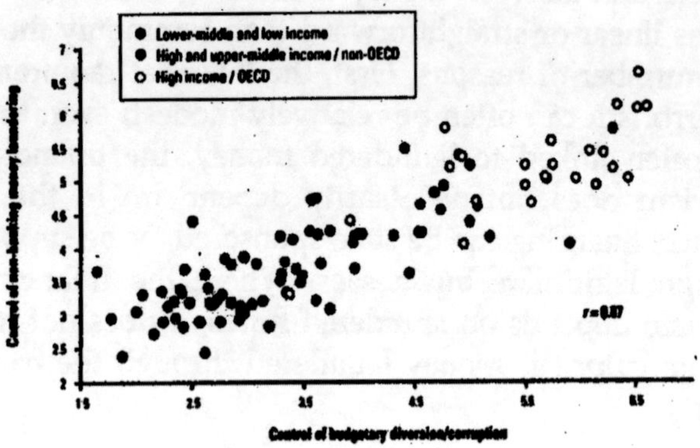

Figure 11. Non-banking money laundering vs. budgetary leakages

Thus, this initial empirical inquiry suggests that the costs and threat of terrorism cannot be easily explained by focusing on simplistic financial variables, such as money laundering through the banking system, or by merely concentrating on domestic developmental factors. Instead, more promising avenues are offered by probing more deeply, and empirically, into the set of countries where quasi or full-fledged state failure has taken place, at the one extreme, and into the powerful countries of the OECD, on the other, and to their complex interface.

In terms of quasi, or actual state failure, a developmental and basic governance approach provides potential insights, complemented by the challenge of non-democratic regimes. Finally, insufficient attention has been paid to the problem of unequal distribution of wealth worldwide; the fact is that worldwide wealth and income inequality across countries is much more severe than the already gross inequities existing within countries.

7

Threats of Economic Crime

Economic crime remains a significant threat to companies across all industries and territories. Well over a third of respondent companies worldwide (37%) said they had suffered from one or more serious frauds during the previous two years.

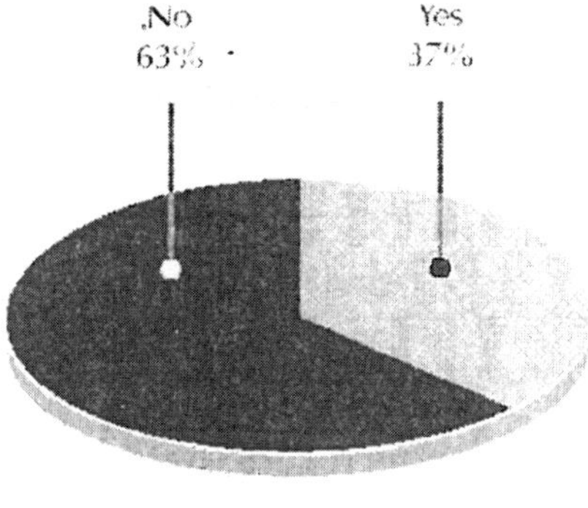

Figure 1. Victims of fraud

The number of organisations reporting fraud in Western Europe has grown from 29% to 34%, and in Central and Eastern Europe from 26% to 37%. This increase appears to reflect two factors:

— greater awareness of fraud leading to heightened detection rate; and

— a growing desire for transparency, particularly in European Union 'accession countries'.

The highest levels of economic crime were reported by respondents in Africa (51%) and North America (41%). In contrast, respondents in Russia and Turkey reported no economic crime at all. There is clearly some way to go in both these countries to either improve detection or to promote greater transparency.

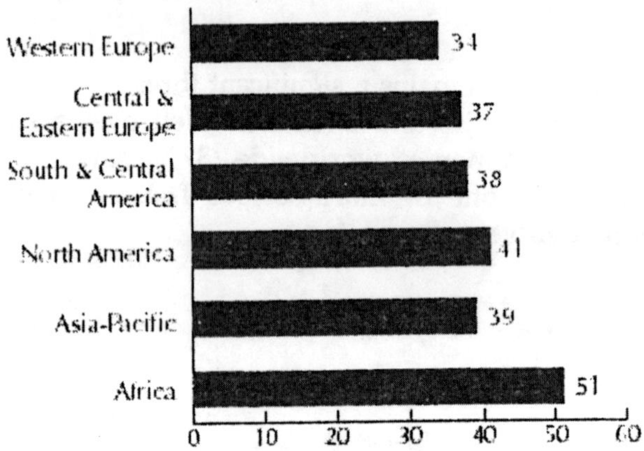

Figure 2. Victims of fraud

Direct relationship between company size and the likelihood of economic crime. Only 37% of smaller companies (less than 1,000 employees in territory) reported economic crime, compared to 52% in larger companies (over 1,000 employees in territory). Possible reasons for this higher incidence among larger companies include their greater devolution of operational responsibility, tendency to pursue opportunities in unfamiliar markets, higher transactional complexity, and greater opportunities for collusion amongst employees. Staff in larger corporations may also be less concerned about the financial well being of their employer, regarding fraud as a "victimless crime". Larger companies also generally invest more in fraud risk management systems. This will increase detection rates for most economic crimes.

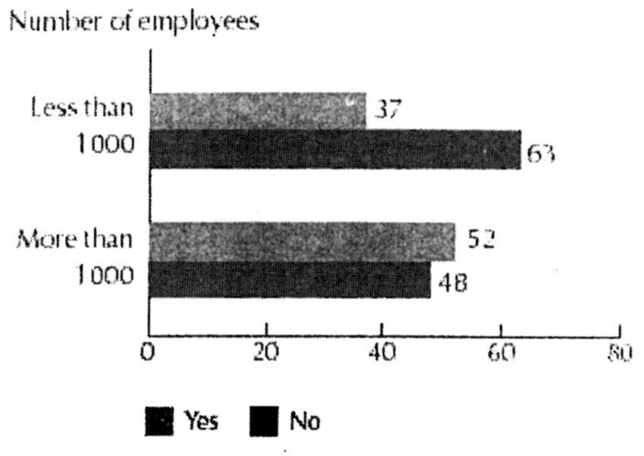

Figure 3. Victims of fraud by organisation size (worldwide)

While all commercial activity is vulnerable to economic crime, its incidence varies between industries. Financial services (banking, insurance) have reported more incidences of economic crime than other industries. The financial services industry is an obvious target for any fraudster, given the significant quantities of physical assets held, and access to financial transactions, many of which may be complex. It is also noteworthy that other highly regulated industries, such as telecoms, appear at the top of this league table.

Due to their regulation, these companies have usually developed more sophisticated control and compliance systems. The financial services sector in particular is more acutely aware of the threat from economic crime. So the higher reported levels of fraud in these sectors partly reflect higher sensitivity to - and detection of - economic crime.

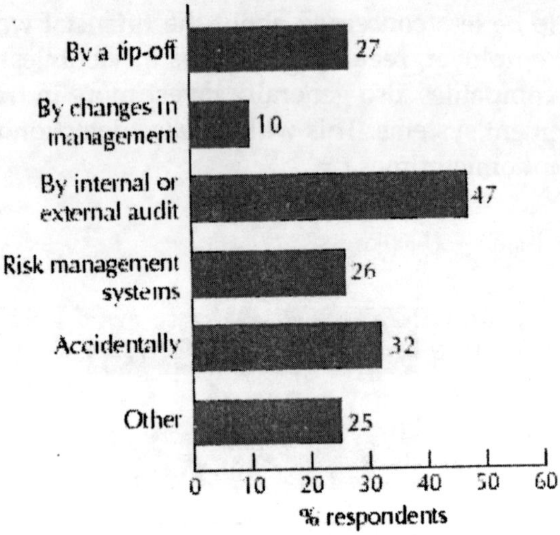

Figure 4. Victims of fraud by industry (worldwide)

The lower end of the chart contains less regulated industries such as manufacturing and construction. Whilst these industries are prone to economic crimes ranging from asset misappropriation to product piracy, they may often have less sophisticated control and detection mechanisms, or may accept losses through fraud as inevitable.

Different Types of Economic Crime

By far the most commonly reported fraud is asset misappropriation, with 60% of those reporting economic crimes claiming this was among them. This type of fraud is generally the easiest to detect, as it involves the theft of tangible items with a defined value. This may help to explain why it is the most commonly reported.

Perception and reality

Further insights can be gained by comparing the perceived prevalence of each type of economic crime with its actual incidence. With asset misappropriation and, product piracy, the perceived prevalence and actual incidence are very similar. This is likely to be due to their greater visibility: lost assets can be counted, counterfeit products seen in the market. However, with both financial misrepresentation and corruption & bribery, the perceived prevalence is much higher than the reported incidences. With financial misrepresentation, this gap appears to reflect two factors:

— higher awareness following the corporate scandals in North America and Europe; and

— an understanding that it is likely to have an especially dramatic impact on a business.

Given the serious implications of financial misrepresentation, it should be worrying that one in 10 organisations reported incidences. The high perceived prevalence of corruption & bribery reflects the hard work of governments, regulators, and certain NGO's to raise public awareness; an important factor in helping to reduce actual incidence. 199 respondents reported suffering corruption & bribery. 46% were solicited with or received a bribe, and 36% of those 4 or more times! 44% were required to offer or pay a bribe - 49% of those 4 or more times! The remaining 10% refused to comment. These reported incidences of corruption & bribery have a regional bias towards the developing markets of Africa, South and Central America, and Asia Pacific.

In these regions such acts are often viewed as an acceptable element of doing business. Increasing pressure from developed economies is forcing many countries to promote increased awareness of corruption & bribery, and many companies operating in those markets to carefully review their procedures. It is inevitable that the overall figure for Money Laundering incidence will be low. In order to get a realistic impression of the level or impact of money laundering, it should be assessed according to its incidence within the financial services sector.

One in six banks reported having uncovered money laundering during the previous two years. 216 financial services organisations worldwide said they had reported suspicious transactions during the two years, with one in five reporting more than 10 suspicious transactions. This almost certainly reflects the well publicised and ongoing efforts to raise awareness of money laundering and stop movements of illegally obtained funds by convincing countries to adopt internationally accepted anti-money laundering regulations, as well as regularly monitoring their performance.

Financial Cost of Fraud

Over 1284 companies that reported losses due to economic crime in the last 2 years. 813 of these companies were able to quantify their loss. Even when companies know that they have suffered economic crime, they find it difficult to quantify the financial impact on their business. Almost a third of victims cannot even guess how much it cost them. It is clear that the financial cost of less tangible economic crimes, such as bribery & corruption and cybercrime can be especially hard to quantify. Even with a more quantifiable crime such as asset misappropriation, 22% of victims could not put a figure on their losses. Among the remaining two thirds (813 companies), we estimate the average loss from fraud was US$2,199,930.

The Collateral Cost of Fraud

The damage inflicted by economic crime goes far beyond direct monetary loss. Intangible assets including business relationships, staff morale, reputation and branding are critical to any business. These can all be undermined by the occurrence or even the perception of fraud. The reported impact varies depending on the nature of the crime committed. Incidence of economic crime in an organisation invariably raises questions in employee's minds about its leadership and governance, its ethics, or as a secure environment to work. Repeated exposure to such issues can undermine years of carefully built up staff loyalty.

The second most common concern is the effect of economic crime incidence on external business relationships. It is noteworthy that both asset misappropriation and cybercrime are perceived to inflict less damage in this area than the other forms of economic crime. It may be that organisations accept exposure to these types of crimes as part of the everyday risks of dosing business, whereas financial misrepresentation, corruption and bribery may be indicative of wider company issues. Business relationships and brand image also suffer significantly where product piracy is at play.

As a crime extremely prevalent in Africa and Asia Pacific, companies operating in those markets need to be aware of the major impact product piracy can have on product and brand licensing deals by diluting the underlying asset value and creating mistrust among business partners. The relationship between economic crime and share performance is a complex issue. A relatively small number of victims felt that fraud had affected their share price - even where financial misrepresentation has potentially called previously disclosed information into question.

However, the proportion of respondents who reported an impact on share price as a result of economic crime has doubled since 2001, perhaps indicating that the financial markets no longer view economic crimes as a historical offence with limited future relevance. Overall, a failure to tackle - or at least manage the risk of - economic crime effectively can store up long-term operational problems for any enterprise. The safeguarding of valuable intangible assets such as brand, client relations, and staff morale should be a key objective.

Asked to consider whether the collateral damage had a short or long-term impact on their business, most respondents believed the impact to be short-term (less than one year). This should not disguise the fact that approximately one third of respondents reported long-term effects of economic crime on their business, and in the case of share price 47%. A sure sign that collateral damage should be considered on a par with monetary loss when determining economic crime risks.

Detecting Economic Crime

Fraudsters invariably take great pains to conceal or remove evidence of their crimes. As companies can only report crimes that have been detected, it is not possible to judge how much fraud goes unnoticed. What we can analyse is the means by which fraud is brought to light.

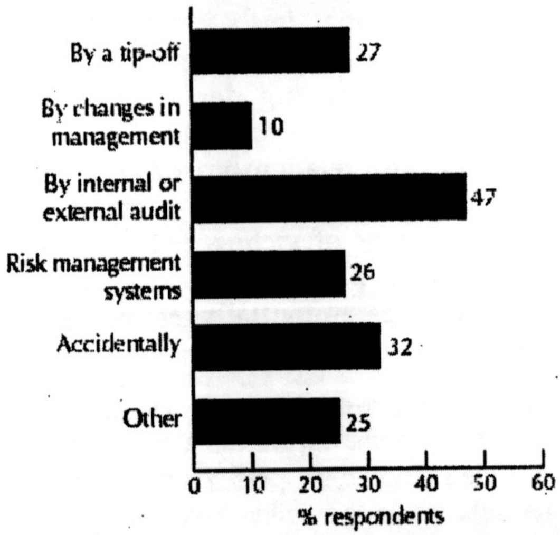

Figure 5. How economic crime is detected (worldwide)

The results vary considerably depending on the size of the organisation concerned. Within larger organisations a combination of factors are likely to be involved in the detection of an incident. Control and risk management systems often detected fraud. However, in many cases this was accompanied by a finding from the internal or external audit function or from a tip-off. Smaller organisations detected a far greater proportion of economic crime through audit processes than by other means. Given the respective size of the organisations this is most likely to be via the external auditors - a worrying finding that suggests smaller companies may be placing too little attention on the development of effective controls and alternative checks and balances. Over-reliance on a single annual review to root out problems may be playing into the fraudster's hands.

Reliance on luck is not a basis for an anti-fraud regime. However, even where companies have control systems to detect economic crime, these can often be rendered ineffective by management override or collusion. Companies need to do more in terms of:

— Assessing the real risks and vulnerabilities to fraud within the organisation

— Communicating actively the company's stance on fraud and "walking the talk"

— Proactively monitoring risky areas

— Developing policies to encourage (and protect) "whistleblowers"

— Expecting the worst and being prepared - devising a robust fraud response plan

Economic Crime Managing

Respondents assign primary responsibility for managing

economic crime issues to the board of directors. 61% of respondents stated that the board must be informed of all instances of economic crime. There are significant regional variations however. Within Asia-Pacific (83%) the responsibility is vested firmly with the Board. Significantly fewer companies in North America (54%) and Central & Eastern Europe (47%) rely on the Board to fulfill this duty. In both these regions, company management is just as likely to have responsibility for managing the issues. Regardless of where the primary responsibility lies it is surprising that only 29% of organisations have implemented any fraud-related training for the Board or management.

Given the increasing focus on corporate fraud with regulators, ratings agencies and others now scrutinising companies for signs of misdeed, Boards and management need to consider making this type of training part of their corporate governance regime. Respondents' opinions varied on how economic crimes should be dealt with once detected. Overall 64% of respondent organisations said they had a requirement to report frauds to an external body. Once more though, regional variations are significant. In the Asia-Pacific region only 48% of companies had a requirement to involve the authorities. In Africa and Central & Eastern Europe at least 80% of companies said that they applied this policy.

PricewaterhouseCoopers experience in investigating economic crime for corporations suggests that there are many reasons why an organisation may choose not to report a fraud to an external body. These include the potential impact of negative publicity on business relationships or staff morale. In addition, companies often fear the costs of a drawn-out judicial process, or simply believe there is little chance of recovering the stolen assets. It may well be that companies have a public face supporting a policy of reporting all matters to the authorities, but reconsider when faced with an actual event.

Even if economic crime is detected and prosecuted, it can still prove impossible to recover the assets. Of respondents who had experienced fraud, only 9% had succeeded in recovering more than 80% of their losses, whilst almost threequarters recovered less than 20%. There are many reasons for this relative failure to recover lost assets. Companies are reluctant to embark on long recovery processes with no certainty of success, especially where the assets have been moved across borders. However, there may be good reasons to pursue the assets regardless - firstly because it is not always possible to form a realistic view of the chances of recovery until the process gets under way, and secondly because a policy of always attempting recovery helps to create the right culture of deterrence.

Insurance

Surprisingly, given the high awareness of economic crime, just over half the organisations surveyed had taken out insurance against fraud losses. This may be due to management indifference or scepticism over how much insurance could actually recover. However, insurance can have a significant impact on recoveries. Companies with insurance reported being 3 times more likely to recover more than 60% of their losses. Preventing Economic Crime Not surprisingly, companies that have suffered economic crime are more concerned about the strength and effectiveness of their systems to prevent fraud. They are also more likely to have taken proactive measures to reduce future exposure.

Our findings illustrate the impact of fraud on an organisation's mindset. Those that had not suffered fraud tended to rely on more intangible prevention tools such as codes of conduct or ethical policies. In contrast, fraud victims instituted more tangible measures such as management training and whistleblowing programmes. They also invested greater effort in raising awareness of the potential for economic crimes.

Organisations that take practical measures to combat fraud, and that effect change on the ground rather than creating the appearance of addressing the problem, will develop a stronger culture of prevention. As a result of such action, companies that had reported economic crime are "quite" or "very" confident that their anti-fraud controls are stronger now than they were two years ago.

Future of Economic Crime

Most organisations expect the threat of economic crime to increase over the next five years, with respondents in Africa being especially pessimistic. However, companies in Central & Eastern Europe and South & Central America expect the risk to decrease. In the last two years however, the respondents in Central & Eastern Europe reported significantly more economic crime. In the view it is unrealistic to expect decreases in economic crime risks without substantial actions to tackle the roots of all economic crime: motive, opportunity and a clearly perceived benefit of reward over punishment.

Asset misappropriation is most noticeably seen as a threat in Africa (48%) and North America (48%). And cybercrime is still seen as a key risk for the future in North America (38%) and Western Europe (37%). However, respondents in Africa (48%) believe that the issues of corruption & bribery will remain one of their greatest economic crime threats.

8

Confiscating the Proceeds of Crimes

A confiscation is a measure. The confiscation is not considered as a punishable sanction; it just transfers illegal benefits of a crime from a criminal to society. There is three legal purpose of confiscation. The first legal purpose of the confiscation is to ensure that a crime does not pay. The confiscation tries to eliminate the monetary benefits of the crime. The second purpose of the confiscation is that it prevents investing the illegal gain to new crimes. It may also be so that the illegal proceeds of the crime will be reinvested in illicit activities.

By confiscating the illegal proceeds of the crime to the society ensure that the illicit benefits of the crime will be reinvested in legal activities. Society can for instance reinvest the confiscated money in crime detection, and this way reduces the level of the crime. The third purpose of the confiscation is to prevent for a firm to get illegal competitive advantages. By confiscating the proceeds of a crime may remove unfair advantages that the firm have obtained over competitors.

If the benefits of a crime are equal to harms of victims, a criminal need not to pay the confiscation, the compensation is primary. Thus, whenever the criminal has to pay the compensation, the monetary amount of the compensation will be diminished to the monetary amount of the confiscation. Therefore, it can be considered that the compensation takes over the confiscation. Although, sometimes it can be considered that the confiscation replaces compensation. For offences such as theft, the criminal can be required to return stolen goods or to pay compensation to the victim of the crime. But for victimless crimes like living off immoral earnings the harm caused by a crime is experienced by society at large than by individual victims, and no compensation is paid.

Nevertheless, the confiscation is possible, and the confiscation can be considered to replace the compensation since the society can be regarded as the victim of the crime. The socially undesirable actions are actions in which criminal's benefits of the crime is less than social costs of the criminal action. Then it is for social point of view efficient to deter the criminal action.

Legal Aspects

From legal point of view, the confiscation is not a punitive sanction. The confiscation is a reparative measure which seeks to recover from an offender the benefits of the crime. Confiscating the proceeds from a crime can ensure that the crime does not pay. The following types of confiscation legislation can be distinguished:

— *In personam*: a person must be convicted of a crime and then it must be proven on criminal criteria that specific property was proceeds from that crime. For instance, in Finland a prerequisite for a forfeiture order is an act criminalised by law (offence). A forfeiture order may be based on an act criminalised by law also where the person committing the act has not attained the age of fifteen years at the material time, or is without criminal capacity.

- *In rem*: property can be confiscated if it can be proven by civil criteria (i.e. beyond reasonable doubt) that the property was the proceeds of a crime or instrumentality to commit a crime. This kind of confiscation legislation is in force for example in the United Kingdom.
- *Mixed systems*: once a person is convicted of a crime, property can be confiscated using civil criteria. A variety of confiscation systems is found in Europe. Almost all countries in the Europe have provisions in their legislation allowing for the confiscation of proceeds; many of them modified the relevant legislation in the second half of the 1990s. Most countries in Europe have systems:allowing for the confiscation of both, specific items of property or items based on the value corresponding to proceeds, providing for the confiscation of proceeds related to all serious crimes requiring a conviction before confiscation (although there are exceptions in several countries) . requiring criminal standards of proof (exceptions include Ireland and the United Kingdom where civil standards are applied).

So, in Europe mainly the confiscation can be forfeited under criminal procedure. In that case, the principle of legality sets a limitation for the use of the confiscation. The confiscation is possible only and only if it is enacted in the law. Hence, in the case of the confiscation there must be a connection between a criminal act and the property being confiscated. The principle of legality makes possible that the confiscation is predictable. Individuals know when the confiscation will be convicted, and how severe it will be. In spite of all, one problem, if we wish to keep to the principle of legality, is how it is possible to establish whether someone came into possession of his property legally or illegally.

In some cases, it is easy to establish that the property is obtained by illegal conduct. For instance, in the case of environmental crimes since in most countries environmental crimes are of the abstract endangerment type, whereby the mere violation of for instance emission standards is criminalized, it is quite easy to show that a firm has achieved illegal benefits by for instance not investing the needed environmentally friendly technology. Some severe crime cases - often drug offences - there has a reversal burden of proof to show the origin of the property which means that the owner of property has to prove that he has obtained the property by legal conduct in order to avoid the confiscation.

In Ireland and the United Kingdom confiscation provisions will be applied when an offence has been proved to a criminal standard (i.e. beyond reasonable doubt). The amount confiscated is then determined according to the calculated benefit of the crime to a civil standard (i.e. on the balance of probabilities). Nevertheless, the criminal confiscation can only follow a conviction. Once guilty is proven, the questions of the confiscation - such as the amount of assets deemed to be the proceeds of the crime - are decided in the balance of probabilities (the civil standard of proof). So, the confiscation of the proceeds of the crime needs lower standards of proofs than the criminal standards of proof.

However, applying the lower standard of proof will inevitably mean that more mistakes and miscarriages will occur: a greater number of assets are taken from unfairly. In many European countries, like Finland, German, Switzerland, the United Kingdom, Denmark, and Norway, there are two types of the confiscation of the proceeds of the crime. The first there is the confiscation of benefits from particular criminal conduct. The court may confiscate the benefits of the crime of which the criminal has just been convicted. Secondly, there is the confiscation of the benefits from general criminal conduct. The court may then calculate and confiscate the criminal's benefits from his entire past criminal conduct. This kind of extended forfeiture of the proceeds of the crime is often used with severe crimes and with crimes like drug trafficking offences and money laundering offences.

For instance in Finland the extended forfeiture of the proceeds of the crime may be ordered "on a person who is found guilty of an offence which carries a possible penalty of imprisonment for at least four years, a punishable attempt of such an offence, or an offence referred to a concealment offence, a money laundering offence, a smuggling offence, a drug offence, a promotion of a drug offence, or a smuggling alcohol or spirits, and on a participant in this offences and on a person on whose behalf or to whose advantage the said offence has been committed, provided that the nature of the offence is such that it may result in considerable financial proceeds and that there is reason to believe that the property is fully or partially derived from criminal activity that is not to be considered insignificant."

It can be considered that the extended forfeiture of the proceeds of a crime will be used with severe crime cases. Whereas, when there is lenient crime case, the extended forfeiture of the proceeds of a crime cannot be used. In the lenient cases, normal forfeiture of the proceeds of a crime is efficient. Using the extended forfeiture of the proceeds of a crime only with severe cases increases marginal deterrence of a crime so that it is not profitable to commit a severe crime instead of lenient crime.

Usually, in the extended forfeiture of the proceeds of the crime cases the benefits from the crime will be confiscated unless the criminal can prove that he has received them from some non-criminal source. So, there is a reversal burden of proof unlike usual criminal cases where the prosecution have to prove that an accused person is guilty. The protection of the innocent is one of the main concerns of criminal trial. The principle is that the accused person is innocent until proven guilty. Although, the purpose of the confiscation is not seek to determine criminal guilt or innocent of any person, but it will focus on whether the property can be shown to have been obtained through some person's/firm's unlawful conduct.

The proceeds of the crime will be confiscated to society if the person is found guilty of an offence. Thus, the reversal burden of proof will be used to show did the assets have derived from criminal conduct or not. And it is usually so that the accused person has the best possibility to prove that his property is obtained by legal conduct. Thereby, the reversal burden of proof can be considered to be cost effective, since the owner of the property can more easier than authorities show the noncriminal source of the property.

Whereas, if the accused person should prove that he has not committed a crime, the costs could be (very) high. To prove guiltlessness would require that a person should keep a diary in order to prove what he has done in that day when the crime has been committed. Instead, if the prosecution have to prove that the accused person is guilty, he can take advantage of the economics of scale in settling crimes. Therefore, the unit costs to a criminal case for the prosecution are decreasing.

At least in Finland, the procedure can waive a confiscation claim if the benefits of a crime are insignificant or if the detection of the grounds for the claim or the hearing would create unreasonable costs in view of the nature of the crime and the other circumstances. This is increase in efficiency of confiscation legislation from economic point of view. Whenever the social cost of confiscation legislation is greater than the social benefits of confiscation legislation, it is optimal not to enforce the confiscation legislation.

The confiscation is not a punitive sanction in legal point of view. The main purpose of the confiscation is to recover the proceeds of the crime from a criminal so that the crime would not pay. Almost all European countries have confiscation legislation but the confiscation systems vary between countries. In some severe crime cases there may have a reversal burden of proof - a criminal have to show that his property is achieved by legally for that the property would not be confiscated to society. The reversal burden of proof when it has been used within crimes like drug offences and money laundering may increase the efficiency of the confiscation system since the owner of the property has the best opportunity to show how he has obtained the property.

Economic Models

The main purpose of the confiscation is that a criminal should not be left with illegal proceeds from a crime. For instance, when a firm gets an illegal benefit committing a crime it may also reflect competitive advantages. The firm may achieve illegal competitive advantages by diminishing the costs in an illegal way. When the economic benefits of the crime will be confiscated, it may also remove unfair advantages which the criminal firm may have obtained over competitors. The forfeiture of the benefits derived from the crime should put the criminal in the situation with an identical competitor who did not commit a crime. Thus, the confiscation is not considered to be punitive, i.e. it only seeks to recover from criminals the proceeds of the crime.

In the illegal competitive advantages situation the purpose of the confiscation should be that it does not allow the criminals to manufacture and sell products in the market more cost-effectively, and achieve short-term and long-term economic advantages through illegal improved market position. The criminal firm shall not obtain benefits at the expense of competing firms. For instance, criminal cost saving which reduce criminal's marginal costs can affect to the criminal's behaviour, resulting in a profit increase greater than the costs savings. Reducing marginal costs by the criminal action may help the criminal firm to be able to sell its products at a lower price than its competitors and thus gain market share. So, it is important that society wants to deter completely this kind of action which may affect harmfully to the market situation.

Most firms commit a crime since they want to make profit, not cause a harm. Increasing profit by illegal way usually hurts competitors, and if there were no ability to the confiscation, competitors may have to follow the criminal firm and commit a crime which is not socially desirable. Thus, the confiscation is important, and the net benefits of the crime should be confiscated to society. The optimal confiscation is the net benefits of the crime. If the criminal have to pay compensation or rehabilitation costs then the amount of these costs should be taken away from the amount of the confiscation. For example, if a firm have gotten illegal benefits by illegal waste disposal the firm left its' waste on the gravel pit.

The legal waste disposal costs would have been 63,800 euros, so the achieved net illegal benefits are then 63,800 euros minus the expected compensation and rehabilitation costs. If the rehabilitation cost and compensation is 10,000 euros then the net benefits of the crime is 53,800 euros and it should be confiscated to society. A firm may achieve illegal benefits by obtaining extra income, saving costs or gaining interest yield. For example, if the de jure project is delayed, the firm does not get cost saving. In this kind of situation the illegal benefit is the interest yield of not invested capital. But in the case of failed project, the illegal benefits are the saved investment and operating costs multiplied by the interest rate.

According to the basic economic model of the crime, a potential criminal will commit a crime if the expected utility of the crime (i.e. the revenue of the crime (= the benefits of the crime) minus the expected punishment (= the expected costs of the crime)) is greater than zero, i.e. $E(U) = Y(x) - P(x)f(x) = 0.4$ So, the economic model of the crime implies that the potential criminals can be deterred from committing a crime by raising the expected costs of the crime, i.e. increasing the probability of being convicted or severity of punishment, or reducing the revenue of the crime. The confiscation fits very well to this deterrence model of the crime. The confiscation diminishes the revenue of the crime. The idea of the confiscation is that criminals should not be left with the benefits they have made by committing the crime.

The confiscation removes the illegal gain from the wrongdoer to society, so it reduces the expected utility of the crime. If the expected utility of the crime is equal to $E1(U) = Y(x) - P(x)f(x)$ and when the confiscation (k) is included in the function, the expected utility of the crime is $E2(U) = Y(x) - P(x)[f(x) + k]$. Usually $k = Y(x)$ so the expected utility of the crime is $E2(U) = [1 - P(x)]Y(x) - P(x)f(x)$. Comparing E1(U) with E2(U) it is clear that the E1 is greater than the E2. Nevertheless, the confiscation is not an efficient measure alone. If the confiscation is only sanction or measure, then the expected utility of the crime would be positive, and it would be efficient to commit a crime. Thus, there is needed other criminal sanctions with confiscation to make a criminal action not profitable.

The confiscation directly reflects the amount of the benefits of the crime; so the higher is the benefits of the crime, the higher is the confiscation. The confiscation increases also the deterrence effect, because it reduces the benefits of the crime and therefore it fits very well in the deterrence model of the crime. In the case of the confiscation the marginal deterrence is also fulfilled. If the benefits of the crime are zero, for example because the criminal could not commit the crime, only attempt is done, the confiscation is also zero. Therefore, the confiscation makes it possible that punishments for attempt is lenient than for fulfilled crimes. It is also so that the greater the proceeds of the crime is, the more probable the crime is more severe.

Thus, the confiscation can be good proxy to the severity of the criminal action. It might be so that the confiscation may get it possible that there is no need use prison sanction, the fine within the confiscation may be efficient. Using the confiscation increase the deterrence, and it is part of efficient policy since it may enable that the probability of being convicted can be set at lower level than in the situation where the confiscation has not been used to achieve the wanted deterrence effect. The confiscation is also very cost-effective, since through the confiscation society can collect money for itself. The confiscation is quite costless transfer from a criminal to society. International experience (especially in Ireland and the USA) shows that the confiscation generates significant revenue flows to society that reduce the net costs of the criminal justice system.

For example, the US Asset Forfeiture Reinvigoration Programme has returned a surplus of up to 140 million euros annually. When criminals know that the proceeds of the crime will be removed to society, they have an incentive to avoidance activities to make it difficult for society to identify and evaluate the monetary benefits of the crime. This increase the enforcement costs and makes the confiscation not to be costless transfer from the criminal to society.

COMPENSATION

The net proceeds of a crime should be confiscated to the society, and therefore the monetary amount of compensation is taken away from the monetary amount of the proceeds of the crime. The compensation reflects the amount of a harm and makes an injurer to internalizes the harm he is caused. A perfect compensation will make a victim to be indifferent between an accident and a non-accident. But in reality the perfect compensation is not very realistic one.

The compensation actualizes only if the harm will occur, whereas the confiscation comes into account if the crime gives benefits to a criminal. Then in the case of the compensation the injurer will compare the prevention cost to the expected compensation (i.e. the probability of being convicted to pay the compensation multiplied by the monetary amount of the compensation) together, and the injurer will choose the one of these which is lower, e.g. if the cost of preventing the harm is greater than the expected compensation cost, it is optimal for the injurer lets the harm actualizes.

The confiscation reduces the benefits of the crime and the potential criminal will commit a crime if the expected utility of the crime is positive, i.e. the difference between benefits of the crime and the expected punishment is positive. If the confiscation is only sanction, the criminal will commit a crime since the probability of being convicted is less than one $E(U) = Y(x) - P(x)Y(x) = (1 - P(x))Y(x) > 0$ if $P(x) < 1$.

The confiscation is not therefore an efficient sanction alone: there is needed other sanction within the confiscation so that the expected utility of the crime would be negative. The sanction equal to the proceeds of the crime will not deter enough an undesirable behaviour as criminals lose no more than their benefits of the crime. The economic models of the crime usually expect that the social costs of the crime are the harm caused plus the costs of preventing crimes. These models assume that the benefits of the crime are counted in social welfare.

9

Corporate Crime in the Digital Age

Digital technologies are present throughout all aspects of business activity-new companies are able to be registered and official documents lodged with regulators electronically; investors are able to obtain prospectuses and information about companies from the Internet; business records are able to be maintained electronically and archived on computerised databases; many Stock Exchanges now offer electronic trading systems from dedicated terminals which enable securities to be bought and sold on-line; and personnel matters are able to be carried out electronically such as through the use of video-conferencing for job interviews, analysing working patterns though the use of neural networks, and paying staff electronically through the use of electronic funds transfers.

There are many other examples of how digitisation-or the process of reducing information to electronic streams of '0s and 1s'-has monopolised corporate existence. As one writer has asserted, everything now depends on code. The benefits of digitisation are clearly apparent. People are able to communicate more effectively and at lower cost than in the past. It has also meant that geographical boundaries are able to be crossed more easily which has enhanced the process of globalisation of economic and social life enormously. These same technologies that have provided so many benefits have, however, created enormous opportunities for offenders.

Criminals are able to communicate with each other in secret, disguise their identities in order to avoid detection, and manipulate electronic payment systems to obtain funds illegally. They are also able to perpetrate crime on a much wider scale than in the past, duplicating countless fraudulent invoices, or establishing large numbers of accounts that only exist in cyberspace. Their victims may also be located anywhere in the world.

Finally, the potential losses that could be sustained through electronic corporate crime are enormous-a fact which many enterprising and technologically literate offenders know only too well. The extent to which individuals are using the Internet for business transactions has, for example, increased dramatically. In terms of commercial usage, Forrester Research has estimated that global business-to-business electronic commerce will be worth $2.7 trillion by 2004 while the Gartner Group puts this figure closer to $7 trillion. The market in the Asia-Pacific region is expected to expand considerably over the next few years. In 2005, the Asia-Pacific region will account for 28 percent of the worldwide business-to-business commerce total, with business-to-business Internet commerce transactions amounting to US$2.4 trillion. If even a small fraction of this is lost to fraud, substantial sums will be involved.

Nature and Extent

In recent years, a number of surveys have been carried out to determine the extent to which organisations have been victimised through computer-based crime. Although victimisation surveys have been criticised on a number of grounds to do with the unrepresentativeness of the samples they employ and the limited types of activities which they examine, they do provide information which tends not to be recorded in official police statistics which, in this area, are recorded only in respect of the most general categories. Business victimisation surveys have been carried out regularly by some of the large firms of consultants, such as KPMG and Ernst and Young. These surveys have dealt specifically with fraud experiences of large organisations and have provided an indication of the nature of organisational fraud and the extent of losses suffered.

Although the response rate to these largescale surveys has been rather low, they provide a good starting point for documenting the nature and extent of digital crime in recent years. The kinds of computer frauds that presented the greatest concern were those that involved manipulation of data records or computer programs to disguise the true nature of transactions, hacking into an organisation's computer system to steal or to manipulate business information, and unauthorised transfers of funds electronically. Seventy-nine per cent of respondents indicated that a security breach to their electronic commerce system would most likely result from a breach caused via the Internet or other external access.

Risk of damage to the company's reputation was considered by 72 per cent of respondents to be the major damage that could be caused to their electronic commerce system. In March 2001, the Computer Security Institute and the FBIs Computer Intrusion Squad based in San Francisco released its sixth 'Computer Crime and Security Survey'. This was a survey of over 500 computer security practitioners in corporations, government agencies, financial institutions, medical institutions and universities in the United States. Eighty-five percent of respondents (primarily large corporations and government agencies) detected computer security breaches within the preceding twelve months. Sixty-four percent acknowledged financial losses due to computer breaches. Thirty-five percent (186 respondents) were willing and or able to quantify their financial losses. These 186 respondents reported US$377,828,700 in financial losses. In contrast, the losses from 249 respondents in the 2000 survey totalled only US$265,589,940. The average annual total losses sustained over the three years prior to 2000 was US$120,240,180.

As in early years, the most serious financial losses occurred through theft of proprietary information (34 respondents reported US$151,230,100) and financial fraud (21 respondents reported US$92,935,500). For the fourth year in a row, more respondents (70%) cited their Internet connection as a frequent point of attack than cited their internal systems as a frequent point of attack (31%). Indeed, the rise in those citing their Internet connections as a frequent point of attack rose from 59 per cent in 2000 to 70 per cent in 2001. Thirty-six percent of respondents reported the intrusions to law enforcement; a significant increase from 2000, when only 25 per cent reported them (in 1996, only 16% acknowledged reporting intrusions to law enforcement agencies).

In terms of reported incidents relating to electronic commerce, the survey found that of the 47 per cent of respondents that conducted electronic commerce on their Websites, 23 per cent suffered unauthorised access or misuse within the preceding twelve months, while 27 per cent said that they did not know if there had been unauthorised access or misuse of their sites. Twenty-one per cent of those acknowledging attacks reported between two and five incidents while 58 per cent reported ten or more incidents. Eight per cent of respondents reported financial fraud of their electronic commerce sites which had increased from only three per cent in the 2000 survey.

In the United Kingdom, computer crime surveys of large organisations were carried out in 1990 and 1993 by the Audit Commission which found that there had been a thirty eight per cent increase in reported computer fraud during the three year period in question. Total losses due to computer fraud in 1993 were over £3 million which represented the largest category of losses due to any form of computer abuse.

In Australia, KPMG's Fraud Survey examined over 1,800 of Australia's largest businesses in February 1999. 367 replies were received (20%) with information being provided on fraud awareness, the experience and cost of fraud, who perpetrated the fraud, how it was discovered, and why it occurred. Specific data were also obtained concerning computer-related fraud. In all, some 7,280 incidents of fraud generally were reported in the two years preceding the survey and fifty-seven per cent of respondents reported at least one incident during that period. Total losses amounted to $239 million with the average cost per incident of $1.1 million.

Although small in number, between the surveys conducted in 1997 and 1999, there was a seventy-one per cent increase in the percentage of respondents to KPMGs surveys who reported computer-related fraud (7 to 12%). Total reported losses due to computer crime were over A$16 million in KPMGs 1999 survey although these figures are likely to be under-estimates as many organisations were unaware of the extent to which their organisation was being defrauded through the use of computers and some did not define other forms of fraud as computer-related. In 1999, thirty-six per cent of KPMGs respondents who reported computer crime were either unaware of how much they had lost or were unwilling to disclose it.

In November 1998, another survey was carried out of 350 large organisations by the Victoria Police and Deloitte Touche Tohmatsu. Thirty-three per cent of respondents reported unauthorised use of their computers within the preceding twelve month period and one quarter of these attacks were motivated by financial gain. More than one third of those who responded believed that computer theft would have an impact on their organisation over the next five years. High-technology fraud against government organisations is an area of particular concern as agencies become increasingly reliant upon computers for the provision of services and the payment of benefits.

In the survey of computer crime and security conducted by the Office of Strategic Crime Assessments and the Victoria Police Computer Crime Investigation Squad, thirty-six per cent of the eleven government agencies surveyed reported misuse of their computer systems with forty-five per cent reporting external forms of attack, that is remote access to computer systems.

The most frequently reported types of computer abuse reported by the government agencies surveyed related to damage or unauthorised access to, or copying of data and programs. The Internet is also proving to be a great boon to fraudsters. As electronic commerce continues to expand in terms of the range of products and services which are offered for sale on-line, and as the number of users continues to increase, so the opportunities for dishonesty and fraud have also increased. In the United States, the newly established Internet Fraud Complaint Centre-organised by the United States Department of Justice and the Federal Bureau of Investigation-received 19,490 complaints relating to Internet fraud from the time of its establishment on 8 May 2000 to 30 November 2000.

The average monetary loss per complaint was US$665.00 with 49 per cent of complaints relating to auction fraud. In 1999, Internet Fraud Watch reported an estimated 2 million instances of credit card fraud taking place with respect to on-line purchases in Europe, with a 600 per cent increase in Internet fraud complaints occurring in the United States since 1997. Also in the United States, over 18,600 complaints were registered on the Federal Trade Commission's fraud database 'Consumer Sentinel' in 1999, more than double the number in 1998- when 8,000 were registered. In a telephone survey of 1,006 on-line consumers conducted for the National Consumers League in the United States between April and May 1999, 24 per cent said they had purchased goods and services on-line.

Seven per cent, which represents 6 million people, however, said that they had experienced fraud or unauthorised use of credit card or personal information on-line. Another commentator has estimated that as much as ten per cent of on-line commerce may involve consumer fraud. A worldwide clean-up operation, involving the Office of Fair Trading in Britain and its counterparts in twenty-two other countries, identified 1,159 potential 'get rich quick' schemes being advertised on Internet sites. In 1999, a survey was conducted at the University of Utah of Internet trading which was coordinated by Consumers International and funded by the European Union. Representatives of those groups bought more than 150 items from Web sites based in seventeen countries, and then tried to return them.

It was found that eight percent of the items ordered never arrived; many Web sites did not give clear information about delivery charges; a minority disclosed whether the laws of the seller's country or the buyer's country would apply in the event of a dispute, and only fifty-three percent had a return policy. In addition, only about thirteen percent of the sites promised not to sell customers' personal data to a third party and only thirty-two percent provided information on how to complain if there was a problem with a transaction.

Examples of Electronic Crime

In order to understand the nature of the crime risks that

corporations face in the digital age, it is worth considering some specific instances of crimes that have been reported in recent times. The use of computers and E-mail has greatly facilitated the manipulation of sharemarkets during secondary trading of securities. This can occur through the use of rumour, hyperbole, or other forms of misinformation to boost the price of a stock prior to the manipulator's quick and profitable exit ('pump and dump'), or by talks down a stock so that he or she may buy in at a bargain price ('slur and slurp'). Bulk E-mail programs allow stock promoters to send personalised messages to thousands and even millions of Internet users simultaneously. Such so-called 'spamming' can be indiscriminate-in September 1998, the Chairman of the Australian Securities and Investments Commission received an anonymous E:mail message enthusiastically promoting a stock traded in the United States.

In a recent Australian prosecution, a 24 year-old man who lived in a Melbourne suburb, manipulated the share price of an American company by posting information on the Internet and sending E-mail messages around the globe that contained false and misleading information about the company. On 8 and 9 May 1999, he posted messages on Internet Bulletin Boards in the United States and sent more than four million unsolicited E-mail messages to recipients in the United States, Australia and in other parts of the world. The messages contained a statement that share value of the company would increase from the then current price of US$0.33 to US$3.00 once pending patents were released by the company, and that the price would increase up to 900 per cent within the next few months.

The effect of the information was that the company's share price on the NASDAQ doubled, with trading volume increasing by more than ten times the previous month's average trading volume. The offender had purchased 65,500 shares in the company through a stock broking firm in Canada several days before he transmitted the information. He sold the shares on the first trading day after the transmission of the information and realised a profit of approximately A$17,000. The offender was prosecuted by the Australian Securities and Investments Commission for distributing false and misleading information with the intention of inducing investors to purchase the company's stock. He pleaded guilty and was sentenced to two years' imprisonment on each of three counts, to be served concurrently.

The Court ordered that twentyone months of the sentence be suspended upon his entering into a two-year good behaviour bond with a surety of $500. In a separate prosecution, Wayne Loughnan, of Cawarral in central Queensland, who assisted Hourmouzis in the sharemarket manipulation, was sentenced to two years' imprisonment, wholly suspended, in the County Court of Victoria on 22 May 2001.

Identity-Related Crime

One of the most frequently used strategies to perpetrate crime is the creation of false documents used to misrepresent one's identity. Once a convincing identity has been fraudulently established, it is then possible to steal money or otherwise to act illegally and then to evade detection, investigation, and arrest. Australian police services have recently found an increase in such misrepresentations which have been used for money laundering and tax evasion, to obtain personal loans from banks, enter into hire-purchase agreements, and deal in stolen motor vehicles.

Often counterfeit documents have been created by a single person to support multiple identities, each being used once only for a specific illegal enterprise, and then discarded. In the past, forgery of documents used to provide evidence of identity was a highly skilled task which few criminals were able to undertake convincingly.

Since the advent of digital technologies, however, it is much easier to scan an official document electronically, alter the image as it appears on a screen, and print out a counterfeit version using high quality laser, colour printers. In Victoria, for example, between August 1995 and March 1996, an offender used desk-top publishing equipment to create forty-one birth certificates, forty-one student identification cards, some containing photographs, each in separate names, and a counterfeit driver's licence.

These were used to open forty-two separate bank accounts throughout the Melbourne metropolitan region, to pay cheques into accounts as wages and make immediate withdrawals before they had cleared, to register a business name, to obtain sales tax refunds, and to defraud various retailers.

The offender was charged with a variety of state and federal offences and sentenced to five years' imprisonment with a non-parole period of three years. He was also ordered to compensation of $41,300 and reparation to the Commonwealth of $458,383. The technology of the Internet makes it relatively simple for users to disguise their identities. Electronic mail and Internet addresses may be manipulated by including details which are misleading or the source of a message may be made anonymous or changed so that it appears to be coming from another user. Similarly, there is no way of knowing the commercial affiliations of those on the Internet. Referees for businesses or products might, in fact, be individuals employed specifically to indicate their approval of the venture or product in question.

Businesses might also choose legitimate-sounding names in order to improve their credibility or include domain names which are misleading. There has recently developed a practice in the United States and Canada of some businesses adopting domain names containing the names of Australian cities in order to improve their marketability and credibility, despite the fact that they have no connection at all with Australia. In one case investigated by the ACCC, an Internet trader used the same domain name as another trader (the original bearer of the name), but with a <.com> suffix, as opposed to the <.net> suffix of the original site. The confusion created as to the identity of the actual proprietor of the site allowed consumers to be misled or deceived. The <.com> site did, however, include an inconspicuous notice stating that the site should not be confused with the <.net> site of the same name, although this could easily have been overlooked by those visiting the site.

Telecommunications Crime

Telecommunications systems may also be manipulated to perpetrate crime. One of the great weaknesses in the past has been PABXs which have been manipulated so as to enable longdistance telephone calls to be charged to organisations without authorisation. Sometimes substantial sums have been involved. In the United Kingdom, for example, a case of PABX fraud cost a government department the equivalent of US$80,000 a day while another department lost US$640,000 over a six week period. In yet another case illegal access was gained to Scotland Yard's PABX system in London by computer hackers based in the United States.

Unauthorised international calls to the value of A$1.29 million were made for which Scotland Yard was liable. Other cases have involved tee-ing into telephone lines and cloning of cellular telephones, many of which have involved employees within organisations disclosing confidential security information to enable the crime to be committed. The Internet has also been used to perpetrate telecommunications crime. One example involved a company which advertised 'free' erotic photographs on the Internet. In order to see the images, the user was required to download software which, once installed, took control of the user's modem, cut off the local Internet Service Provider, and dialled a number in the former Soviet Republic of Moldova in Eastern Europe.

Electronic Funds Transfer Crime

Crime may also take place by manipulating the security systems established to protect electronic funds transfers. These systems are designed to ensure that information cannot be manipulated as it passes over computerised networks and that only authorised users have access to computers. Most of the large scale electronic funds transfer frauds which have been committed in the past have involved the interception or alteration of electronic data messages transmitted from the computers of financial institutions. In many cases offenders have worked within financial institutions or corporations themselves and been privy to the operation of the security systems in question.

One recent example of funds transfer fraud involved a financial consultant contracted to the Department of Finance and Administration in Canberra who, on 25 September 2001 was convicted of defrauding the Commonwealth by transferring $8,735,692 electronically to private companies in which he held an interest. He did this by logging on to the Department's computer network using another person's name and password. He also was able to obscure an audit trial by the use of other employees' logon codes and passwords. He was sentenced in the ACT Supreme Court to 7 years and six months' imprisonment with a non-parole period of 3 years and six months.

In order to secure electronic funds transfers, data are generally encrypted using algorithms which encode messages. These are then decoded using electronic keys known to the sender and the recipient. Digital signatures are also used to authenticate each of the parties involved and hashing algorithms used to ensure that messages have not been altered. The main security risks associated with these systems relate to the possibility that private encryption keys could be stolen or used without authorisation by people who have obtained them illegitimately.

The easiest way to do this would be to submit false identification evidence to Registration Authorities when obtaining a public-private key pair. Alternatively, if a private key were held on a smartcard it might be possible to obtain access to the key simply by breaking the access control device on the card which could simply be a password. Thus it could be possible for someone to make use of another person's private key to carry out transactions and be unable to be traced.

Some Solutions

Some of the solutions simply involve the application of conventional risk management strategies while others entail the adoption of new technological approaches, or reliance on traditional legal responses.

Effective Corporate Governance

In the first place it is important for those who manage companies to have a proper understanding of the risks that are present within their organisation. This requires manages to know precisely how their business operates. Often those in charge of a company may not understand how their organisations function in sufficient detail to be fully aware of the risks of fraud that exist. This is particularly the case with respect to information technologies. In Ernst and Young's survey of large organisations, for example, less than one third of the Australian respondents considered that their directors had a good overall understanding of their business for fraud prevention purposes. Although managers may not be able to understand the technicalities of all the computer software and hardware that their organisation makes use of, they should be in a position to understand the areas where fraud risks arise and instruct appropriately trained personnel to monitor these areas regularly.

Fraud Control Policies

It is also important for organisations to have clear and transparent fraud control policies in place. These are necessary in the digital environment no less so than in the terrestrial world. Australian Standard No. AS 3806-98 Compliance Programs provides guidelines for both private and public sector organisations on the establishment, implementation and management of effective compliance programs. The Standard also provides principles which organisations are able to use to identify and to remedy any deficiencies in their compliance with laws, industry codes and inhouse company standards, and to develop processes for continuous improvement in risk management.

Establishing principles on, for example, the ethical use of information technologies and how to respond to instances of fraud are essential in conducting a business of any kind, whether or not it makes use of electronic commerce. Of particular importance is the need to develop specific policies on computer security along with appropriate guidelines on reporting computer misuse and abuse. Policies need to deal with specific on-line behaviour of employees such as security of user authentication systems (e.g. passwords), access to and use of the computers for private purposes, personal use of electronic mail, downloading software, and the use of copyright material. Principles also need to be established to ensure that those who report illegal conduct are not disadvantaged by their conduct.

Personnel Monitoring

There is also a need for organisations to be confident that the staff they are employing are reliable and trustworthy, as electronic fraud often involves confederates with inside knowledge of a company's security and computer procedures. The administration of modern technologically-based security systems involves a wide range of personnel- from those engaged in the manufacture of security devices to those who maintain sensitive information concerning passwords and account records. Each has the ability to make use of confidential information or facilities to commit fraud or, what is more likely to occur, to collude with people outside the organisation to perpetrate an offence.

Preventing such activities requires an application of effective risk management procedures which extend from pre-employment screening of staff to regular monitoring of the workplace. Longterm employees who have acquired considerable knowledge of an organisation's security procedures should be particularly monitored, as it is they who have the greatest knowledge of the opportunities for fraud which exist and the influence to carry them out.

Caution is also needed when organisational disputes develop. A case heard before the New South Wales District Court on 27 March 1998, for example, concerned an unsuccessful applicant for a position with an Internet Service Provider (ISP). When he was refused the job he took revenge by illegally obtaining access to the company's database of credit card holders and publishing details relating to 1,225 cardholders on the Internet as a demonstration of the security weaknesses of the company. As a result, the business lost more than $A2 million and was forced to close its ISP activities.

Computer Usage Monitoring

Employees' use of computers and their on-line activities can be monitored through the use of software which logs usage and allows managers to know, for example, whether staff have been using the Internet for non-work-related activities. Ideally, agreed procedures and rules should be established which enable staff to know precisely the extent to which computers are able to be used for private activities, if at all. If staff are permitted to make use of computers for private purposes, then procedures should be in place to protect privacy and confidentiality of communications, subject, of course, to employees obeying the law.

Where certain on-line activities have been prohibited, it is possible to monitor the activities of staff, sometimes covertly such as through video surveillance or checking electronic mail and files transmitted through servers. Filtering software may also be used to prevent staff from engaging in certain behaviours. 'Surfwatch', for example, can be customised to deny employees access to specified content. When the employee requests a site, the software matches the user's ID with the content allowable for the assigned category, then either loads the requested page, or advises the user that the request has been denied. The software also logs denied requests for later inspection by management. The use of computer software to monitor business activities also provides an effective means of detecting fraud and deterring individuals from acting illegally.

Institutional Responses

Where corporations have experienced electronic crime, managers are faced with difficult choices as to how they should respond. On the one hand, they may choose to 'exit' the situation-to use a term adopted by sociologists of law -and to dismiss the employee responsible, or cease doing business with the individual who perpetrated the offence. On the other hand, they may seek legal avenues of redress, either employing civil proceedings to recover compensation or criminal proceedings to punish the offender and to deter others from acting similarly. Many organisations prefer not to report crime to the authorities.

A survey of organisations victimised through fraud conducted by Deakin University found that fraud was not reported officially because the matter was not considered to be serious enough to warrant police attention, a fear of consumer backlash, bad publicity, inadequate proof, and a reluctance to devote time and resources to prosecuting the matter. The reasons for the reluctance to report fraud are often due to a fear of 'sending good money after bad' as experience may have shown that it will be impossible to recover losses successfully through legal avenues and that the time and resources which are required to report an incident officially and to assist in its prosecution simply do not justify the likely financial returns. Prosecution may entail countless interviews with the police, extensive analysis of financial records, and lengthy involvement in court hearings for staff.

The other disincentive to taking official action lies in the reluctance of organisations to publicise the fact of their victimisation through fear of losing business or damaging their commercial reputation in the marketplace. Government agencies might also believe that adverse publicity may result in a loss of confidence in voters, whilst financial institutions might believe that publicity of security weaknesses might result in acts of repeat victimisation taking place using the same techniques as those being investigated.

Finally, where crime has been committed by those in positions of responsibility within organisations, they may not wish to draw undue attention to their own illegal activities. As a result, many organisational victims simply take no official action preferring instead to warn or to dismiss the perpetrator and to take steps to prevent a recurrence of the incident by tightening security procedures. On some occasions a desire to 'save face' may result in the perpetrator being allowed to resign with no further action being taken.

Although some of these strategies are understandable, failure to take action creates an undesirable atmosphere in the organisation indicating that fraud is tolerated. It may also may result in the offender in question being able to reoffend, either in the same organisation or elsewhere. Failure to report crime also means that new forms of crime do not receive publicity and thus others may be victimised in the same way. Finally, if crime is not reported then it is not possible to gather statistics on the nature and extent of incidents that takes place.

Technological Solutions

A wide range of technological solutions have been devised in order to reduce the risks of electronic crime in business.

Hardware Security

At the outset, computer hardware needs to be adequately secured. This extends from computer workstations through servers operated by ISPs, to the hardware maintained by merchants and financial institutions. The extent of the security precautions used will be determined by the level of risk present. Terminals located in Internet kiosks may need only basic access controls such as through the use of passwords or smartcard tokens, whilst servers maintained by banks might need to be shielded against electro-magnetic radiation (EMR) scanning. The threat of EMR scanning should not be taken lightly. Although the risk is remote, the possibility exists. In one case in England, for example, a computer eavesdropper scanned electronic transaction information transmitted by a bank.

Despite the fact that the information was encrypted, the code was defeated and the individual successfully obtained £350,000 by blackmailing the bank and several customers by threatening to reveal certain information to the Inland Revenue. If payment systems are in place which make use of digital signatures and encrypted data transmissions, then the need to protect computer cables from interception would not arise as any data would not travel in clear text. At present, however, a good deal of sensitive information travels across networks in unencrypted form making it vulnerable to interception and subsequent disclosure. The adequacy of encryption as a security measure depends, of course, upon the strength of the encryption system used and the determination of the attacker.

Card Security

Plastic cards may be used in conjunction with business activities in a variety of ways. Primarily they will be used to store access devices such as cryptographic keys or other user authentication devices. They may also be used to store value in Mondex-type smart card systems. The most sophisticated security features should be built into plastic cards in order to prevent counterfeiting, alteration or unauthorised access to the data which they hold. There are various crime prevention strategies which have been used to prevent plastic card counterfeiting including the use of security printing, micro-printing, holograms, embossed characters, tamper-evident signature panels, magnetic stripes with improved card validation technologies, and indent printing. Smart cards, of course, are much more difficult to copy than ordinary magnetic stripe cards.

Unfortunately, all of these card security features have been overcome by organised criminals including computer chip circuitry in smart cards. On-line payment systems which do not rely upon plastic cards will, presumably, be much more secure and it may also be possible for these to operate in conjunction with biometric user identification systems.

User Authentication

Passwords used as a means of authenticating the identity of users are popular at present but frequently misused and abused. It is possible to guess passwords, particularly if little or no thought has been given to their selection, or to use various forms of social engineering to trick users into revealing their passwords for subsequent improper use. The use of brute computing force has also been used to break passwords. Password cracking programs are available by which computers are able systematically to search entire dictionaries in search of a password. Even if passwords are encrypted so as to prevent them from direct exposure, encryption keys have been broken through the use of massive computing resources.

There are various ways of enhancing access security through the use of passwords. Appropriate education of users is an initial first step in which information is given concerning ways of ensuring that passwords are not disclosed, guessed, or otherwise compromised by the user in question. Systems should be used which change passwords regularly, or which deny access after a specified number of consecutive tries using invalid passwords. Terminals should have automatic shutdown facilities when they have not been used for specified periods, such as five minutes. Single use passwords, where the password changes with every successive login according to an agreed protocol known to the user and system operator, could also be used. Challenge-response protocols may also be used as a means of carrying out user authentication.

The server generates a random number which is sent to the card. In a public key system, the card digitally signs the number and returns it to the server. The server then validates the digital signature. Alternatively, call-back devices may be used. After the user dials into a computer through a modem and gives his or her identity, the system disconnects the user and then telephones the user on a number previously registered with the server. After the user is verified, the transaction can then proceed. Such a system is, however, able to be overcome through the use of call-forwarding arrangements. Another user authentication system makes use of space geodetic methods to authenticate the physical locations of users, network nodes, and documents.

One company, CyberLocator, involves the use of a location signature sensor which uses signals transmitted by satellite to provide a location on earth at any given time. Users are thus able to be located at the time they attempt to gain access to the system, which provides a safeguard against individuals pretending to be legitimate users who are located in a different physical location. Biometrics One way in which problems of password and token security may be overcome, is for users to identify themselves biometrically. Already there are a wide variety of such systems being used which make use of an individual's unique physical properties. Common biometric identifiers today include fingerprints, voice patterns, typing patterns, retinal images, facial or hand geometry, and even the identification of a person's subcutaneous vein structures or body odours.

Fingerprint identification systems are now being used in retail stores and for access to ATMs, whilst in California, a company 'Identix', has developed a system which has fingerprint recognition sensors on mobile telephones, computer keyboards, and plastic cards. The Bank of Texas has also recently introduced iris recognition systems for its ATM network. The costs and volume of data required to be stored online to enable comparison for any potential user may, however, be prohibitive and there is always the possibility that computer security systems could be compromised by reproducing data streams which correspond with the biometric characteristics in question. An additional problem is that users must be required to provide samples of their personal characteristic and that the security of these samples could be compromised. Recognition systems are also, at present although not presumably in the future, costly and sometimes slow to use.

Digital Signature Security

The use of public key encryption systems also have their security risks. Public key systems require that cryptographic key pairs be issued to individuals who are able to establish their identity to an appropriate degree of assurance by supplying multiple and independent sources of identification such as those required when accounts are opened with a financial institution. Primary documentation (such as a passport, birth certificate etc) along with matching secondary documentation (such as a bank statement, car registration papers etc) would be required in order to satisfy the degree of documentary evidence of identity required.

This, however, may prove to be one of the system's weakest points in terms of security. Already systems which require the identification of individuals when they open accounts with financial institutions have been circumvented by offenders producing documents which have been forged or altered through the use of computerised desk-top publishing equipment (see above). Similar problems may arise when verifying the identity of individuals to whom cryptographic key pairs are issued. In addition, security risks arise in the process of generation of key pairs and in communicating key pairs to individuals, whether electronically or physically such as on a smart card token.

The possibility also arises that smartcard tokens themselves may be altered or counterfeited. Already this has taken place in relation to smartcards used for small value commercial transactions. Where keys are stored on personal computers or servers, their security may be compromised in which case appropriate risk management measures need to be taken.

Fraud Detection Software (Neural Networks)

If one is unable to prevent electronic crime from taking place entirely, then at least it may be possible to identify the presence of fraudulent transactions quickly in order to reduce the extent of any losses which are suffered or the occurrence of repeat victimisation.

A number of organisations are now providing software for use in the prevention of electronic funds transfer fraud. Software has been devised to analyse transaction patterns in order to alert individuals to the presence of fraud. Action can then be taken to determine how the incident occurred and to prevent a recurrence of the problem. The success of such an approach depends, however, upon the extent to which the software cannot be interfered with or modified.

Legal Responses

The use of criminal prosecution and punishment is one of the principal means of deterring criminal conduct in both digital and non-digital environments. Although the process may be time consuming and costly, the publicity which a criminal conviction and sentence of imprisonment attracts can be beneficial in terms of ensuring that potential offenders take the consequences of acting illegally seriously. The extent to which lengthy terms of imprisonment constitute a deterrent to criminal conduct is, however, open to debate. Whilst many property offenders behave more or less impulsively, computer criminals are relatively more likely to engage in rational calculation, making some assessment of the prospective benefits and costs of a given fraudulent course of action. In these circumstances, the greater the perceived likelihood of conviction and the more severe the expected punishment, the less the inclination to offend.

Prison, however is not a panacea. Rather than increase spending on the wider use of incarceration, prospective offenders would more effectively be deterred through increased efforts at crime prevention and enhanced rates of detection and reporting of offences. Increased spending on law enforcement activities might first be directed at detecting crime quickly and with certainty, and publicising this fact. In addition, increased spending on education, training in business ethics, and crime prevention initiatives would produce benefits in terms of reducing crime to complement expenditure on the incarceration of individuals. Financial considerations have also meant that only the most serious cases involving substantial monetary losses are likely to be fully investigated and tried, with the attendant possibility of convicted offenders receiving the most severe sanction of a term of imprisonment. The legal response to crime control has, therefore, been severely restricted, although the possibility of criminal prosecution and sanction has always remained open.

Investigation and Policing

Many problems arise in investigating cases of electronic crime as they often involve the use of highly sophisticated techniques of deception and planning. Offenders often go to considerable lengths to disguise their identity and to make financial trails of evidence difficult to follow. Those who seek to mask their identity through the use of computer networks are often able to do so, by means of 'looping', or 'weaving' through multiple sites in a variety of nations. Electronic impersonation, colloquially termed 'spoofing', can be used in furtherance of a variety of criminal activities, including fraud. Anonymous re-mailers and encryption devices can shield one from the scrutiny of all but the most determined and technologically sophisticated regulatory and enforcement agencies.

As a result, some crimes may not result in detection or loss until some time after the event, thus making the process of investigation even more challenging. Other issues which may complicate the investigation of computer-based crime, entail the logistics of search and seizure during real time, the sheer volume of material within which incriminating evidence may be contained, and the encryption of information, which may render it entirely inaccessible, or accessible only after a massive application of decryption technology. Although computer technologies may make some aspects of fraud investigation difficult, they may also be able to assist law enforcement officers. Computers, for example, are able to handle with ease substantial quantities of evidence and complex financial records which cases of serious fraud entail, and are also able to record patterns of conduct used in previous cases which facilitate the identification of repeat offending by the same individual or others utilising the same fraudulent techniques.

Trans-Jurisdictional Problems

Because digital crime often does not involve face-to-face communication, it is possible for offenders and victims to be located in more than one jurisdiction. More sophisticated conspiracies may involve individuals in three or more jurisdictions within Australia or overseas. Few remedies are available to corporations that fall victim to such activities. Even if one is able to mobilise the law, the chances of locating the fraudsters, obtaining extradition, mounting a prosecution, or recovering compensation may be impossible.

Even where a perpetrator has been identified, two problems arise in relation to the prosecution of offences which have an international aspect: first, the determination of where the offence occurred in order to decide which law to apply; and, secondly, obtaining evidence and ensuring that the offender can be located and tried before a court. Both these questions raise complex legal problems of jurisdiction and extradition. Although many of the legal and procedural impediments to the successful prosecution of electronic forms of crime have been removed, a number of practical difficulties still remain. The most problematic relate to cost and delay in cases of extraterritorial law enforcement which makes some prosecutions practically impossible. Moreover, cooperation across international boundaries in furtherance of such enforcement usually requires a congruence of values and priorities across nations which, despite prevailing trends towards globalisation, exists only infrequently.

Court Processes

There are also numerous problems associated with conducting criminal trials in cases involving electronic crime. The principal difficulties relate to the presentation of computerised business and accounting records to a court, the difficulty of presenting complex financial transactions to a jury in such a way as to permit lay people, perhaps unfamiliar with the technologies used, to understand the factual issues involved, and the length of time which such trials take, which is often exacerbated in cases of criminal conspiracy by having multiple defendants and multiple charges.

Various reforms to court procedures have been introduced throughout Australia in recent years to reduce the length, complexity and cost of prosecutions, particularly those which involve substantial sums of money or complex factual circumstances. Computer technology, for example, has greatly facilitated the presentation and analysis of complex business dealings. In addition, legal practitioners are now closely regulated with respect to the length, manner and nature of material which they present to the courts.

In view of the complexities associated with the conduct of criminal trials involving allegations of digital crime, it is necessary for all those involved to be thoroughly trained in carrying out their various duties in an efficient and effective way. Witnesses, particularly forensic accountants, need to be trained in the presentation of technical information to courts and juries in much the same way as expert medical witnesses have specialised in presenting complex medical testimony in clear and simple terms to courts.

Legal practitioners also need to be trained not only in the particular evidentiary and procedural rules which apply in such cases, but in liaising effectively with accountants and financial advisers, particularly when presenting lengthy and complex computer-based financial records. Just as a specialist Bar now exists for dealing with such cases, so a specialist Judiciary needs to be established in order to ensure that judges with appropriate experience and financial and information technology skills are allocated to these trials. Finally, jurors and those lay witnesses who give evidence in such cases should be provided with information which will enable them to understand the latest court procedures and arrive at decisions in an efficient manner.

Legal Problems in Electronic Crime

A variety of legal problems also arise in prosecuting electronic crime. These relate to the multiplicity of rules that exist in the various jurisdictions and the fact that many of the rules are complex, unclear and contradictory. In the Commonwealth, the criminal law relating to economic crime has recently been amended by the Criminal Code Amendment (Theft, Fraud, Bribery and Related Offences) Act 2000 (Cth). Various offences are specified including the offence of obtaining property or a financial advantage by deception and certain other offences involving fraudulent conduct.

A range of different approaches have been taken to law reform in order to accommodate electronic transactions with some parliaments enacting highly specific reforms to define words such as 'documents', 'writing', and 'signatures' as well as to specify the rules which govern the attribution of communications. In Australia, a more generalised approach has been adopted with the enactment of broad, technology-neutral provisions which constitute a basis for more specific legal changes which will be introduced subsequently.

10

United Nations Action Against Corporate Crime

Action Against Corruption

Several questions arise in connection with the increased interest in action against corruption at both the national and international levels. In such interest due to the higher occurrence of corrupt practices, higher detection rates or lower levels of (public, official and business) tolerance. The available evidence suggests that the answer may lie in a combination of these explanations. If each of them is examined separately, it will be easier to understand not only the eruption of scandals, but also the explosion of anti-corruption sentiments and how the two can be mutually reinforcing.

There are good reasons to believe that in a world of relative turmoil produced by radical changes in the post-cold-war era, there are new opportunities and incentives to engage in corrupt practices. Although characteristics of particular people can be found that make them more prone to misconduct than others, the problem of corruption is a problem of systems and institutions rather than one of individuals. The structural roots of corruption may be examined under four interrelated categories.

First, there may be monopolistic or oligopolistic situations, in which one or a handful of companies control a given market. The State may wish to engage private companies to perform specific tasks or public works or provide services. To the extent that only a very small number of companies can practically carry out the work, the ground is fertile for corrupt practices (such as overcharging, providing low-quality work or delivering the work late). Such a condition obtains, for example, in the field of defence projects.

Indeed, with regard to defence projects, oligopolistic conditions may be desired: no one wishes to see the proliferation of certain types of weaponry or technology that affect both national and international security. In this field, then, it is warranted to devote special attention to transactions and to have special bodies overseeing them. In other cases, oligopolies may be created by rules requiring specific conditions that companies must meet for eligibility, or may be introduced by rules dictating preferential treatment for some companies (for example, domestic versus foreign). Analytically, the same type of situation arises when a party or regime monopolizes power and decision-making for very long periods.

Secondly, very wide discretionary powers in the hands of individuals or organizations can generate temptations and motives for corrupt practices. Whenever there are few or no mechanisms of checks and balances, people will have plenty of opportunities to take undue advantage of their power. Examples of this corrupt-inducing situation are found in authoritarian regimes where powers are concentrated in the hands of very few persons. Another example is the power conferred to people with extremely specialized skills and knowledge. By definition, there are not too many of them, and therefore their powers are to a large extent unchecked. Again, the defence industry may be a concrete illustration of this situation. Additional examples of such a risk can be found in the field of physics, medicine, etc.

Thirdly, lack of transparency reduces the ability to control those in positions of authority. The lack of transparency may be caused by factors ranging from the banking secrecy to dictatorial regimes disallowing the questioning of authority. The same problem arises as a result of rare and specialized skills and knowledge. If a given public work or special warship entails such complex and incomprehensible details that only a few individuals can understand the whole project, transparency is effectively lacking. Whenever regulations of a particular sector are unclear, ambiguous and technically complicated, reporters, the public and lay persons may be completely unable to exercise effective control. The regulation of agricultural subsidies, price supports and loan guarantees in many countries provides a good example of the problem.

Finally, the genesis of corruption may be analysed through the concept of asymmetries. Asymmetries are discrepancies or disjunctions that occur at the legal, administrative, cultural, economic or political level. Although they are either domestic or international, the latter are more consequential in a global community. Asymmetries are conducive to corruption both directly and indirectly through the creation of illegal markets that operate best with the collusion of authorities. Examples of problematic legal asymmetries can be found in banking and tax regimes of different countries. This asymmetry invites many individuals and corporations to seek the most convenient jurisdiction to engage in certain transactions, even if that constitutes a violation of domestic laws. It also provides a shield against the discovery of corrupt practices.

Another example is the differential treatment of bribes paid to foreign officials. It is a serious crime in some countries, but a tax-deductible business expense in others.

This makes it easy for people to rationalize their corrupt practices as technical violations. Administrative asymmetries fuel the payment of speed money as well as clientelage and patronage systems. When some administrations function better and faster than others, bottlenecks and frustrations will certainly generate motives and rationalizations for illicit payments to "get the job done" or avoid the unnecessary costs of delays. Economic and political asymmetries can produce systematic frustrations in large parts of the population. They underlie and fuel capital flight, as well as the smuggling of aliens into countries where a better future appears possible. In another way, such asymmetries foster attitudes justifying corruption as functional to local economies and as a way of redistributing wealth.

The globalization and liberalization processes of the 1990s have increased the number and types of such asymmetries, or they have generated more awareness of their existence. Therefore, the criminologenic effect can be expected to be higher during the 1990s than before. Law enforcement asymmetries are also increased, at least temporarily, as borders are being redefined or renegotiated in different parts of the world. Lofty expectations in former centrally planned economies are frustrated by disappointment and disillusionment. The wave of privatization processes offer considerable opportunities for misconduct and corruption. Technological advances have made the contact between different countries easier and faster, and this increases the possibility of clashes of traditions or lifestyles, as well as the feelings of relative deprivation. All these reasons suggest that the problem of corruption may indeed be greater now than before.

The momentum of democratization and economic liberalization processes fosters attitudes strongly opposed to discrimination and market distortions caused by corruption. Higher awareness and lower tolerance of the problem, combined with expected increases in the incidence of corruption, account for the intensity of debates and the large number of initiatives against this scourge. Large numbers of people have come to realize the real extent of its negative consequences. All the more so in developing countries, where it has hampered national, social, economic and political progress.

Where corruption involves the transfer of funds outside the country, it seriously undermines economic development. This in turn leads to political instability as well as poor roads, schools, medical services, lower education standards and the non-completion of projects. The way funds are allocated is distorted and inefficient; competent and honest citizens feels frustrated, and the general population's level of distrust rises. As a consequence, much foreign aid disappears, productive capacity is weakened, administrative efficiency is reduced and the legitimacy of political order is undermined.

The same effects, if somewhat less acute, can be found in industrialized countries. Individuals who wish to conduct their affairs fairly and honestly are demoralized and lose faith in the rule of law. Corruption breeds distrust of public institutions, undermines ethical principles by rewarding those willing and able to pay bribes, and perpetuates inequality. Economic competition is distorted and public funds are squandered. As institutional and market reforms may lose credibility in the eyes of the public, processes of democratization (which should eventually reduce inequalities and improve transparency and accountability) risk losing momentum.

Because of the substantial amounts involved in corrupt practices every year, the international financial system is also affected. The risk include what has been termed competitive deregulation, whereby jurisdictions seeking to attract these proceeds relax their regulations and enhance secret provisions. Money-laundering becomes an even more lucrative business with a potential corruptive effect, in turn leading to increased dependency of financial systems on such funds. International conflicts and tensions are another risk, as States attempt to repatriate some of the funds, institute extraterritorial investigations that may be injure national pride or raise issues related to sovereignty, while others may be compelled to exert increased pressures on some States to amend their legislation and provide mutual assistance in corruption cases.

The global risks are even higher when links between corruption and organized crime become clearer. Several recent examples have highlighted how the illicit relationships between organized criminal groups and public officials have the potential to cause serious damage to the socio-economic structure of States (1). It is essential to note that serious and profitable illicit activities - whether related to ancient sculpture, nuclear material, drugs, illegal aliens or prostitution - invariably rely at some point in time on the support of corrupt public officials. Corruption is a necessary condition for organized criminals to operate. The risk is that, because of the immense power that some groups command, organized criminals may come to acquire such great power that they would completely undermine and destroy institutions, with dire consequences for democracy and the rule of law.

Corruption and Typology of Illicit Activities

Over the years, considerable debate has been carried out in both academic and international forum on the definition of corruption. On the basis of the report of the Italian Minister of Justice at the 19th Conference of European Ministers of Justice (organized by the Council of Europe at Valletta, Malta, from 14 to 15 June 1994), the Multidisciplinary Group on Corruption of the Council of

Europe established the following provisional working definition of corruption: "

Corruption as dealt with by the Council of Europe's GMC is bribery and any other behaviour in relation to persons entrusted with responsibilities in the public or private sector which violates their duties that follow from their status as public official, private employee, independent agent or other relationship of that kind and is aimed at obtaining undue advantages of any kind for themselves or for others". In other words, corruption could be said to constitute the combined effect of monopoly of power plus discretion in decision-making in the absence of accountability. This means that officials will have the opportunity to collect corrupt benefits as a function of their degree of monopoly over a service or activity, their discretion in deciding who should get how much, and the degree to which their activities are accountable. Accountability then becomes one of the key issues of international discourse, as well as the ultimate goal of international cooperation.

Large scale corruption may be transnational. Even when a large scale fraud is perpetrated entirely within one country, the necessity to transfer funds overseas introduces an international element. The danger posed by corruption are magnified and exacerbated by its reciprocal relationship with organized transnational crime. In a world that is constantly changing and becoming more interdependent, the long-term consequences of that relationship merit attention and action.

Organized criminal groups have demonstrated their preference towards "systemic" corruption designed to ensure the preservation of a congenial and low-risk home base or a comfortable environment in host countries. Such a method of operation may be characterized by widespread use of bribery and favours to ensure the malleability of key positions and agencies; political funding to ensure that politicians elected to office will be indebted to the criminal organizations; carefully targeted "payoffs" to law enforcement personnel to provide intelligence; and the provision of financial incentives to members of the judiciary to ensure that the penalties for criminal activities are either not imposed or are modest. Indeed, systemic corruption is one of the ways in which criminal organizations develop a symbiotic relationship with the State.

A growing awareness that corruption is a serious problem has galvanized support for an international and coordinated fight against it. In spite of this awareness, corruption remains a highly complex phenomenon. Conceptually, it is generally agreed that at the core of the problem lies some form of abuse of power. A generic conceptualization could be the abuse of public office for direct or indirect personal gain. Indirect personal gain would include benefits that someone secures improperly for his or her organization (for example, a company, a political party or a non-profit organization). Given the need for a common understanding of what is at stake and what kind of practices are to be eradicated, it is worthwhile to list several specific questionable or illegal acts that are criminalized in various States. The list is, of course, not exhaustive. This empirical approach towards corrupt practices would avoid culture-bound conceptions, thereby enhancing consensus-building and allowing anti-corruption efforts to gain further momentum.

All the offences dealt with below are frequently differentiated depending on whether the offender is a low-level or high-level official. Distinctions are also made on the basis of the gravity of the offence and the amounts involved. Systemic, large-scale and high-level corrupt practices are more severely punished. Nevertheless, all types and all levels of corruption need to be equally addressed and at the same time, since, the cumulative effect of petty corruption can be just as significant in monetary terms. In addition, it serves to maintain a culture that facilitates corruption, constantly frustrating and demoralizing the public.

Bribery

The penal laws of most countries include the offence of bribery, where private parties offer or promise money or advantages to officials in order to influence their decisions. Variations exist as to the attempt, promise, giving, solicitation or acceptance of a bribe (active and passive bribery). The crime of extortion generally consists in the demand of a benefit by an official. One of the main sources of recent global initiatives springs from the concern that public officials in many countries accept illicit payments or other advantages in order to extend contracts or offer business deals to particular corporations.

The criminalization of the direct or indirect offer or actual giving of anything of value to a foreign official in order to assist a company in its international business has become a model that may guide national lawmakers and multinational efforts. This offence is not a new concept, and involves little more than the extension of domestic bribery laws to cover bribery committed in a foreign country. The logic remains the same: no one should be required or allowed to exercise improper influence on the decision of officials in any jurisdiction. Another way in which such practices are dealt with is by resorting to unfair trade or anti-trust regulations. A company or individual that obtains a contract because of illicit payments has gained an unfair advantage over other competitors. Rules governing competition in domestic or international markets address this problem.

Some States equally criminalize and penalize the offeror and the recipient of bribes or other illegal payments. In some States the offence and the penalty are different, depending on whether public officials are or are not involved. In other States, such distinctions have no legal consequences. Also, laws cover the role of intermediaries, if the benefit was provided to a public servant through a nominee or agent.

Fraud

An alternative way of dealing with corrupt payments, especially in transactions between the private and public sector, is through the crime of fraud (as is the case in the United Kingdom of Great Britain and Northern Ireland). When corrupt intentions cannot be proved easily or at all, it may still be possible to demonstrate beyond reasonable doubt that the overpricing of a project is due to the effort of a company to recuperate the cost of bribes. The same applies to cases of providing work of inferior quality than that specified in the contract, charging for goods or services never delivered, altering the specifications or the timing of completion etc.

Other illicit payments

Observers have often referred to "speed money", amounts paid to officials in order to expedite a decision-making or other process. In such cases, officials receive illicit benefits to do what they are supposed to do anyway. In certain cases, advantages are conferred or promised in order to cut the red tape. Although some might rationalize this practice by thinking that it is valuable and in the best interests of their community, such payments are commonly outlawed.

Another act worthy of consideration is the payment of money to politicians to influence not only their vote in parliament or committees of which they are members, but also for asking particular questions or raising issues. In democratic societies, such practices may be regarded as undermining the principle of one person, one vote, and of equality and fairness - those who do not have the means to influence the political process in this way will not be sufficiently listened to and their interests may not be adequately represented. An offence that may be used to prosecute many of the above-mentioned practices is that of trading in influence, which is currently being considered by the Council of Europe working group on criminal law.

Buying and delivering of votes

A related type of misconduct, also undermining democratic principles, is the direct or indirect purchase of votes. Those able and willing to pay voters to vote for them gain an unfair advantage over those who follow the rules and do not wish to or cannot resort to similar practices. This offence may be committed not only through direct payments, but also though "clientelism" and patronage, whereby favours and jobs may be offered only to those who voted for the official in power.

Votes may be delivered in the sense of accepting favours or other advantages from a public official or representative of a party to ensure that people over whom the deliverer has control in a geographical location, company or other organization will vote for the corrupt candidate.

Illicit political contributions

Some States disallow contributions to political parties or candidates, while others criminalize them when they exceed a certain amount or violate disclosure rules. Sometimes the contributions are outlawed only when they are made by certain categories of persons (for example, by foreigners). If the intention of the contributor is to exert undue influence on a political party or candidate, the offence of bribery can be used in the absence of specific laws regarding such contributions.

Abuse of power and breach of trust

A host of malpractices can be considered as examples of exploitation of a public office and abuse of power or breach of trust. They range from favouritism and illegal discrimination to abusing sensitive or confidential information. Extortionate demands may be made for favourable treatment or for simply not discriminating against a private person. Demands may include payments, gifts or sexual intimacy.

Abuses of power may take place in the process of liberalization of economies as State-owned companies are privatized. Opportunities exist in this process for officials to undervalue the price of a company, so that it is sold very cheaply to private interests. The value of the company and, consequently, the price of its shares may go significantly higher within a short period of time. Officials can then be rewarded in a variety of ways. Officials who have special knowledge about pending or not publicity announced decisions may commit insider trading, by engaging in commercial or business activity in an unauthorized and improper fashion on the basis of non-public information.

For instance, they may buy the stock of companies that they know will be awarded a contract by the Government (the price of the stock is likely to go up when a big order is publicly announced, and corrupt officials can then sell the shares at a substantial profit). This trading, again, may occur through relatives, nominees or shell corporations. Inside knowledge may be abused by disclosing to a company representative the secret details of a competitor's bid for a public construction work. The company thus obtains the order by being able to prepare its own proposal with the advantage thus given. In this case, unfair competition laws may apply. The corrupt official may be given something of value in exchange.

Some observers have noted the case of deferred bribery, a type of misconduct that is not easy to criminalize but worth considering because of its harmful effects. This type of bribery occurs when the official is simply given a very well-paid position in a company that he favoured while in office shortly after he retires from public service. Because the elements of bribery in such cases are hard to prove, some States have introduced, or are considering the introduction of, laws prohibiting officials from working for companies that they regulated, or which were involved in transactions with the officials' department while these officials were in office. Other States opt for a waiting period during which former officials cannot accept employment from entities in such cases as mentioned above - two or more years. Disallowing the use of "revolving doors" can help strengthen public perceptions of the integrity of their government and officials.

Officials with powers of control over revenue departments or social agencies have the opportunity to interfere improperly with the work of those bodies. They may orchestrate persecutions of political opponents, organizations or companies for ideological of profit-motivated reasons. They may direct the selective prosecution of certain offenders, or systematically turn a blind eye to other offenders. They may arbitrarily undercharge or overcharge taxes and duties on commercial transactions to the point of extortion. Obstruction of justice is an offence that may be used against officials who seek to hide or cover up such illegal activities by misdirecting investigations or destroying evidence. Such misconduct is often linked to the operation of illegal enterprises and markets - what is usually considered organized crime.

The best-organized crimes perpetrated discreetly, without risking scandals and public attention, and with the collaboration of officials. Whenever there is suspicious of serious drug trafficking, arms trafficking or other smuggling operations on a grand scale, it can be expected that the collusion and illicit enrichment of some official will be found. In dealing with such practices, legal tools used against organized criminal groups, such as the Racketeer Influenced and Corrupt Organizations (RICO) statue in the United States of America, may prove useful in the punishment of corrupt officials.

Misappropriation of public funds

The offences of abuse of power and breach of trust can also be used against practices that involve the misuse and misappropriation of public funds or resources. Public officials may divert public money to their accounts or those of a partner. Some autocratic rulers are known for the systematic looting of their countries' wealth. Additional offences that may be used in those cases include embezzlement and theft, both of which are quite common among Member States. States that apply currency restrictions and controls may use the violation of those rules to prosecute corrupt officials who export the proceeds of their illicit profits overseas. Other States may resort to laws prohibiting tax evasion, given that this illegal income is neither declared nor taxed. In the event that an official is unable to explain his or her net worth and level of spending, prosecutors may be able to use this as an evidence of tax evasion.

Conflict of interest

Public officials have the obligation to be fair, impartial and efficient in their public roles. The legislation of many States provides that it is not appropriate for officials to make decisions significantly affecting companies in which they are shareholders or directors. Such conflicts, in some States, are outlawed entirely. In others, the officials must declare the conflict and withdraw from the decision-making process with respect to the area of potential conflict. In yet other States, mere disclosure of the conflict is considered sufficient to prevent improper decisions by an official. In those cases, non-disclosure of related interests is a punishable offence. The same would apply to violations of routine obligations of public servants to place their assets on public records (sometimes including the assets of their close family members).

Action against Corruption and Bribery

The United Nations has been concerned with the problem of corruption for more than two decades. The matter has been discussed by the quinquennial United Nations congresses on the prevention of crime and the treatment of offenders, particularly with reference to new forms of crime and crime prevention planning in the context of development. The Fifth Congress on the Prevention of Crime and the Treatment of Offenders, held in Geneva in 1975, focused on crime as business at the national and international levels, bringing particular attention into organized crime, white collar crime and corruption. The working paper prepared by the Secretariat and titled: "Changes in Forms and Dimensions of Criminality - Transnational and National", recognized the increasing threat posed by economic crimes, and in particular by corruption, to many countries in the world. The Fifth Congress also considered the role of the police in the prevention of crime, in accordance with a specific request made by the General Assembly in 1974 (resolution 3218 - XXIX).

In the working paper on: "The Emerging Role of the Police and Other Law Enforcement Agencies, with Special Reference to Changing Expectations and Minimum Standards of Performance", the Secretariat noted that when corruption occurs in high places, it is a problem for those who are expected to keep order to maintain standards different from those respected by their superiors. For this reason, corruption within the police depends largely upon the influence, guidance and interest of the total society on the police. Nevertheless, it is still true that a police force is in a unique position and a police officer cannot be regarded simply as an ordinary citizen in so far as his conduct is concerned. By virtue of his appointment, he is expected to behave in a manner that is at least one level higher than that of most persons.

In preparation for the Fifth Congress, the United Nations convened a working group of police experts from several regions of the world in January 1975 to help draft an international code of ethics for the police and related law enforcement agencies. The working group, after reviewing the methods used in setting standards for law enforcement officials in various parts of the world and studying a variety of models, prepared a draft international code of police ethics, which was subsequently presented to the Congress, as part of the above mentioned working paper prepared by the Secretariat.

On the basis of the above, the Fifth Congress, which is remembered mainly for having offered the Declaration on the Protection of all Persons from Being Subjected to Torture and Other Cruel, Inhuman or Degrading Treatment or Punishment, discussed the scope and content of the international code of conduct and recommended the General Assembly be requested to establish a committee of experts to study the question of an international code of police ethics and within one year prepare a new document to be considered by the competent organs of the United Nations, including the feasibility of regional groups drafting preliminary documents, consisting of representatives who would reflect the cultural and legal system of each region.

The General Assembly, by resolution 3453 (XXX) of 9 December 1975, requested the Committee on Crime Prevention and Control "to elaborate, on the basis of, inter alia, the proposal presented to and conclusions arrived at by the Fifth United Nations Congress on the Prevention of Crime and the Treatment of Offenders, a draft code of conduct for law enforcement officials and to submit this draft code to the General Assembly".

The Fourth session of the Committee on Crime Prevention and Control (New York, 21 June-2 July 1976) elaborated, on the basis of the proposals presented to and conclusions arrived by the Fifth Congress a draft code of conduct, for submission to the Assembly. Further its consideration, the Assembly established in 1977 an intersessional working group of the Third Committee to achieve universal consensus on its text.

In finalizing the working of the code, much attention was devoted to the question of police professionalism and accountability. Regarding the problem of corruption among police officials, the code states that: "Corruption being intolerable in all phases of life, and inasmuch as Governments cannot expect to enforce the law among their citizens if they cannot, or will not, enforce the law against their own agents and agencies, it is incumbent upon law enforcement officials to rigorously oppose and pursue all acts of corruption coming to their attention". At its thirty-fourth session, in 1979, the General Assembly adopted the Code of Conduct for Law Enforcement Officials, by resolution 34/169. The Assembly decided to transmit the Code to Governments with the recommendation that favourable consideration should be given to its use within the framework of national legislation or practice as a body of principles for observance by law enforcement officials.

While assisting Countries in the implementation of the above mentioned code, the United Nations has also devoted substantial energy to develop proposals on practical steps that States can follow in their efforts to devise and implement strategies and reforms. In this connection, for example, the Eighth Congress considered a draft resolution on international co-operation for crime prevention and criminal justice in the context of development, to which were annexed a series of recommendations on the subject. Recommendation 8 reads as follows: "Because the corrupt activities of public officials can destroy the potential effectiveness of all types of governmental programmes, hinder development, and victimize individuals and groups, it is of crucial importance that all nations should:

— (a) review the adequacy of their criminal laws, including procedural legislation, in order to respond to all forms of corruption and related actions designed to assist or to facilitate corrupt activities, and should have recourse to sanctions that will ensure an adequate deterrence;

— (b) devise administrative and regulatory mechanism for the prevention of corrupt practices or the abuse of power;

— (c) adopt procedures for the detection, investigation and conviction of corrupt officials;

— (d) create legal provisions for the forfeiture of funds and property from corrupt practices; and

— (e) adopt economic sanctions against enterprises involved in corruption.

The Crime Prevention and Criminal Justice Branch should co-ordinate the elaboration of materials to assist countries in these efforts, including the development of a manual to combat corruption, and should provide specialized training to judges and prosecutors that would qualify them to deal with the technical aspects of corruption, as well as with the experience derived from specialized tribunals handling such matters".

Almost one year early, and also as part of the preparation activities for the Eighth Congress, the Crime Prevention and Criminal Justice Branch (now Division), in cooperation with the Department of Technical Cooperation for Development (now part of the new Department for Development Support and Management Services) organized an Interregional Seminar on Corruption in Government, hosted by the Government of the Netherlands at The Hague. The Seminar was attended by high-level officials from 18 developing countries from all the regions and by observers from eight developed countries, non-governmental organizations, academic institutions, independent anti-corruption bodies and ombudsman's offices.

A first draft Manual to Combat Corruption, prepared for submission to the Eighth Congress, was circulated for comments. The Seminar conducted in-depth discussions on the forms of corruption in government, and its causes, consequences, and relationships with organized crime; and it assessed the existing measures against corruption, as well as appropriate actions to be taken against it at the national, regional and international levels. At the same time, the role of international cooperation in the prevention, detection, investigation, prosecution and sanctioning of corrupt practices and enforcement in the public management system, was highlighted. The need for better information and expertise, and facilitating technical cooperation and mutual assistance through technical co-operation among developing countries was emphasized. Finally, the possibility of an international convention to deal with transnational corruption and an international code of ethics for public service was also considered.

On the basis of the above, the Eighth Congress received a new version of the Manual on Practical Measures against Corruption. Its purpose was to review the most common problems encountered by policy-makers and practitioners in their efforts to deal with corruption. It highlights possible measures that could be taken and procedures for devising anti-corruption programmes. In suggesting possible courses of action, the manual touches on legal issues whose degree of relevance and difficulty may vary, depending on the legal system of each country. As far as possible, such issues have been taken into account, in order to facilitate the adaptability of the Manual to as many contexts as possible. After that Congress, the Manual was circulated to experts around the world and the comments received were incorporated to produce a revised version, which was published as a special issue in the International Review of Criminal Policy.

The Eight Congress also adopted resolution 7 on "corruption in government" recommending that Member States should devise a variety of administrative and regulatory mechanism for the prevention of corrupt practices, and inviting them to review the adequacy of their criminal laws, including procedural legislation, to respond to all forms of corruption and to actions designed to assist or facilitate corrupt activities. The Eighth Congress requested the Secretariat to provide technical cooperation assistance to requesting Member States in the fields of strategic planning of anti-corruption programmes, law reforms, public administration and management, training of public officials and criminal justice personnel, and in tendering international aid projects.

The Secretariat was also requested to organize regional and interregional seminars, expert group meetings, workshops and other appropriate activities. These were intended to encourage the exchange of information on anti-corruption techniques, laws and research, and in the examination and promotion of improvements in institutional arrangements and processes. In addition, these activities were also directed towards the improvement of the management of the justice process, through the use of databases, to improve decision-making. Finally, the Secretary was requested to develop a draft international code of conduct for public officials, for submission to the Ninth Congress.

The issue of corruption received further attention by the General Assembly, which adopted resolution 45/107 of 14 December 1990 on international cooperation for crime prevention and criminal justice in the context of development, as recommended by the Eighth Congress. The Assembly reiterated the recommendations of the Eighth Congress regarding the measures that should be adopted by Member States and recommended that the Branch coordinate the elaboration of materials to assist countries in their efforts against corruption and to provide specialized training to judges and prosecutors to qualify them to deal with the technical aspects of corruption.

One year later, and as a result of the Ministerial Summit held in November 1991 and the restructuring of the Crime Programme, the Assembly adopted a Statement of Principles and Programme of Action, annexed to its resolution 46/152, in which it decided that the United Nations Crime Prevention and Criminal Justice Programme should be designed to assist the international community in meeting its pressing needs in the field of crime prevention and criminal justice and to provide countries with timely and practical assistance in dealing with problems of both national and international crime. For this reason a new functional interregional body was established: the Commission on Crime Prevention and

Criminal Justice. Among the goals of the programme would be the integration and consolidation of the efforts of Member States in preventing and combatting transnational crime and the promotion of the highest standards of fairness, justice and professional conduct.

At its second session, the Commission on Crime Prevention and Criminal Justice (Vienna, 13-23 April 1993) had before it a number of suggestions regarding possible subjects of workshops to be organized during the Ninth Congress. Corruption was one of those subjects. On the recommendation of the Commission, the Economic and Social Council decided, by its resolution 1993/32 of 27 July 1993, to devote one day of plenary general discussions at the Ninth Congress to the issue.

In pursuance of resolution 7 of the Eighth Congress, the Secretariat elaborated a draft international code of conduct for public officials, which was discussed by the five regional preparatory meetings for the Ninth Congress and by the Commission at its third session. It also prepared a working paper which helped for approaching the discussion in plenary, which was introduced by five panellists. The Economic and Social Council, in its resolution 1994/19, section VI, of 25 July 1994, recommended that the Ninth Congress should consider the desirability of a code of conduct for public officials, and that the Secretary-General should seek comments from Member States and relevant entities, in order to assist the Commission on Crime Prevention and Criminal Justice in its consideration of the matter at its fourth session.

As recommended by the Congress, the draft code was submitted to the Commission at its fourth session (Vienna, 30 May-9 June 1995) for its review and comments. The Commission was of the opinion that the draft code, when finalized, could constitute an important tool for the operational activities of the United Nations Crime Prevention and Criminal Justice Programme, as well as for States wishing to include similar codes in measures to prevent and control corruption.

In its resolution 1995/14 on action against corruption, adopted on the recommendation of the Commission on Crime Prevention and Criminal Justice at its fourth session, the Economic and Social Council requested the Secretary-General to finalize the draft code, on the basis of the comments received from Governments. In the same resolution, the Council urged States to develop and implement anti-corruption measures, to increase their capacities to prevent and adequately control corrupt practices, and to improve international cooperation in this field. The Council also requested the Secretary-General, inter alia, to review and expand the Manual on Practical Measures against Corruption, then published in the above-mentioned double-issue of the International Review of Criminal Policy; to coordinate and cooperate with other United Nations entities and relevant international organizations in the anti-corruption efforts; and to keep the issue of action against corruption under regular review.

The General Assembly, by resolution 50/225 on "Public administration and development", also took note of the fact that the United Nations system, responding to requests from interested Member States, has contributed in support of their public administration to include wider aspect of governance, including democratic, legal and judiciary reform, and strengthening of the civil society and recognized that Governments in all countries should make their procedures transparent in order to avoid and combat all acts of corruption.

Accordingly, on its proposal, and as recommended by the Council in its resolution 1996/8, the General Assembly, in December 1996, adopted the International Code of Conduct for Public Officials recommending it to Member States as a tool to guide their efforts against corruption. The Assembly requested the Secretary-General to distribute the Code to all States and to include it in the Manual on Practical Measures against Corruption, to be revised and expanded pursuant to Council resolution 1995/14. The Assembly further requested the Secretary-General to continue to collect information and legislative and regulatory texts from States and relevant intergovernmental organizations, in the context of his continuing study of the problem of corruption.

According to the Code a public office is a position implying a duty to act in the public interest. As a consequence the ultimate loyalty of public officials shall be to the public interests of their country. The code also focuses on several issues concerning the conduct of public officials, such as: (a) Conflict of interest and disqualification; (b) Disclosure of assets; (c) Acceptance of gifts or other favours; (d) Confidential information; (e) Political activity. Concerning the conflict of interest and disqualification, the Code states that:

1. Public official shall not use their official authority for the improper advancement of their own or their family's personal or financial interest. They shall not engage in any transaction, acquire any position or function or have any financial, commercial or other comparable interest that is incompatible with their office, functions and duties or the discharge thereof;

2. Public officials shall, in accordance with laws or administrative policies, declare business, commercial and financial interests or activities undertaken for financial gain that may raise a possible conflict of interest;

3. Public officials shall at no time improperly use public moneys, property, services or information that is acquired in the performance of, or as a result of, their official duties for activities not related to their official work;

4. Public officials shall comply with measures established by law or by administrative policies in order that after leaving their official positions they will not take improper advantage of their previous office.

The General Assembly, after the approval, in March 1996, by the Member States of the Organization of American States of the Inter-American Convention against Corruption and aware of the relevant work developed by other regional and international organizations, such as the Council of Europe and the European Union, to combat international bribery, adopted, by its resolution 51/191, the United Nations Declaration against Corruption and Bribery in International Commercial Transactions annexed to the resolution.

The Declaration recognized the importance of promoting social responsibility and appropriate standards of ethics not only in the public sector, but also in private corporations, "including transnational corporations, and individuals engaged in international commercial transactions, inter alia, through observance of the laws and regulations of the countries in which they conduct business, and taking into account the impact of their activities on economic and social development and environmental protection".

The Declaration also urged Member States to take concrete action:

1. to combat all forms of corruption, bribery and related illicit practices in international commercial transactions;
2. to criminalize bribery of foreign public officials in an effective and coordinate manner;
3. to develop or maintain accounting standards and practices that improve the transparency of international commercial transactions;

4. to develop or to encourage the development, as appropriate, of business codes, standards or best practices that prohibit corruption, bribery and related illicit practices in international transactions;
5. to examine establishing illicit enrichment by public officials or elected representative as an offence;
6. to cooperate and afford one another the greatest possible assistance in connection with criminal investigations and other legal proceedings brought in respect of corruption and bribery in international commercial transactions;
7. to enhance cooperation to facilitate access to documents and records about transactions and about identities of persons engaged in bribery in international transactions;
8. to ensure that bank secrecy provisions do not impede or hinder criminal investigations or other legal proceedings relating to corruption, bribery or related illicit practices in international commercial transactions, and that full cooperation is extended to Governments that seek information on such transactions.

The General Assembly also requested the Economic and Social Council and its subsidiary bodies, in particular the Commission on Crime Prevention and Justice:

— (a) to examine ways, including through binding international instruments, without in any way precluding, impeding or delaying international, regional or national actions, to further the implementation of the resolution and the Declaration, so as to promote the criminalization of corruption and bribery in international commercial transactions;

— (b) to keep the issue of corruption and bribery in international commercial transactions under regular review; and

— (c) to promote the effective implementation of the resolution.

As a follow-up of the request to revise and to expand the Manual on Practical Measures against Corruption, the Crime Prevention and Criminal Justice Division of the Secretariat, with the assistance of the Government of Argentina, organized a meeting of experts from all regions at Buenos Aires from 17 to 21 March 1997 to consider ways and means of strengthening international cooperation in this field, as well as to offer suggestions on the revision and expansion of the manual.

The Expert Group Meeting on Corruption brought to the attention of the Commission at its sixth session that action against corruption requires the adoption and revision of legislation and regulatory provisions to ensure that there is in place a set of measures that facilitate the prevention, detection, deterrence, prosecution and adjudication of corruption, fully taking into account the evolving nature of the problem and its various manifestations. The Expert Group Meeting also recommended that consideration should be given to the following specific measures:

1. Disclosure by public officials of assets and liabilities;
2. Guidelines for the performance of duties by public officials;
3. Introducing or strengthening existing independent auditing institutions or bodies that vet public expenditures;
4. Establishment of specialized anti-corruption bodies;
5. Measures to introduce or encourage transparency in the management of public funds and in the decision-making process;
6. Establishment of transparent and competitive procedures for tendering and supervision of public

works contracts and introduction of clear procurement rules;

7. Measures to ensure free competitions, including anti-trust regulations;
8. Measures to prevent improper advantages;
9. Elimination of curtailment of bank secrecy;
10. Measures to ensure and encourage public participation;
11. Measures to ensure accountability and effective disciplinary action;
12. Financing of political parties and campaigns;
13. Guaranteeing freedom of the parties and the right to information;
14. Elaboration and introduction of codes of ethics for certain categories of professions;
15. Elaboration of a programme to encourage the implementation of the International Code of Conduct for Public Officials.

Pursuant to resolutions 51/59 and 51/191, the Crime Prevention and Criminal Justice Division organized the African Regional Ministerial Workshop on Action against Organized Crime and Corruption at Dakar, Senegal, from 21 to 23 July 1997, at the invitation of the Government of Senegal. The Workshop was supported by the Agency for Cultural and Technical Cooperation (ACCT), and in cooperation with the United Nations International Drug Control Programme (UNDCP).

The Dakar Ministerial Workshop was crucial in the translation of declarations of political support into concrete action plans for the implementation of effective regional cooperation, covering investigation and legal assistance, extradition and confiscation of criminal proceeds. In this context, three projects had been prepared covering the fields of organized crime control, an inventory of trafficking routes in Africa and the elaboration of instruments to fight corruption for the consideration and approval of the African Ministers. At its final meeting on 23 July 1997, the Workshop adopted unanimously the Dakar Declaration. In the Declaration the Ministers and Representatives of the African States expressed their concern about the increase and expansion of organized criminal activities, corrupt practices and bribery in international commercial transactions, recognizing the importance of the contribution that the United Nations Crime Prevention and Criminal Justice Programme can make to the implementation of the United Nations New Agenda for the Development of Africa in the 1990s, in particular regarding the intensification of the democratic process and the strengthening of the protection of the civil society. The Ministers and Representatives of African States expressed their commitment to combat corruption and organized crime by:

— Reviewing and strengthening the existing institutions, in particular the criminal justice systems and establishing appropriate mechanisms to coordinate action at the national level;

— Reviewing, modernizing and harmonizing existing substantive and procedural legislation and regulatory regimes, to ensure their continued relevance, efficiency and adaptability to the various forms of corrupt practices, including in the context of international commercial transactions, and to modern manifestations of organized crime;

— Elaborating and adopting new laws and regulations, designed to meet the challenge posed by the complexity and sophistication of organized crime and corruption;

— Upgrading the skills of the law enforcement and criminal justice personnel, increasing their knowledge and expertise, and raising their professional abilities, to enable them to effectively implement relevant legislation and regulations, for the purpose of preventing and controlling organized crime and corruption.

At its sixth session, the Commission on Crime Prevention and Criminal Justice recommended the adoption of five draft resolutions by the General Assembly. One of these draft resolution was the "International cooperation against corruption and bribery in international commercial transactions". The draft resolution stressed the threat posed by the bribery of public officials by individuals and enterprises to the international commercial transactions. The draft resolution also urged Member States "to criminalize, in an effective and coordinated manner, the bribery of public office holders of other States in international commercial transactions and encourages them to engage, as appropriate, in programmatic activities to deter, prevent and combat bribery and corruption (...)".

During the Commission great attention was given to preventive measures, in particular to the establishment or strengthening of already existing auditing institutions or agencies having the authority and the capacity to scrutinize public expenditure, to the elaboration and introduction of code of ethics for certain categories of professions, to measures to ensure accountability and effective disciplinary action, to measures to guarantee the independent status of officials working within the public sector or in charge of fighting against corruption and bribery, and educational programmes to promote ethical values and training programmes for law enforcement officers. Particular importance was attached to measures taken at the national level to promote transparency in the expenditure of public funds by allowing or encouraging public access to and monitoring of the related decision-making process.

Activities of the Crime Prevention and Criminal Justice Division

Technical Cooperation

The Crime Prevention and Criminal Justice Division has also made efforts to provide its technical cooperation services to requesting Member States to enable them to enhance their capacity to develop and pursue anti-corruption policies and strategies effectively and to combat corrupt practices and related activities.

In this connection, the Division undertook a number of needs assessment missions at the request of Member States (Angola, Gambia, Romania, Senegal, Sierra Leone, the former Yugoslav Republic of Macedonia and Togo). As a follow-up to those missions, five projects proposals have been elaborated and are either awaiting funding or are in the first stages of implementation.

The first project is aimed at strengthening the institutional capacity of Angola to prevent and fight corruption. The project accords high priority to the improvement of the effectiveness of Angolan legislation in combatting activities related to corruption by introducing new and more effective measures. The project includes the provision of assistance in improving the capacity of Angola for international cooperation in criminal matters, mainly through promoting the harmonization of its various penal laws with those of other countries in the subregion. Further, the project includes practical measures such as establishing a national commission on corruption with the tasks of coordinating action and setting up database in this field.

The aim of the second project is to provide advisory services and training to assist the Government of the former Yugoslav Republic of Macedonia in its efforts against corruption. The project also aims at elaborating anti-corruption legislation and envisages the introduction of basic concepts of community policing and the provision of training to improve police skills in the prevention and control of criminal activities related to corruption.

The objective of the projects for Gambia, Guinea and Sierra Leone is to build and strengthen the institutional mechanism of those States for preventing and fighting corruption, initially through introducing new legislative tools, as well as setting up a national commission on corruption and an interministerial unit aimed at coordinating national and subregional efforts in the fight against corruption. The projects provide for assistance in facilitating cooperation within the subregion through the conclusion of agreements on extradition and mutual assistance with neighbouring countries. The projects also envisage a training programme for judges, prosecutors and law enforcement officers, as well as the provision of technical assistance for the establishment of a central database to store and retrieve relevant information on corruption activities to be run by the interministerial unit. Finally the projects seek to strengthen the exchange of information and experience between the States concerned and international agencies.

The Crime Prevention and Criminal Justice Division has also elaborated practical tools for technical cooperation activities in the field of corruption, such as the model law on corruption. In 1996, the interregional advisor of the Division was asked by the authorities of Romania, to identify possible areas of activities in the field of corruption. As a result of that mission, undertaken jointly with UNDCP and UNDP, the Division elaborated a project proposal for building and strengthening the capacity of the Romanian criminal justice system to prevent and fight corruption and organized crime activities. As a first step in the implementation of the project, the Parliament of Romania is going to discuss a law on corruption drawn upon the model law and tailored to local needs with the assistance of the Division. The project for Romania also pursues the establishment of a national commission against corruption to coordinate national policies in this area, assistance on providing a training programme and the development of the capacity for the exchange of information and experiences.

As a follow-up to the signature of a memorandum of understanding with respect to the provision of technical assistance in the area of crime prevention and criminal justice between the Division and the Ministry of Justice of Bosnia and Herzegovina, the Division, in cooperation with Department for Development Support and Management Services and UNDP, has developed a project for strengthening the administration of justice in Bosnia and Herzegovina. One of the main objectives of the project is to provide advisory assistance on anti-corruption strategies, thereby strengthening the criminal justice mechanism of the State in this particular area.

UNDP has become increasingly interested in corruption as part of the work of its Management Development and Governance Division (MDGD). Programmes that explicitly attempt to reduce malfeasance in government are complementary to the MDGD's broader mandate to help countries reform their institutional structures. As a result of the new partnership between the Division and UNDP, a memorandum of understanding with the Regional Bureau for Eastern Europe and the Commonwealth of Independent States was signed in 1996. This memorandum of understanding will provide opportunities for joint needs assessment missions and fund-raising and the actual funding or co-funding of projects in crime prevention and criminal justice, particularly with regard to action against corruption.

The Division is also cooperating closely with the Inter-Parliamentary Union, with a view to addressing issues of mutual concern and exchanging experiences and expertise, particularly considering the intense interest of that organization in action against corruption and its ongoing work in this area.

Further, the Division continued to cooperate and interact with the scientific and research institutions involved in criminological activities, such as the International Society of Social Defence, which held its thirteenth international congress at Lecce, Italy, from 28 to 30 November 1996, on the theme of "Social defence, corruption, and the protection of public administration and the independence of justice". The international congress was an occasion to carry out an in-depth examination of available legislative options, whether in criminal, administrative or constitutional law, to prevent and control corruption and ensure fairness, equity and justice in both the public and private sectors.

In view of the growing needs of States and the consequent increase in requests for technical assistance, the Division plans to continue developing operational activities in this area. In this context, the Division could collect and analyse national anti-corruption strategies, in order to elaborate compilations of best practices, which would form the basis for training programmes. Further, the Division could undertake the elaboration of comparative studies, which would assist States in designing, formulating and implementing joint strategies and collaborative arrangements to prevent and control corruption. The technical cooperation activities of the Division could also include model courses for universities and schools of business and public administration, as well as the provision of assistance in organizing public campaigns to promote good governance, for the purpose of enlisting public support for necessary anti-corruption resources and legislation. In addition, the Division could provide assistance in the establishment of special anti-corruption entities, including by elaborating feasibility studies and making available the required expertise. The need for such entities, is of high priority, particularly in the case of transnational bribery and corruption, where the sensitive nature of the transactions, the usually high level of the officials involved and the diversity of sophisticated techniques for the transfer and concealment of the proceeds make detection of corrupt activities extremely difficult.

United Nations
Resolution 1998/16.
44th plenary meeting 28 July 1998.

UNITED NATIONS ACTION AGAINST CORRUPTION

The Economic and Social Council,

Concerned about the seriousness of problems posed by corruption, which may endanger the stability and security of societies, undermine the values of democracy and morality and jeopardize social, economic and political development,

Convinced that existing arrangements for combating corruption at the national and international levels must be periodically reviewed and modernized to ensure that the specific contemporary problems of fighting all forms of corruption are being effectively addressed at all times,

Recalling General Assembly resolution 51/59 of 12 December 1996,

Recalling also its resolution 1995/14 of 24 July 1995,

Recalling further General Assembly resolution 52/87 of 12 December 1997, in which the Assembly requested the Secretary-General to invite each Member State to provide a report on steps taken to implement the provisions of the United Nations Declaration against Corruption and Bribery in International Commercial Transactions (1),

Taking note of the report of the Secretary-General on action against corruption and bribery, (2)

Recalling the manual prepared by the Secretariat on practical measures against corruption, (3)

Aware of recent multilateral initiatives to combat corruption, including the United Nations Declaration against Corruption and Bribery in International Commercial Transactions(3), the International Code of Conduct for Public Officials (4), the Inter-American Convention against Corruption, adopted by the Organization of American States on 29 March 1996 (5), the Organisation for Economic Cooperation and Development on Combating Bribery of Foreign Public Officials in International Business Transactions done at Paris on 17 December 1997, the Convention on the protection of the European Communities' financial interests and the Protocol and Second Protocol to that Convention drawn up by the Council of the European Union on the basis of article K.3 of the Treaty on European Union, the Convention on the fight against corruption involving officials of the European Communities or officials of member States of the European Union, the ongoing work of the Council of Europe to elaborate a criminal law convention against corruption, the programmes of the Council of Europe targeting that form of criminality, and recommendation 32 of the recommendations elaborated and endorsed by the Senior Experts Group on Transnational Organized Crime, which met at Lyon, France, from 27 to 29 June 1996, which are contained in annex I to Economic and Social Council resolution 1997/22,

Convinced that updating the manual on practical measures against corruption by incorporating into the manual a section describing recent developments will contribute to increased efficiency in combating that form of criminality,

Determined to ensure that United Nations materials to assist States in their efforts to combat corruption remain as useful and up to date as possible,

1. Requests the Secretary-General, in his efforts update the manual prepared by the Secretariat on practical measures against corruption, to include in the text a section describing recent developments in combating corruption, in particular the practical impact of recent multilateral initiatives in this area, such as the above-described activities of the United Nations, the Organization of American States, the Organisation for Economic Cooperation and Development, the European Community, the Council of Europe and the Senior Experts Group on Transnational Organized Crime;
2. Decides to convene an open-ended meeting of governmental experts, using extrabudgetary resources offered by the Government of France for that purpose, to explore means of ensuring that the initiatives described in paragraph 1 above are effective and that an appropriate international strategy against corruption, including the proceeds thereof, is formulated in consultation with other intergovernmental organizations active this area;
3. Requests the Secretary-General, to submit a report on the implementation of the present resolution, including on the work of the intergovernmental experts, to the Commission on Crime Prevention and Criminal Justice at its ninth session.

Annex 1

Action against corruption and International Code of Conduct for Public Officials

General Assembly - Resolution 51/59
Date: 12 December 1996
Meeting: 82
Adopted without a vote
Report: A/51/610

The General Assembly,

Concerned at the seriousness of problems posed by corruption, which may endanger the stability and security of societies, undermine the values of democracy and morality and jeopardize social, economic and political development,

Also concerned about the links between corruption and other forms of crime, in particular organized crime and economic crime, including money-laundering,

Convinced that, since corruption is a phenomenon that currently crosses national borders and affects all societies and economies, international cooperation to prevent and control it is essential,

Convinced also of the need to provide, upon request, technical assistance designed to improve public management systems and to enhance accountability and transparency,

Recalling the Inter-American Convention against Corruption, adopted by the Organization of American States at the Specialized Conference for Consideration of the Draft Inter-American Convention against Corruption, held at Caracas from 27 to 29 March 1996,

Recalling also its resolutions 45/121 of 14 December 1990 and 46/152 of 18 December 1991, and Economic and

Social Council resolutions 1992/22 of 30 July 1992,1993/32 of 27 July 1993 and 1994/19 of 25 July 1994,

Recalling in particular its resolution 50/225 of 19 April 1996, adopted at its resumed session on public administration and development,

Recalling Economic and Social Council resolution 1995/14 of 24 July 1995 on action against corruption,

Recalling also the work carried out by other international and regional organizations in this field, including the activities of the Council of Europe, the European Community, the Organisation for Economic Cooperation and Development and the Organization of American States,

1. Takes note of the report of the Secretary-General on action against corruption, (11) submitted to the Commission on Crime Prevention and Criminal justice at its fifth session;

2. Adopts the International Code of Conduct for Public Officials, annexed to the present resolution, and recommends it to Member States as a tool to guide their efforts against corruption;

3. Requests the Secretary-General to distribute the International Code of Conduct to all States and to include it in the manual on practical measures against corruption, to be revised and expanded pursuant to Economic and Social Council resolution 1995/14, with a view to offering both those tools to States in the context of advisory services, training and other technical assistance activities;

4. Also requests the Secretary-General to continue to collect information and legislative and regulatory texts from States and relevant intergovernmental organizations, in the context of his continuing study of the problem of corruption;

5. Further requests the Secretary-General, in consultation with States, relevant intergovernmental and non-governmental organizations, as well as in cooperation with the institutes comprising the United Nations Crime Prevention and Criminal Justice Programme network, to elaborate an implementation plan and submit it to the Commission on Crime Prevention and Criminal Justice at its sixth session, in conjunction with his report to be submitted pursuant to Economic and Social Council resolution 1995/14;

6. Urges States, relevant intergovernmental and non-governmental organizations, as well as the institutes comprising the United Nations Crime Prevention and Criminal Justice Programme network, to extend to the Secretary-General their full support in elaborating the implementation plan and in implementing paragraph 4 above;

7. Urges Member States carefully to consider the problems posed by the international aspects of corrupt practices, especially as regards international economic activities carried out by corporate entities, and to study appropriate legislative and regulatory measures to ensure the transparency and integrity of financial systems and transactions carried out by such corporate entities;

8. Requests the Secretary-General to intensify his efforts to closely cooperate with other entities of the United Nations system and other relevant international organizations and to more effectively coordinate activities undertaken in this area;

9. Also requests the Secretary-General, subject to the availability of extrabudgetary resources, to provide increased advisory services and technical assistance to requesting Member States, in particular in the elaboration of national strategies, the elaboration or

improvement of legislative and regulatory measures, the establishment or strengthening of national capacities to prevent and control corruption, as well as in training and upgrading skills of relevant personnel;

10. Calls upon States, relevant international organizations and financing institutions to extend to the Secretary-General their full support and assistance in the implementation of the present resolution;

11. Requests the Commission on Crime Prevention and Criminal Justice to keep the issue of action against corruption under regular review.

ANNEX 2

INTERNATIONAL CODE OF CONDUCT FOR PUBLIC OFFICIALS

General Assembly resolution 51/59, annex.

I. General Principles

1. A public office, as defined by national law, is a position of trust, implying a duty to act in the public interest. Therefore, the ultimate loyalty of public officials shall be to the public interests of their country as expressed through the democratic institutions of government.

2. Public officials shall ensure that they perform their duties and functions efficiently and effectively, in accordance with laws or administrative policies, and with integrity. They shall at all times seek to ensure that public resources for which they are responsible are administered in the most effective and efficient manner.

3. Public officials shall be attentive, fair and impartial in the performance of their functions and, in particular, in their relations with the public. They shall at no time afford any undue preferential treatment to any group or individual or improperly discriminate against any group or individual, or otherwise abuse the power and authority vested in them.

II. Conflict of Interest and Disqualification

4. Public officials shall not use their official authority for the improper advancement of their own or their family's personal or financial interest. They shall not engage in any transaction, acquire any position or function, or have any financial, commercial or other comparable interest that is incompatible with their office, functions and duties or the discharge thereof.

5. Public officials, to the extent required by the officials' position, shall in accordance with laws or administrative policies, declare business, commercial and financial interests, or activities undertaken for financial gain that may raise a possible conflict of interest. In situations of possible or perceived conflict of interest between the duties and private interests of public officials, they shall comply with the measures established to reduce or eliminate such conflict of interest.

6. Public officials shall at no time improperly use public moneys, property, services or information that is acquired in the performance of, or as a result of, their official duties for activities not related to their official work.

7. Public officials shall comply with measures established by law or administrative policies in order that after leaving their official positions they will not take improper advantage of their previous office.

III. Disclosure of Assets

8. Public officials shall, in accord with their' position and as permitted or required by law and administrative policies, comply with requirements to declare or to disclose personal assets and liabilities, as well as, if possible, those of their spouses and/or dependents.

IV. Acceptance of Gifts or Other Favors

9. Public officials shall not solicit or receive directly or indirectly any gift or other favours that may influence the exercise of their functions, performance of their duties or their judgement.

V. Confidential Information

10. Matters of a confidential nature in the possession of public officials shall be kept confidential unless national legislation, the performance of duty or the needs of justice strictly require otherwise. Such restrictions shall apply also after separation from service.

VI. Political Activity

11. The political or other activity of public officials outside the scope of their office shall, in accordance with laws and administrative policies, not be such as to impair public confidence in the impartial performance of their functions and duties.

Annex 3

United Nations Declaration against Corruption and Bribery in International Commercial Transactions

The General Assembly,

Recalling its resolution 3514 (XXX) of 15 December 1975, in which it, inter alia. condemned all corrupt practices, including bribery, in international commercial transactions, reaffirmed the right of any State to adopt legislation and to investigate and take appropriate legal action, in accordance with its national laws and regulations, against such corrupt practices, and called upon all Governments to cooperate to prevent corrupt practices, including bribery,

Recalling also the further work carried out by the General Assembly and the Economic and Social Council on the issue of illicit payments and on elaborating a code of conduct for transnational corporations, consideration of which helped call attention to and raise international awareness of the adverse consequences of bribery in international commercial transactions,

Recalling further its resolution 50/106 of 20 December 1995, in which it recommended that the Economic and Social Council consider the draft international agreement on illicit payments at its substantive session of 1996 and report to the Assembly at its fifty-first session,

Welcoming the steps taken at the national, the regional, and the international level to fight corruption and bribery, as well as recent developments in international forums that have further advanced international understanding and cooperation regarding corruption and bribery in international commercial transactions,

Noting the adoption in March 1996 by States members of the Organization of American States of the Inter-American Convention against Corruption, which includes an article on transnational bribery,

Noting also significant continuing work relevant to and consistent with the objectives of the present resolution in other regional and international forums, such as the continuing work of the Council of Europe and the

European Union to combat international bribery, as well as the commitment by the States members of the Organization for Economic Cooperation and Development to criminalize bribery of foreign public officials in international commercial transactions in an effective and coordinated manner and further examine the modalities and appropriate international instruments to facilitate criminalization, and to re-examine the tax deductibility of such bribes with the intention of denying such tax deductibility in the member States that do not already do so,

1. Adopts the United Nations Declaration against Corruption and Bribery in International Commercial Transactions, the text of which is annexed to the present resolution;

2. Notes the work being undertaken by the United Nations and in other international and regional forums to address the problem of corruption and bribery in international commercial transactions, and invites all States concerned to pursue the completion of such work;

3. Invites Member States, in accordance with the Declaration, to take appropriate measures and cooperate at all levels to combat corruption and bribery in international commercial transactions;

4. Requests the Economic and Social Council and its subsidiary bodies, in particular the Commission on Crime Prevention and Criminal Justice:

   — (a) To examine ways, including through legally binding international instruments, without in any way precluding, impeding or delaying international, regional or national actions, to further the implementation of the present resolution and the annexed Declaration, so as to promote the criminalization of corruption and bribery in international commercial transactions;

— (b) To keep the issue of corruption and bribery in international commercial transactions under regular review;

— (c) To promote the effective implementation of the present resolution;

5. Invites other bodies of the United Nations system, including the United Nations Conference on Trade and Development, whose competence extends to this matter to take action as appropriate within their mandates to promote the objectives of the present resolution and the Declaration;

6. Encourages private and public corporations, including transnational corporations, and individuals engaged in international commercial transactions to cooperate in the effective implementation of the Declaration;

7. Requests the Secretary-General to inform Member States, the relevant bodies and the specialized agencies of the United Nations system, and international, regional and non-governmental organizations, of the adoption of the present resolution, to encourage action towards making its provisions widely known and to promote its effective implementation;

8. Also requests the Secretary-General to prepare a report, for consideration by the General Assembly at its fifty-third session, on the progress made towards implementation of the present resolution and the steps taken by Member States, international and regional organizations and other relevant institutions to combat corruption and bribery in international commercial transactions; on the results of the work in this regard undertaken by the Commission on Crime Prevention and Criminal Justice and other bodies of the United

Nations system; and on measures taken in accordance with the present resolution to promote social responsibility and the elimination of corruption and bribery in international commercial transactions;

9. Invites Member States and competent international, regional and non-governmental organizations to provide relevant information to assist the Secretary-General in preparing the above-mentioned report;

10. Decides to include in the provisional agenda of its fifty-third session, under the item entitled "Business and development", a review of the report of the Secretary-General concerning the implementation of the present resolution.

Annex 4

United Nations Declaration Against Corruption and Bribery in International Commercial Transportation

The General Assembly,

Convinced that a stable and transparent environment for international commercial transactions in all countries is essential for the mobilization of investment, finance, technology, skills and other important resources across national borders, in order,inter alia, to promote economic and social development and environmental protection,

Recognizing the need to promote social responsibility and appropriate standards of ethics on the part of private and public corporations, including transnational corporations, and individuals engaged in international commercial transactions, inter alia, through observance of the laws and regulations of the countries in which they conduct business, and taking into account the impact of their activities on economic and social development and environmental protection,

Recognizing also that effective efforts at all levels to combat and avoid corruption and bribery in all countries are essential elements of an improved international business environment, that they enhance fairness and competitiveness in international commercial transactions and form a critical part of promoting transparent and accountable governance, economic and social development and environmental protection in all countries, and that such efforts are especially pressing in the increasingly competitive globalized international economy,

Solemnly proclaims the United Nations Declaration against Corruption and Bribery in International Commercial Transactions as set out below.

Member States, individually and through international and regional organizations, taking actions subject to each State's own constitution and fundamental legal principles and adopted pursuant to national laws and procedures, commit themselves:

1. To take effective and concrete action to combat all forms of corruption, bribery and related illicit practices in international commercial transactions, in particular to pursue effective enforcement of existing laws prohibiting bribery in international commercial transactions, to encourage the adoption of laws for those purposes where they do not exist, and to call upon private and public corporations, including transnational corporations, and individuals within their jurisdiction engaged in international commercial transactions to promote the objectives of this Declaration;

2. To criminalize such bribery of foreign public officials in an effective and coordinated manner, but without in any way precluding, impeding or delaying international, regional or national actions to further the implementation of this Declaration;

3. Bribery may include, inter alia, the following elements:

   — (a) The offer, promise or giving of any payment, gift or other advantage, directly or indirectly, by any private or public corporation, including a transnational corporation, or individual from a State to any public official or elected representative of another country as undue consideration for performing or refraining from the performance of that official's or representative's duties in connection with an international commercial transaction;

   — (b) The soliciting, demanding, accepting or receiving, directly or indirectly, by any public official or elected representative of a State from any private or public corporation, including a transnational corporation, or individual from another country of any payment, gift or other advantage, as undue consideration for performing or refraining from the performance of that official's or representative's duties in connection with an international commercial transaction;

4. To deny, in countries that do not already do so, the tax deductibility of bribes paid by any private or public corporation or individual of a State to any public official or elected representative of another country, and to that end, to examine their respective modalities for doing so;

5. To develop or maintain accounting standards and practices that improve the transparency of international commercial transactions, and that encourage private and public corporations, including transnational corporations, and individuals engaged in international commercial transactions to avoid and combat corruption, bribery and related illicit practices;

6. To develop or to encourage the development, as appropriate, of business codes, standards or best practices that prohibit corruption, bribery and related illicit practices in international commercial transactions;

7. To examine establishing illicit enrichment by public officials or elected representatives as an offence;

8. To cooperate and afford one another the greatest possible assistance in connection with criminal investigations and other legal proceedings brought in respect of corruption and bribery in international commercial transactions. Mutual assistance shall include, as far as permitted under national laws or as provided for in bilateral treaties or other applicable arrangements of the affected countries, and taking into account the need for confidentiality as appropriate:

   — (a) Production of documents and other information, taking of evidence and service of documents relevant to criminal investigations and other legal proceedings;

   — (b) Notice of the initiation and outcome of criminal proceedings concerning bribery in international commercial transactions to other States that may have jurisdiction over the same offence;

   — (c) Extradition proceedings where and as appropriate;

9. To take appropriate action to enhance cooperation to facilitate access to documents and records about transactions and about identities of persons engaged in bribery in international commercial transactions;

10. To ensure that bank secrecy provisions do not impede or hinder criminal investigations or other legal proceedings relating to corruption, bribery or related illicit practices in international commercial

transactions, and that full cooperation is extended to Governments that seek information on such transactions;

11. Actions taken in furtherance of this Declaration shall respect fully the national sovereignty and territorial jurisdiction of Member States, as well as the rights and obligations of Member States under existing treaties and international law, and shall be consistent with human rights and fundamental freedoms;

12. Member States agree that actions taken by them to establish jurisdiction over acts of bribery of foreign public officials in international commercial transactions shall be consistent with the principles of international law regarding the extraterritorial application of a State's laws.

11

Corporate Crime in a Globalised World

On the threshold of the twenty-first century, we are living in a world of increasing economic interdependence where global markets provide attractive opportunities for firms to do business on six continents, 24 hours a day. The increase of foreign investment has created a myriad of opportunities for expansion within developing countries where the legal and regulatory frameworks governing working conditions radically differ, posing many new challenges for corporations, governments and communities. These challenges have drawn increased public attention and apprehension in recent years, particularly surrounding business activities in zones of conflict.

In an era of increasing economic interdependence, what role are corporations playing in conflict, and moreover, its prevention? Are international laws adequate in ensuring companies are accountable for human rights abuses when operating outside of their home state, particularly in zones of conflict? Is national legislation in host state countries with weak government structures and repressive regimes strong enough to control and challenge corporate behavior? Is the increasing effort towards self-regulation a progressive path toward addressing fundamental human rights concerns? Evidence will be summarized that suggests a serious governance gap currently exists in the extraterritorial operations of corporations, leaving them unaccountable for violations of international human rights and humanitarian law.

While international and multilateral efforts aimed at promoting the incorporation of social accountability for corporations is notable, it is not sufficient in ensuring private sector activity is not a source or support for instability. Businesses can play an important role in contributing to long-term peace and the protection of human rights, especially in conflict-prone areas. However, in light of the growing power and mobility of corporations, legally binding regulations for industry are necessary in order for this role to be realized.

A paper produced by International Alert, the Council on Economic Priorities and The Prince of Whales Business Leaders Forum on The Business of Peace reported that in 2000, there were 72 countries where the security risk for the majority of locations in which foreign business operates was rated medium, high, or extreme. Multinational companies were also reported to be investing more than US$150 billion annually in "nearly 50 countries which fall below the intermediate point in Transparency International's Corruption Perception Index - in other words countries which may be confidently described as fairly to very corrupt."

There is a widespread assumption that corporations have a vested interest in preventing and managing conflict as it typically negatively disrupts private investment and business activity. However, as a workshop on Private Sector Actors in Zones of conflict summarized, "not all corporations share the same level of interest in ethical practices or assessment of risk." While corporations generally prefer to operate in politically and economically stable regions, in certain sectors, particularly the natural resource extraction sector, "asset specificity, long production cycles, and the expected returns on investment may simply outweigh the reputation and security costs of continuing to operate in areas of conflict."

Petroleum, natural gas, mining and other extractive industries are particularly reluctant to withdraw as they have extensive financial and physical investments within the region and are often tied to concession agreements which may carry time-frames of several decades. Not surprisingly, then, extractive multinationals operating in conflict zones have gained pressing international and domestic concern in recent years.

Canadian "junior" mining companies such as Rex Diamond, AmCan Minerals, and DiamondWorks operating in Sierra Leone during the 1990's are but a few of the handful of companies whose operations have been targeted for their role in exacerbating conflict. Michael Renner, a senior researcher with Worldwatch Institute in Washington, reports that in 2001 approximately one quarter of the roughly 50 wars and armed conflicts had "a strong resource dimension". In these cases "legal or illegal exploitation of resources helped trigger or exacerbate violent conflict, or financed its continuation." Renner further calculates that from these resource wars, roughly 5 million people have been killed, 6 million have become external refuges and 11 to 15 million have been internally displaced.

Corporations in Conflict Prevention

With the influx of capital and cross-border operation of major corporations, new opportunities have been presented for private sector actors to play an influential role in addressing some of the structural issues which underpin conflict. While there is no proven formula for conflict prevention, research has shed light on structural factors, including economic and social conditions, which are more conducive to the prospects of peace. As a 2002 Development Dimensions of Conflict Prevention and Peace-Building report notes,

> Certain levels of achievement and improvement in conditions of life, such as economic well-being, freedom and choice, social stability and social justice, seem to be a necessary part of such development, as so do trusted mechanisms of open, responsive governance, and the respect of individual and minority rights. At some point, these supporting beams, working together, do seem to provide a solid foundation for internal peace, and ultimately to be more conducive to peaceful relations with others - as well as being manifestly desirable in themselves.

Indeed, statistics have indicated a correlation between economic, political and social instability, and conflict. A recent study by Jonathon Goodhand on the links between poverty and violence found that horizontal inequalities and social exclusion, particularly when they coincide with identity or regional boundaries, may increase a society's predisposition towards violent conflict. Poverty was also shown to play a role in sustaining wars, as crime and violence become the only viable livelihood strategy for the poor. Generally speaking, the risk for violent conflict increases when people are marginalized from economic opportunity and access to social services, when they have no means for providing for themselves or their families, and when they have no voice within the political arena.

In light of the aforementioned evidence, the concept of Conflict Prevention has begun to shift focus over the last decade from "preventative diplomacy," which includes a limited set of diplomatic or military initiatives, toward structural interventions, which seek to address the underlying causes of conflict itself. This is reflected in the 2001 Report of the Secretary General on Prevention of Armed Conflict, when "an effective preventive strategy" is defined as a comprehensive approach that "encompasses both short-term and long-term political, diplomatic, humanitarian, human rights, developmental, institutional, and other measures taken by the international community, in cooperation with national and regional actors."

While this approach is still relatively recent, it is potentially of great benefit to both developing countries, which are the sites for most contemporary conflicts, and to corporations, who are playing an increasingly prominent role within them. As Kofi Annan stated in 1999 at an address to the United Nations, The private sector and security are linked in many ways, most obviously because thriving markets and human security go hand in hand. Global corporations can do more than simply endorse the virtues of the market, however. Their active support for better governance policies can help create environments in which both markets and human security flourish.

Through the adoption of conflict-sensitive internal management strategies and through policy dialogue and institutionbuilding, corporations can help to maximize their contribution to peace. The following suggests policies and initiatives that could be undertaken.

Table 1. Conflict-Sensitive Policies and Initiatives for the Private Sector

I.	Internal Management Policies
1. Risk and Impact Analysis	Corporations can examine their impact on local communities by undertaking social impact studies.
2. Process of Dialogue and Consultation	Corporations can implement a system that ensures corporations regularly engage and consult with community members and key stakeholders. Rather than perspectives of stakeholders merely being taken into account, they need to be actively incorporated into the policy process. As Fletcher notes, Operation Policy Manager for the International Business Leaders Forum, "the result is that a

	participative policy-making process can be nurtured which allows the community to have an element of ownership in the activities of the company."
3. Recruitment and Human Resources	Corporations can ensure minority or oppressed groups are given an equal chance as employees. This may include the active recruitment and encouragement of these groups through affirmative action programs.
4. Security Policies	Corporations can coordinate security policies with other groups, which may include the local community themselves. Amnesty International and Human Rights Watch have drafted recommendations on security policies to ensure they do not result in human rights abuses.
5. Building Trust and Support	Corporations can promote diversity and inter-dependency in the workplace by providing places of worship for different religious groups and/or offering workshops to educate employees on different religious and cultural traditions.
6. Anti-Corruption	Corporations can help to improve the lack of transparent government and business transactions that fuels conflict by implementing anti-corruption policies within business operations, and making public the clear condemnation of accepting or paying bribes.
7. Improving Transparency	Corporations can be required to report information about their investment activity, including their social and environmental impact in the community of operation, based on a "welldeveloped concept of "disclosure."
II.	Policy Dialogue and Institution Building
1. Good Governance and Democracy	Corporations can pay an advocacy role in improving local governance by promoting local and national government institutions to adopt democratic and transparent practices.
2. Tax revenues and Land compensation	Corporations can use their leverage to encourage land reform and fair distribution of tax revenues.

3. Provision of social services	Corporations can pressure national governments to improve provision of education and health services, particularly to neglected communities.
4. Judicial Reform	Corporations can pressure national governments to ensure a fair and transparent judicial system.

Corporate Accountability under International Law

At present, corporations that operate extraterritorially cannot be held accountable for violation of international human rights standards under international law. Transnational and multinational corporations are under no direct obligation to respect, nor ensure respect, of human rights within their sphere of influence. While new initiatives toward addressing corporate social responsibility issues are developing within the UN and various free trade agreements, no substantial progress has been made in monitoring and enforcing corporate accountability for complicity in, or perpetuation of human rights abuses.

On December 10, 1948 the General Assembly of the United Nations adopted and proclaimed the Universal Declaration of Human Rights (the "UDHR"). The declaration set an international precedent, aiming to recognize responsibility of states and individuals to respect human rights. As the preamble states:

> Every individual and every organ of society, keeping this Declaration constantly in mind, shall strive by teaching and education to promote respect for these rights and freedoms and by progressive measures, national and international, to secure their universal and effective recognition and observance. Respect for these rights and freedoms and by progressive measures, national and international, to secure their universal and effective recognition and observance, both among the peoples of Member States themselves and among the peoples of territories under their jurisdiction.

The final article in the document further clarifies obligation of groups as well as individuals to "do no harm," and specifically includes corporations. This provision, also echoed in the International Covenant on Civil and Political Rights and many regional human rights treaties, states:

> Nothing in this Declaration may be interpreted as implying for any state, group or person any right to engage in any activity or to perform any act aimed at the destruction of any of the rights and freedoms set forth herein.

While the obligations outlined in the Declaration have become the framework for many other human rights treaties and corporate rights doctrine within free trade agreements, the Declaration itself is not legally binding or enforceable for corporations. As the 2003 report on Corporate Self-Regulation notes, "respecting (or under) the UDHR, the best that can be said is that TNC's have a moral and social obligation to respect the universal rights enshrined in the Declaration." While the UDHR is clearly a highly authoritative statement by UN member states, and establishes a model of expected moral behavior, it remains an unenforceable ideal in a world motivated by economic profit.

Corporate Accountability under National Law

Home state responsibility

There exists no legislation within international law that makes national governments liable for extraterritorial acts of its national corporations. Although states "are in certain circumstances liable for the acts or conduct of private actors," there is no imposed duty by which states attempt to prevent, or punish corporations that are complicit in human rights abuses in host states. The US Foreign Corrupt Practice Act stands as an example of states attempt at extending criminal legislation to national corporations, however, most nations have been highly resistant to this approach, due to the fear of "the potential costs to diplomatic cooperation and access to markets, investment sites, and raw materials." There exists also a serious political barrier to establishing corporate boundaries of responsibility, as many wield considerable influence with host governments.

In a 2002 report by Amnesty International entitled Environmentalist Under Fire, four companies, which include ExxonMobil, Chevron and Texaco, Occidental Petroleum and Freeport-McMoRan, were highlighted for committing grave human rights violations. The report argues the companies were able to significantly influence the U.S. government's response due, in large part, to their collective contribution of more than $2.8 million during the 2002 election cycle.

Host State Responsibility

There is a pervasive argument in public dialogue on corporate accountability that regards receiving states as the necessary regulatory body. This conception also holds significant weight on a legal basis. International human rights law does recognize host states as being responsible for preventing abuses by private actors, including companies. This is confirmed in several human rights treaties, and has been recognized by an overwhelming majority of governments through UN declarations. As specified by the UN Committee on the Elimination of Discrimination against Women in 1992, "Under general international law and specific human rights covenants, states may also be responsible for private acts."

While states are clearly not expected to be held responsible for every crime committed by private parties, they can be held accountable when "they fail to exercise due diligence in protecting the rights of people within their jurisdiction." Yet, in reality this approach toward corporate accountability remains highly problematic, as governments operating in a world of global markets are now less capable than formally of effectively challenging and changing corporate behavior. Through mergers, corporations have grown remarkable quickly, and currently the largest six corporations are larger than all but the seven largest nation states, comparing corporate revenues with states revenues. Investor pressure, new international trade rules, weakened government tax bases and budget cuts have all combined to weaken regulation at the national level.

As exemplified by the cases of Unocal, Total and Premier Oil in Burma, and Talisman Energy, major barriers exist which obstruct the willingness of government authorities to adopt or enforce remedial regulation. Often governments either lack the physical capacity or political motivation to confront corporate abuses, or they may be themselves prime perpetrators of violence. This is particularly true for corporations operating in conflict zones. As David Petrasek notes, Research Director for the International Council on Human Rights Policy,

> If companies engage in systematic discrimination in the workplace, knowingly work in a manner that supports repressive state institutions, show little concern for hazardous production processes that destroy people's livelihoods (and lives), or suppress freedom of association, it is of little help to the victims of such abuses that, in theory, duties to respond lie with the national government. Of course, individual governments should put in place the legal structure (laws, courts etc.) that would prevent such abuses, or act quickly against perpetrators. The fact is, however, that there are real obstacles to effective action at the national level. Even well intentioned governments may find resource and other constraints work to the advantage of those companies that are abusing rights.

Due to the aforementioned factors, it is unlikely that host states will be effective for ensuring constructive corporate engagement in conflict-settings.

Conception of Ethical Business

Due to the widespread media attention gained by recent corporations' extraterritorial activities, the "bottom line" of the corporate stance has come under increasing scrutiny; the conventional view that held corporations' two sole responsibilities to be profit maximization and responsibility to a company's shareholders has been uprooted from its historically solid ground. As Aron Framer, Vice President at Business for Social Responsibility articulates, "there is a fundamental shift taking place. Human rights principles were really written with governments in mind. (But) it's clear that more and more, the (public) is looking at what the private sector is doing on human rights."

At issue is the responsibility corporations have as global citizens and members of the local communities in which they operate. Even if the legal duties of a company remain solely with its shareholders, there is a growing acceptance that companies need to be more accountable to other stakeholders, such as employees, customers, suppliers, creditors, governments and the community. The heightened expectations of what companies can or should contribute in terms of social progress has shed light on the corporate governance conundrum that currently exists, and has, moreover, raised serious concerns over how and if corporate accountability should be practically implemented in the future.

Voluntary Standards and Self-Regulation

Accompanying the recent public shift in perspective toward increasing corporations' scope of responsibility has been a growing initiative within the business sector itself to develop and implement policies and practices that ensure compliance with human rights. Several companies have begun to adopt corporate codes of conduct and create new corporate functions dedicated to addressing human rights and labor practices. Most of the new voluntary codes adopted by corporations state broad objectives and values of the organization, and specify commitments the company has toward stakeholders, consumers and often host governments. Employing inspirational language ("strive", "work towards", "try to minimize") many of the codes attempt to project the companies' values, ethical standards and expectations.

Critical of national investment rules and international regulations, pro-business voices have advocated for self-initiated voluntary codes arguing they reflect an effective move toward corporate accountability and responsibility in the new millennium; however, as will be shown below, this remains to be proven. While responsibility for governing behavior remains in individual corporate hands, the voluntary efforts are often based upon an over-arching framework of values and corporate standards. The United Nations and the International Labor Organization (ILO) have already established several codes of conduct and international principles that outline private-sector human rights responsibilities.

Similar global initiatives have also taken hold, including the Global Reporting Initiative, Social Accountability 8000, the Ethnical Trading Initiative, the Fair Labor Association, and the Global Sullivan Principles. These guidelines have allowed companies to remain flexible and innovative in their operating contexts, and do not involve enforceable commitment mechanisms or punitive measures for non-compliance. The International Chamber of Commerce (ICC), also coined the World Business Organization, along with its supporters, have presented an adamant argument in support of self-monitoring and voluntary regulation. As one of the organization's spokesperson states,

> To be effective, business principles should be developed and implemented by the companies themselves... Clearly,

> the way to ensure a greater business contribution to environmental and social progress is not through prescriptive codes and regulations imposed from outside, but by persuasion and peer pressure.

From this perspective, the existence of an external regulating framework is unlikely to be a viable alternative to voluntary principles developed by companies themselves. This argument rests upon two central points. First, it is essential that company principles be appropriate to the vastly different conditions which corporations face. Highlighting the culturally and geographically diverse climates in which corporations operate, the organization has argued government-mandated or other external codes that employ a "one-size-fits-all" approach are ineffective. Voluntary codes are seen to be more "flexible" than regulatory rules in a rapidly changing and dynamic environment, as they can be adopted more swiftly and are far less expensive to administer.

Also, the diversity within voluntary business initiatives and principles acts as a "source of innovation in defining responsible business conduct." While a notable argument, flexibility is a double-edged sword, and results in codes being vague statements of principles that rarely provide reliable guidelines for behavior in concrete situations. Codes are often neither transparent nor accountable, and they "do not generally include complaint procedures, nor any basis for legal claims or redress, and thus provide little scope for individuals to be compensated for corporate violations that cause harm." A second argument presented in favour of self-regulation is that voluntary codes are essentially in business's best interest.

In 1998, the UN Human Rights Commissioner, Mary Robinson asked: 'Why should business care about human rights?' She replied, 'because business needs human rights and human rights need businesses. The rational behind her statement rested firstly on the assumption that corporations would be hampered in an environment where fundamental human rights were not respected, and secondly being implicated in human rights would lead to consumer discontent and loss of "band value," thereby jeopardizing economic profitability. While Non-governmental organizations (NGOs) and public scrutiny have undoubtedly made some notable progress in pressuring corporations in a few important cases, it is still of fundamental concern whether all corporations will implement voluntary standards which respect human rights, and moreover whether they adhere to the internal codes which they have implemented.

A study conducted in 1998 by the Natural Heritage Institute found that fewer than ten percent of US- based TNC's adopt codes at all. Since the threat of public pressure and negative publicity act as the driving force behind motivating corporate conduct, only a few sectors that are especially vulnerable to consumer pressure are adopting codes. This has been empirically shown as the "consumer products and natural resource industries represent the lion's share of codes, predominantly in the apparel and petroleum sectors."

The few companies that do adopt conflict prevention and management strategies or codes of conduct may actually find themselves at a comparative disadvantage if they put the codes into practice; Firstly, they may lose out on lucrative contracts and access to markets, and secondly, they face a "free-rider" problem, by privately bearing the costs of supplying the public good which others may benefit from.

As an International Peace Academy Workshop on Private Sector Actors in Zones of Conflict notes: "a single corporation is unlikely to make decisions which place it at a disadvantage vis-à-vis its competitors, such as placing conditions upon its investment, particularly when competition is high." Indeed this has been shown to lessen the incentive to adhere to self-implemented codes. A report released in 1999 by the UN Research Institute for Social Development (UNRISD) entitled 'Visible Hands', argues that many companies have "mastered socially responsible rhetoric," but only a few have taken concrete action to addressing human rights concerns.

The fact that the threat of negative publicity acts as the only deterrent to hold companies back from committing human rights abuses is particularly concerning with corporations operating in zones of conflict. As articulated by Broadhurst,

> Serious problems are posed by abuses occurring in countries where public protest is prohibited, where the press is controlled and where the legal system and/or the government are corrupt... In the case of companies located in North America, Japan and Western Europe, legal systems of enforcement and restraint operate within the context of abundant state resources and high levels of education. In countries where these systems and structures are not yet in place, national and local businesses can function without regard to formal and legal codes of conduct.

Perhaps more significantly, contrary to conventional conceptions, evidence has shown that the failure of corporations to pursue a human rights strategy is unlikely to be reflected in the markets. According to a study by Zadek and Forstater, while Shell, Nestle, Monsanto and Nike were identified as having a poor human rights record and subjected to public boycotts, no demonstrable effect appeared on their share prices or dividends. Even when Nike chief executives were claiming a negative effect on share prices, the empirical evidence did not support this claim. Due to the aforementioned challenges, it is unlikely that voluntary codes will be effective for ensuring constructive corporate engagement in conflict-settings.

International Efforts at Corporate Accountability

In order to assess the effectiveness of voluntary standards

in the global context, the two most renowned voluntary guidelines for multinational corporations in existence; the United Nations Global Compact and the OECD initiatives, will be examined.

The united nations global compact

One half century after the UN Declaration of Human Rights was drafted, at an address to the World Economic Forum on 31 January 1999, United Nations Secretary-General Kofi Annan called on business leaders, trade unions and NGO's to consolidate efforts in developing and implementing a set of principles in the areas of human rights, labour standards and the environment. His call was well received by the international community, and resulted in the launching of the UN Global Compact at UN headquarters on July 26 2000. The Compact received widespread enthusiasm from the business community, and within the first six months the number of participants rose to over two-hundred-and-fifty. The Global Compact encompasses nine central principles and asks "companies to act on these principles in their own corporate environment." These principles include:

— *Principle 1*: support and respect the protection of international human rights within their sphere of influence;

— *Principle 2*: make sure their own corporations are not complicit in human rights abuses.

— *Principle 3*: freedom of association and the effective recognition of the right to collective bargaining;

— *Principle 4*: the elimination of all forms of forced and compulsory labour;

— *Principle 5*: the effective abolition of child labour; and

— *Principle 6*: the elimination of discrimination in respect of employment and occupation.

— *Principle 7*: support a precautionary approach to environmental challenges;

— *Principle 8*: undertake initiatives to promote greater environmental responsibility; and

— *Principle 9*: encourage the development and diffusion of environmentally friendly technologies.

This Global Compact has become a general framework for UN cooperation with the private sector, and is argued to reflect a unique space for dialogue and learning, "with few formalities and no rigid bureaucratic structures." As the Secretary-General's report to the General Assembly articulates, "the Global Compact is not intended as, and does not have the capacity to be, a corporate code of conduct or global standard." Although an important precedent in portraying international interest in corporate citizenship, the Global Compact's voluntary nature and lack of monitoring mechanism makes it little more than a public relations exercise, and may in fact act as a veil for corporate irresponsibility.

Most crucially, it remains questionable whether the poetic mandate of the Compact stated by Kofi Annan to "unite the powers of markets with the authority of universal principles" will be achieved. As will be explored below, in several instances the Compact has not led to a concrete commitment to the core principles by corporations, and fails to reflect businesses' desire to enhance and support the awareness of societal values and concerns. Due to the lack of monitoring mechanisms in place to ensure adherence to its principles, the Global Compact has encountered serious difficulty in producing real changes in company performance. As Making Corporation Accountable points out, "corporations signing up are able to claim the legitimacy of a wide-ranging code under the prestigious United Nations, while only having to adhere to it symbolically."

Several renowned international NGO's, including Amnesty International and CorpWatch, have publicly announced violation of the Principles of the Compact by several Global Compact companies since it was launched. Nike was pronounced as violating Principle 3 in Vietnam, China, Indonesia, Cambodia and Mexico; Rio Tinto was targeted for violating Principle 3 and 8 at the PT kelian gold mine in Indonesia; and Norsk Hydro was targeted for violating Principle 1 and 2 at their bauxite/alumina joint venture in India.

Although the Guidelines on Cooperation Between the United Nations and the Business Community issued on July 20 2000 states that "businesses entities that are complicit in human rights abuses... are not eligible for partnership," this has clearly not been the case. More recently, the inclusion of Shell in the Global Compact, a company renowned for human rights abuses in Ogoni land territory in Nigeria, has seriously undermined the credibility of the initiative.

Another skepticism of voluntary corporate responsibility, as CorpWatch points out, is that it can "become an obstacle when used as a diversion from attempts to hold corporations accountable." With the implementation of the Global Compact and other voluntary measures, there is a distinct possibility that corporations will use these as a leverage point to negate the necessity of a legal framework to hold corporations accountable internationally.

As the United Nations Research Institute for Social Development (UNRISD) report warned, "there is a danger that corporate self-regulation, as well as various partnership arrangements, are weakening the role of national governments, trade unions and stronger forms of civil society activism." Unfortunately, this seems to be the case. As previously mentioned, the ICC, representing the interests of corporations across the globe, has publicly stated external corporate monitoring to be unnecessary, proposing voluntary self-regulation as the most effective path toward the protection of human rights.

The Global Compact does, no doubt, reflect a significant focal shift by the international community. The UN human rights system, which traditionally focused exclusively on the responsibilities of government, is now addressing the role of the business sector in achieving public goals. However, there is so far little convincing evidence that this has been an adequate measure in ensuring human rights norms are more influential, effective and enforceable in today's globalized world.

Adopting the principles of the declaration, several corporate rights and accountability measures are being incorporated, most significantly within the OECD and the International Labor Organization (ILO) Tripartite Declaration. However, these agreements hold similar weaknesses as the Global Compact, as none specify a legal obligation of corporations to respect human rights in the conduct of business.

In 1976, the OECD adopted the Declaration on International Investment and Multinational Enterprises. It was designed primarily to protect the rights of investors, yet also included Guidelines for Multinational Enterprises. A revised version of these OECD Guidelines was adopted by member states in June 2000. Standards were proposed in the guidelines for multinationals that covered worker's rights and industrial relations, environmental protection, bribery, consumer interests, payment of taxation, science and technology, and most significantly, respect for human rights. As paragraph II.2, states:

> [Enterprises should] respect the human rights of those affected by their activities consistent with the host government's international obligations and commitments.

As the document states, it is a "non-legal recommendation that companies are invited to follow voluntarily," it is highly questionable whether it will have a significant impact on changing corporate behavior. The agreement also fails to include mechanisms that allow for citizens or groups, whose human rights may have been violated by business practices, to express their concerns. This places into question how the rights guaranteed under the agreements can be adequately enforced.

While currently the OECD agreement displays little hope for enforceability of human rights norms, it does set a significant precedent in public policy. The OECD is composed of 29 countries, which collectively produce two-thirds of the world's goods and this reflects an important recognition by the world powers that businesses do play a role in social responsibility. As the OECD Secretary-General expressed at the June 2000 ministerial meeting:

The Guidelines are the only multilaterally endorsed and comprehensive code that governments are committed to promoting. The Guidelines' recommendations express the shared values of governments of countries that are the source of most of the world's direct investment flows and home to most multinational enterprises. The Guidelines aim to promote their positive contributions to economic, environmental and social progress. In this respect, the agreement might have some impact as a set of "soft laws." This results when several states are unable to reach a legally-binding treaty and so compromises are made in order to structure behavior around a set of norms. "Soft laws" have shown to have an impact in directing international conduct, and may have at least some "anticipatory effect in judicial or quasi-judicial decision-making and in shaping new, binding, international norms."

However, this remains an inadequate measure in ensuring corporations play a constructive, rather than destructive, role in conflict settings.

Corporate Citizenship

The pervasiveness of the problems associated with voluntary codes and national legislation implies that corporations' behaviour in conflict zones can only be modified if a framework for corporate accountability is established at the global level. Adopting and enforcing binding regulations can play the essential role of providing a universal standard against which corporate conduct can be judged, and can complement and strengthen both voluntary efforts and national regulation. As Petrasek states, "if human rights are not to remain abstract and intangible, there must be systems in place to ensure individuals whose rights have been abused can seek redress. This in turn implies that there be legal remedies and, further, that those individuals and institutions which have the duty to protect the right are clearly identified."

Binding legal regulations are wide-ranging, consistent and demand adherence, removing the competitive problems faced by voluntary codes. Features of compulsion, which includes fines, withdrawal of licenses and other penalties, can also be ensured by a public authority. As Peter Utting, research co-coordinator at the UNRISD, highlights, "while multinational corporations would prefer to comply through voluntary initiatives, the public interest can only be fully served through stronger regulation and monitoring." A statement made by Human Rights Watch to the UN Sub- Commission on the Working Methods and Activities of Transnational Corporations in August 2002, echoed these concerns stating, "only when binding standards are combined with the possibility of punitive sanctions for their violations can corporations be uniformly prevented from having a negative impact on the enjoyment of human rights."

While global society has been slow to build internationally harmonized regulations for corporate behavior, the dramatic changes in both the corporate landscape and governance philosophy in the past decade represents a positive possibility of the increased importance of international law in the near future. Concerned citizens are raising the issue of a new rule-based global economic system and the conditions for its existence are beginning to take root.

The increased commitment to corporate accountability is reflected in several new UN human rights bodies that are dedicated to the behaviour of transnational corporations, including the Working Group on Transnational Corporations of the Sub-Commission on the Promotion and Protection of Human Rights and the Committee on Economic, Social and Cultural Rights. More recently, the cumulative effort by the Security Council to pass new resolutions on conflict diamonds, the arms trade, finance, oil, and smuggling has set new rules for corporate conduct and accountability in zones of conflict.

Creating a Regulatory and Legal Framework

A global framework for ensuring the integration of socially responsible policies and practices into mainstream business activities can play an essential role in preventing and stabilizing conflict, particularly in conflict-prone or conflictridden countries. A rule-based approach can help to ensure the private sector acts as a partner in conflict prevention and resolution rather than exacerbating tensions. The following suggests important steps to strengthening international criminal and liability action against corporations in exterritorial operations.

1. Improve research on the consequences of private sector activity and corporate decision-making in conflict settings.
2. Improve international cooperation of judicial institutions in gathering evidence, questioning of suspects and witnesses, and related access to critical information.
3. Expand the funding and staffing of UN human rights bodies.
4. Create an intergovernmental agency that is committed to addressing issues of corporate accountability and monitoring.
5. Draft new rules, by means of the UN Security Council, to manage and control the potentially negative impacts of corporate policy on peace and security crises.
6. Develop global consumer protection rules that ensure fundamental product safety and reliability, and ensure restrained, truthful and un-manipulative advertising, based on strengthened UN guidelines.
7. Improve the availability of legal protection for employee whistleblowers and NGO watchdogs. This may include creating a stronger relationship between the UN and NGO groups.

Index